CANADA AND OTHER MATTERS OF OPINION

REX MURPHY

CANADA

AND OTHER MATTERS OF OPINION

Library and Archives Canada Cataloguing in Publication

Murphy, Rex
    Canada and other matters of opinion / Rex Murphy.—Updated.

ISBN 978-0-385-66727-2 (pbk.)

    I. Title.

AC8.M918 2010   082   C2010-902546-6

Printed and bound in the USA

Published in Canada by
Anchor Canada, a division of
Random House of Canada Limited

Visit Random House of Canada Limited's website: www.randomhouse.ca

BVG   10   9   8   7   6   5   4   3   2   1

To Harry

CONTENTS

INTRODUCTION: Inclusive Me Out

Ah, Mordecai, thou should'st be living at this hour!

All On Board for the Follies Express. The lunacies multiply.

Just after takeoff from La Guardia airport a passenger jet flies into a flock of birds. Both the jet's engines—and it has only two—shut down, immediately. The pilot, a man with the wonderful name of Chesley "Sully" Sullenberger, has but seconds to react.

There are 137 passengers on board. He chooses to attempt to land his powerless aircraft on the Hudson River. Such attempts to glide-land modern jets on flowing water have a limited and discouraging history. Chesley Sullenberger, however, is not daunted. Chesley Sullenberger, cool as whole crateloads of the frostiest cucumbers, brings his plane down, skims it miraculously over the crowded Hudson River until, intact, it halts.

The passengers—women and children first, note you—emerge, and stand, crouch and cling on or to the jet's wings. All are rescued. Chesley B. Sullenberger—O, hero of another age and time!—is the last to emerge. We learn later that Sullenberger went up and down the aisles of his rapidly sinking craft—twice—

checking that there was absolutely no one still on board before he ever so calmly—shall we say—deplaned.

Everyone is safe. Hardly anyone is even seriously injured. One hundred and thirty-seven people, whom chance and the cruel gods of ornithology had thrown in the way of almost certain death, are alive. Throw a ticker-tape parade for Sully!

Barely two weeks pass by, however, before a miserable handful of those passengers, or rather a handful of truly miserable passengers, announce that they're *suing*. Some want more than the $5,000 all have received for their luggage, which crash inspectors must keep for the duration of their necessary investigation. One magnificently doltish ingrate whom a *USA Today* account tells us "suffered some bumps and bruises" is suing because, he says, he "wishes to be made whole for the incident."

He wishes to be made whole for the incident. Someone should tell him he is *already* a complete idiot. No bits of his perfect idiocy fell off during the incident. He has them all. One hundred per cent of a dolt and an ingrate walked on that jet: one hundred per cent, unfortunately, was saved.

The markets of the whole world are crashing, Al Gore's hysterical legions are raving about the impending global warming apocalypse, the Middle East is in one of its periodic showdowns, Iran is close to getting the nuclear bomb, the world is spinning off its axis—and a handful of people who have been saved from almost statistically certain death sue the airline that had the wit to have the world's most competent pilot on duty at the time when competence was all. And, of that handful, one in particular utters as justification for his miserable ingratitude in pitch-perfect therapy-speak the ultimate Oprah-bleat: *I want to be made whole.* Well, cry me a Hudson River, and throw in a jet.

I cannot speak for other people, but stories such as this one flood me with something like a manic urge to ram my head into the nearest concrete wall—repeatedly, until consciousness retreats and the pain from the spectacle of such typical idiocy recedes into the welcoming darkness.

It is the typicality of these stories, the number and frequency of them, that ignites the pain. There are far, far too many of them. We have long passed the balance point where satire or mockery can keep pace with their targets. That great Gandalf of twentieth-century journalism, Malcolm Muggeridge, long ago noted that the age we live in has voided the power of satire to castigate it. Our reality is far more absurd than any satirist's imaginings. What Swift could invent Flavor Flav or Nancy Grace? Where is the Molière who could draw from his mind's own store the daily councils of *The View*? Larry King probing Sean Penn on the geopolitics of Iraq? One void probing another. Shaw would retire gibbering into the darkness at the challenge of conjuring such a scene.

The follies and hypocrisies of the world multiply and breed, at a pace and with an extravagance far beyond satire's ability to keep up with them. Every day's newspaper carries stories that defy the sternest credibility, and wrench common sense from its tether. Reading them invokes the cry: can such things be? They are items in some huge Diary of a World Gone Mad. Before this great flood of inanity, self-contradiction and megalomaniacal self-righteousness, satire lies disarmed and exhausted, bleeding and in wounded retreat from a million headlines or television lead items.

Fifteen thousand frantic environmentalists jet in to Gabon or Rio to lay a group curse on the world's carbon-consuming ways. They who anathematize the Alberta oil sands fly locust-like in great swarms to yet one more gargantuan "world-gathering" of planet-savers to natter on in first-class five-star hotel-spas about the world's "oil addiction," heedless that their venue, their flights, their meals, and the near equal swarm of the international press which is there to beam their empty jeremiads to the televisions and presses of a yawning world—that all of it is enabled, is made possible by, that "toxic" petroleum and the wealth that it generates, and that they so sanctimoniously deplore.

Heather McCartney wafts her shrewish way to the ice-packs off Labrador, with her bank-account (husband) Paul in sheepish tow, to rub noses with a baby seal and rattle on about cruelty and barbarism, days before she launches her dementedly bitter divorce action and displays herself to the world as one of the most callous and self-centred human beings ever to set a pack of lawyers loose to maul another human being. McCartney was her baby seal.

Lip-synching pop-singers, bling-smothered rappers, fourth-rate standup comics, and geriatric passé rockers dedicate a day, or an hour of a day—time is money—to Make Poverty History. These ludicrous, shallow, vain, shameless preeners wear rubber-bands on their wrists to show their "solidarity" with the world's poor. They arrive on private jets, attended by mile-long "entourages" of sycophants and fixers, scratch each other's eyes out to determine who gets top billing—most of them "earn" more in a hour, or wear around their neck some gaudy trinket that is worth far more, than any poor family anywhere in all the world will make in several lifetimes—and they expect to be, and are, applauded for their "commitment," for "caring," for—may they choke on the phrase—"making a difference."

Were Swift alive what would he say or write, what new Modest Proposal could hope to take the measure, stay the excesses, plumb the hypocrisies of these monumental farces? He could write nothing. Say nothing. There is no new Modest Proposal, however savage its premise or imaginative its scorn, that could challenge the extravagant waywardness of our present moment. Poor Swift would retire silent from the scene, overwhelmed by reality.

Madonna is a Kabbalahist. And I'm Isaac Newton. In Vancouver, the Eumenides of anti-smoking forbid a furtive draw anywhere within seven metres of any doorway, while simultaneously offer an "inclusive" welcome to three new hookah parlours. Inclusive me out, if I may update Samuel Goldwyn. Inclusiveness—how many are the sins done in thy name? An "inclusive" principal in a school in New Brunswick bans the daily singing of *O Canada*. The anthem is the song of all of us, I thought. What could be—what is—more inclusive of Canadians than the anthem of all Canadians? Not in the diversity-respecting head of one principal of a school in an east coast province. So in the name of inclusiveness, our all-including *O Canada* was for a while thought too stressful, too divisive, for morning observance.

Eventually we will tolerate and "inclusive" ourselves into oblivion. We will smudge or abrade our every common characteristic, violate all common sense in doing so, till "being Canadian" is a little more than a vague cloud of barely formed attitudes, a mere mist of politically correct half-thoughts empty of any content.

In some gazetteer of the future there will be an asterisk next to the Canada entry directing the reader to a footnote: *"Canada was unique among twentieth- and twenty-first-century nations in developing a code of such advanced civic sensitivity that its own national anthem was understood, certainly by the most enlightened of its population, to be an instrument of national division. Sexism and Godism were the ancient and now-abandoned anthem's principal defects. That it might, too, be seen as advancing Patriotism was thought too vilely obvious to merit comment."*

Muggeridge was right. Satire cannot catch up with reality. And bear in mind that Muggeridge, despite a lifetime of witness and experience, made his observation when what we call news was less "full" than it is now, more neat and defined. Muggeridge, and his saintly spirit is surely smiling with gratitude for the consideration, died well before the advent of the 24-hour news cycle and multi-channel universe, before "reality television," and the "entertainment-news" buckets/shows, before the twisted inception of remorseless talk-therapy afternoon shows—the bottomless vulgarity and shamelessness of Dr. Phil and his tacky gibberish may stand for all of these—before too, of course, the rise and spread of the Internet, which overlays all other modes of public communication and which multiplies and intensifies all that is *outré,* stark and witless in the daily diet of bulletins from the world that is modern journalism.

The Internet, let me be clear, doesn't "create" the craziness of the world's news. There are in fact on the Internet, if one cares to look for them, some of its most acute diagnosticians. But the Internet came upon the world of news as it was like a vat of adrenalin and—in tandem with the explosion of cable channels and continuous, 24-hour news—exponentially accelerated our exposure to news, and its abundant, unfailing absurdities.

It is probably clear that I don't subscribe to that outdated and cozy description of journalism as the "first draft of history." It's a far too grand and finished a phrase under which to file the massive jumble and sprawl of modern newsmaking. It carries with it too the implication that someone, somewhere, sometime is going to do a rewrite. I wish that sad he or she good luck. It is of course just not going to happen.

In a tidier time, now so long past, when news outlets were relatively few, reporters reported and commentators wrote dutiful, grey expositions on the public announcements of the government of the day, when events had, or seemed to have, a self-contained quality about them, it may have been possible to entertain the notion that what one read on the front page or heard on the prestige news hours of the great networks was a sketch, however tentative, of what Walter Cronkite called in his nightly sign-off "the way it is."

News then was just news, so to speak. News stories had a fixed and familiar shape. In fact, as I remember them from my earliest dips into journalism in the Newfoundland of the sixties, they all had a similar sound as well. They were as rigid in form and flow as pop songs, and oftentimes nearly as dreary. They were like little packets or pellets of "news-stuff": A. Announcer reads lead sentence. B. Voice clip of premier or newsmaker. C. Announcer reads factoid.

"Mr. Smallwood today announced that construction would begin on the new Linerboard mill." Voicer of Smallwood: "Total cost of the project will be $30 million, and provide 400 desperately needed jobs in the Stephenville area." End of item. Or as things heated up in my always volatile province, as heat up they did when John Crosbie staged a revolt against Smallwood, they took on the flavour of an exchange of gunfire—pellets of a different kind, but still pellets, neatly organized and discrete: Announcer: "Premier Smallwood today alleged that several of the Crosbie delegates to the upcoming Liberal leadership convention had their Liberal membership cards 'paid for' by the Crosbie leadership team." Voicer of Smallwood: "John Crosbie is trying to buy the Liberal leadership. Well, I'm here to tell Mr. Crosbie that he won't succeed. Mr. Crosbie can't buy the leadership because I won't let him. And if he can't buy it, he won't win it." Announcer: "Mr. Crosbie is expected to respond to the allegations at a news conference at the Holiday Inn, Portugal Cove Road, tonight."

This would have been followed by some story, say, about a "raffle that raised over $2,440 for the Janeway Children's Hospital," newscast's movement from politics to philanthropy a kind of silent cue that the "serious" stuff, for now anyway—Crosbie's return fire was yet to come—was over.

That world of news is as ancient as Marco Polo. News as a discrete category of information comprising calamity, government announcement, and extraordinary event, is dead. News is everything we hear, watch or read. Everything.

All the convenient categories have dissolved and blended into one another. What was entertainment is now news; what was news is entertainment. Bono sits in on the G8 summit. Sarkozy trails in the wake of his supermodel wife Carla Bruni. Hollywood is Washington: Washington is Hollywood. Is Obama the President of the United States, or the biggest celebrity in all the world? Is he a star or a politician?

Court cases are ersatz scripts for daily talk shows, the blindfolded goddess daily mocked and mutilated by the unspeakable Nancy Grace.

The last days of the Clinton presidency dissolved into a kind of infinite mass soap opera that fed every conceivable form of programming: late-night monologues, the political-comedy half-hours, news panels, afternoon talk, open-line programs, endless front-page revelations and infinite column inches. Everyone was welcome and nothing was off limits: sex-consultants traded "insights" with high-brow Washington insiders on Sunday panels; Hollywood's A, B and C lists trooped dutifully from the green rooms to the interview couch to gloss every day's minutiae; presidential historians shared the aura with prominent psychics; the *National Enquirer* elbowed out *The New York Times*. It was therapy, politics, soap opera, drama, comedy, farce, law and sex. All of it was news I suppose, or news as now we have it. News today is the huge swirl of everything that is.

We hear, God how often do we hear, that "young people get their news from Jon Stewart and *The Daily Show*." This is most often said as if it were a good thing. But, of course, what Jon Stewart, or his twin Stephen Colbert, delivers isn't news at all. It is merely a thin comedic overlay on the "hottest" tidbits of the day. Stewart and Colbert offer comedy as a masquerade for commentary; they are in fact the master practitioners of that "truthiness" they claim to be so expert in exploding. They illustrate what is, to my mind, the other great turn in our understanding of news. People go to certain television shows, read certain newspapers, have favourite web sites because these shows, newspapers, web sites offer them confirmation—not of what they know about the news, but of how they already feel. People seek out confirmation more than information. News, in this new, loose understanding of the term, is that which authenticates feelings or attitudes already held.

Environmental news is, by far, the best illustration of this. Environmental "reporting"—the scare quotes are most necessary here—is so wretchedly somnolent on the major controversies of environmentalism, global warming itself being the principal one, as to constitute a form of evangelism. Environmental reporting is, in the main, a mix of conscious or unconscious advocacy. If business journalists reported on business, if political journalists reported on politics, in the manner that most environmental reporters report on environmentalism it would be a scandal.

In such a context, however fruitless the effort—the windmills are so many, the lances so few—it is a rightful task to bark occasionally at the consensus, to highlight the absurdities, mock the vain celebrities, and puncture the politicians. Which is I hope the point—if I may be permitted to hope, and if I have a point—of much of the writing in my newspaper columns or the "Point of View" for *The National* that I do.

I make no pretense of being earnest in any final sense of that term, and have long since parted with the delusion that my opinions, *because* they are mine, are less hostage to fallibility or walk nearer with truth than those of many others. I subscribe to the spirit of Oscar Wilde's dictum, which should be something of a motto for opinion-mongers: "On . . . occasion[s] of this kind it becomes more than a moral duty to speak one's mind. It becomes a pleasure." The pleasure part is real. It is a pleasure to comment on, rail against, parse, or idly just note in passing the various "occasions" in our national life, or in the broader life of the times, twice a week. To comment on—to coin a title—Canada and other matters of opinion. The occasions are so many, as I've noted above, that for every column or "Point of View" written, ten others have flown by before the fingers reach the laptop.

An Obama win over (we thought then) the indomitable Hillary in one of the early primaries coincides with Stéphane Dion's launch of the leaden lifeboat he called The Green Shift; Mark Steyn, the indefatigable, boldy goes (where no journalist should ever have to go) to plead his case before the Commissars of B.C.'s human rights commission in the same week, say, as Maxime Bernier's fling with the busty Julie Couillard makes the headlines: which boobs to choose? That is always the question. It is always answered, in my case, by whichever of the multiple topics on offer provokes a real itch to respond. If the itch is genuine the chances of the response being fun are greater. It's a simple rule, but about the only real one I have. I hope some of the fun survives in the pieces gathered here. They are, if I may revert to an earlier image, a few pages from my personal diary of a world gone mad.

P.S. I have in many pieces done what time, or absence of industry, did not allow me to do when they were written. I have cleaned up some sentences, unravelled some obscurities. Here and there throughout the book I have appended postscripts in order to underline or add to a point with the benefit of hindsight. What murkiness remains was too thick to be lifted.

Rex Murphy

EMINENT CANADIANS

DON CHERRY, THE PEOPLE'S GG | May 8, 2004

I had not realized how fervently Toronto is a hockey city. The air here was electric with hope for the beloved, hapless Leafs. The dismay following their elimination from the playoffs was palpable. Lord Stanley's cup will grace another city's parade.

But time is a great (actually, the only) grief counsellor. So I guess it's both safe and tactful, from my perch in this city of cruelly procrastinated dreams, to speak of Don Cherry, *arbiter elegantiarum* of *Hockey Night in Canada*, sage of Coach's Corner and straight man for Ron MacLean. He is much in the news; there is talk that his days as the iconic resident of Coach's Corner may be coming to an end. He is also, I gather, by some weird extension of the Canadian bilingualism statutes, under some sort of review. The Commissioner of Official Languages is offering her scrutiny to some of Mr. Cherry's *obiter dicta*.

A strange thing, for a language commissioner to be analyzing the analyzer of Coach's Corner. I'm not sure what business the nation's bilingualism monitor has with the Plato of the playoffs. Whatever Don Cherry—or his faithful dog Blue, for that matter—may be doing, they are not unravelling the two-languages concept.

Parliament, even in its most liberated or unhinged deliberations, did not contemplate the commissioner's office evolving into a freelance inquisition for the furious beadles of political correctness. If this nation is in jeopardy of fracturing, look not to Coach's Corner. Try the sponsorship program.

But it is neither of these matters that has brought the familiar image of the natty, high-collared Homer of hockey onto the front pages and television screens of the country. It is, rather, an active courtship from the newly minted Conservative Party to enroll Mr. Cherry as one of its candidates. I would like to see him in Ottawa in a three-way faceoff against Richard Mahoney and the resuscitated Ed Broadbent. The inevitable candidates' debate would earn higher ratings than the Olympics, and certainly more drama.

But it cannot be. First, because Mr. Cherry has been reported as saying that he has been too long with hockey—I'm paraphrasing here—to dwindle into politics. I agree with him. From Coach's Corner to Question Period would be a subtraction of the great man's zest and energy, and a brutal contraction of his public influence.

Nor, should the Conservatives win, does the thought of Don Cherry at the cabinet table, trying to refashion Stephen

Harper into a reasonable facsimile of Ron MacLean, offer the mind any peace. In any case, politics is a tepid stew of compromise and euphemism, a nest of affectation and posturing—all genetic antimatter to His Outspokenness.

No, I applaud the Conservatives for their nerve and originality, and Stephen Harper for being man enough to contemplate his own eclipse, which would have been inevitable should Mr. Cherry have yielded to the party's entreaty.

I think the time is ripe for a different thought, not original with me, though I have brought it up before.

The co–governor generalship of Their Excellencies Adrienne Clarkson and John Ralston Saul is moving to its flashy close. An eager and anxious nation awaits a worthy successor. These are large, well-heeled and splendidly itinerant shoes to fill.

Well, Don Cherry is the obvious, the blatant, choice. It was said of Diana, that most melancholy of Cinderella-celebrities, that she was the people's princess. I do not think of Mr. Cherry as a princess, but he is the people's governor general.

The Clarkson–Ralston Saul era has left its high-toned and circumpolar imprint. We have had a governor generalship of lofty (and, let us whisper it, bloodless) pretension, a harvest time for the canapé-and-string-quartet set. It has been a Chardonnay era at Rideau Hall. It's time for some beer.

Being as he already is the impresario and master of ceremonies of the national ritual—hockey—Mr. Cherry already carries on his shoulders the mass fealty of this hockey-cherishing country. In every living room and den, in every pool hall and bar, at every checkout counter, in Tim Hortons and at Canadian Tire, Grapes—such is the affectionate diminutive of this man—is the toast of every Canadian heart.

I think he would bring to the office of governor general a kind of profile that has hitherto been only dreamed of, and a popularity not contingent on luring the country's better novelists and musicians to high tea or the annual garden party. Governor General Don Cherry. It has quite a ring to it. The Conservatives' loss will be the country's gain.

Should this come to pass, I have only one wish: to be present when the Swedish ambassador presents his or her credentials.

I see now, more than five years after writing this *homage* (as the French foppishly put it—to borrow from an old comedy album), that my hopes of seeing Grapes as our GG are dim indeed. How dim? They have yet to so much as give Mr. Cherry an Order of Merit pin. A country that does not include Don Cherry on its roll of honour doesn't have a roll of honour.

A BOSWELL'S LIFE | November 13, 2004

You are a very rich and powerful business person, a bit of a recluse, or with a severe distaste for publicity and an allergy to journalists. You hear Peter C. Newman wants to interview you, and the very notion is repellent. What's the best course of action?

Well, if you've had the chance to read *Here Be Dragons*, Mr. Newman's crowded and compelling memoir, the correct, least painful, way out of this quandary is simple. Surrender. Phone him up, right away, and get it over with.

Because if Mr. Newman really wants to interview you, you may be as secretive as a hermit, as elusive as a second-storey man, as disdainful of the press as, well, Conrad Black, but you are going to be interviewed.

He is best known in this country as the Boswell of the A-list corporate overachievers. The four volumes of *The Canadian Establishment* constitute the Debrett's of Canada's entrepreneurs. They constitute, as well, the first, and only, account of the sometimes shadowy, sometimes flamboyant people who own the big companies, live in the big mansions and exercise—by right of the power that large piles of money bestows, and the ego that usually attends the possession of both the piles and power—substantial dominion over the rest of us.

When Mr. Newman set his mind to sketching this set, his first problem was the most basic one: access. The majority of the wealthy and mighty in this country—especially at the time of Mr. Newman's self-assignment—were not (thank God) in the Donald Trump mould. Not, in other words, walking publicity sponges, puerile show-offs and addicts of the dim and dubious pleasure of seeing their names in print or their haughty, smug faces on TV. Most were (the term is seen less frequently of late) WASPs. Reticence and hauteur characterized the majority.

It is one of the delights of *Here Be Dragons* to watch Mr. Newman stalk, seduce, extort, trick and beguile those who had set their teeth against having anything to do with him. The greatest journalistic skill is not the interview; it is *getting* the interview. I've known a few journalists who were more than normally resourceful in coaxing the reluctant to the studio couch or the probing microphone, but Mr. Newman's artfulness and determination are all his own. He is a hedgehog with the cunning of a fox.

Here Be Dragons is the large book of a full life. The chronicler of others comes to the tale of himself. Ever since his flight from Europe at the age of eleven with his parents, from a beach at Biarritz in the early days of the Second World War, Mr. Newman, as he writes in a prologue, "was charged with a sense of purpose. I would search for security and stability, try to find safe haven in causes to follow and heroes to worship. By enlisting myself in the services of worthy men (and later women) who I could believe in, I would never feel so vulnerable or threatened again."

This book is the grand narrative of that search, and in one dimension of the country, ours, in which it was mainly undertaken, and in another the story of himself, the busy, sometimes turbulent professional, of the personal transit of a driven, talented, eager and alert human being. There's not a headline personality in Canada that Mr. Newman's near-half-century career in journalism hasn't encountered and mapped. *Here Be Dragons* is a very lively piece of social and political history. Mr. Newman is a one-man journalistic Niagara (twenty-two books, two million sold—and counting). He has learned this country through the people he has studied; studying himself studying them, he has drawn a thorough portrait of us both.

His signature—apart from the trademark headgear—is the monumental X-ray of our rich and mighty, the early Canadian Establishment. They are the Dragons of the current title, the remote unknown eminences behind or beyond the landscape of Canadian journalism—unknown, that is, until Newman appointed himself their naturalist.

The powerful can be shy. They must be courted to reveal themselves. The story of how he came to lure the reticent rich of the Canadian elite to his journalistic laboratory is not the smallest of this book's many pleasures. For example, he won the keystone interview for *The Canadian Establishment*, with John Angus (Bud) McDougald, by haunting the company of everyone who knew him, and floating to them wild and wilful misapprehensions of Mr. McDougald's financial worth and business dealings. Everywhere Mr. McDougald went, he was hearing of this "journalist" with the crazy estimations of his worth and practice. It took Mr. Newman the best part of a year to win it, but an invitation to Mr. McDougald's Green Pines estate was finally forthcoming. Mr. McDougald had figured out "the trick," but admired the guts behind it.

Mr. Newman's writing had its serious intent. It was not, nor was it ever meant to be, just gossip. He was propelled by a thesis: "I would document my theory that most of our destinies were governed by a shadowy group of financial manipulators I called The Canadian Establishment. I would define and detail their origins, interconnections, rivalries, prejudices, values, strengths, mercenary motives and operational codes. This would not be a bloodless audit of their common strains—this would be a journalist's exposé of who they were, what they did, and how they got away with it."

Not quite Gibbon recalling the origin of his *Decline and Fall of the Roman Empire* ("musing amidst the ruins of the Capitol, while barefoot friars were singing vespers in the Temple of Jupiter"), but there is something of a symmetry of intent here, in the sense of scope and mission, however dissimilar the canvas. Our Caligulas are smaller.

Mr. Newman seems to have come upon his distinct terrain early on. After a stint on *The Financial Post* in Toronto and Montreal, he got work at *Maclean's* in its glory days. His colleagues included Peter Gzowski and Christina McCall (his soon-to-be second wife); Pierre Berton was a senior editor, and celebrated editor Ralph Allen guided the whole rich crew. It was then that he produced his first book, a dozen profiles of prominent businessmen, *Flames of Power*, published on his twenty-ninth birthday.

A handful of zesty reviews, including one in *The Wall Street Journal*, rocketed sales and confirmed him in what turned out to be his vocation: sketching the personalities, aspirations and connections of this country's moneyed elite. He found he loved writing. And he learned he loved success in writing even more.

"Success turns a writer into a praise addict. . . . It becomes a drug, terminally unsettling to mental balance, a price I would willingly pay for the rest of my life."

A comment from one of the luminaries profiled in *Flames of Power*, E.P. Taylor, breathed the note of patterned ambivalence with which Mr. Newman's subjects came to regard him: "Well, we all know Newman is a goddammed Communist, but I'm not taking him off my Christmas card list yet."

He would rise to the editorship of *Maclean's*, and there would be many mighty detours from his dedicated trolling of the guarded waters of Canadian capitalism's master sharks. *Renegade in Power: The Diefenbaker Years*, his second book, was the one that made him. It was a pioneering piece of political journalism. It went for the guts and flavour of politics, spoken in a candour and detail that have become so commonplace it is difficult to see how original and daring they then were. It was also, typically, a monster of research and patient assembly. A thousand interviews, frequent meetings with real insiders, seventeen rewrites, ten galley proofs, and the close, creative oversight of Christina McCall went into its making. Mr. Newman doesn't produce careless books.

Renegade in Power was a publishing home run. John Diefenbaker kept six copies, one annotated on every page, while swearing he had never read it. That he resented it profoundly is understatement's understatement. In the Diefenbaker Centre at the University of Saskatchewan is a note, in the Chief's own hand, the kindest sentence of which reads, "He [Newman] is the literary scavenger of the trash baskets on Parliament Hill."

Newman sets a rich board, but for many I predict the crowning soufflé will be the chapter on Conrad Black and Barbara Amiel. If the subtitle of Newman's memoir—*Telling Tales of People, Passion and Power*—has to earn its keep, the chapter-essay on the Blacks will more than do it.

Mr. Newman has a unique purchase on this great fable of our time. He claims, not without daring, to have "invented" Conrad Black. I suspect the Lord of Crossharbour assiduously asserts that the patent on the great miracle of himself is his and his alone. But Mr. Newman, as *Maclean's* editor and as the earliest biographer of Lord Black, was one of the first amplifiers of the Black persona and had singular access at the initial stages of Lord Black's acceleration into fame, fortune and folly.

Mr. Newman's account is superior to others because he is neither clinically neutral (a rare stance in accounts of The Conrad) nor dripping with glee (a much more crowded assembly) over Lord Black's current miseries and mischiefs. In the early stages of the now-familiar rise, Mr. Newman saw much in Lord Black to admire—the potential to shatter the conventionalities of the dull Canadian business world, intellect in tandem with aspiration. This threads his account with something close to anger that Lord Black turned out to be just another acquisitive egomaniac, one with an absurd itch for archaic status, and distinguished only, as it turns out, by a more generous vocabulary than less-fluent compeers in the greed game—the CEO of, say, Enron.

When Mr. Newman is angry, his light touch and wicked pen take on a degree of flame and sharpness that make for wonderful writing. His thumbnail cameos approach a Muggeridgean callousness. Of Lord Black: "Conrad had turned himself into a latter day Citizen Kane. He looked like a young Orson Welles but behaved like an old William Randolph Hearst."

Of Barbara Amiel: "Even in repose, she was always posing, playing the femme fatale in her own movie. While she kept insisting it was her mind not her body that merited attention, it was widely suspected she was Mother Nature's little helper."

There are many, a wicked many, more. In the caustic-asides department, Mr. Newman is one with Keats: "Load every rift with ore."

Mr. Newman has gulped a lot of life. He has a taste for panorama, but it never overrules detail and individuality, the quirks and quiddities of each personality. This makes him an excellent diarist. He has a zeal for taking in the illu-minating anecdote, and a flair for reproducing it in print.

I have remarked on the frightening industry and vari-ousness of Mr. Newman's career, but there must be time to remark on the writing. He is, on the evidence of this book, a very cheerful fellow. It might seem undistinguished to call *Here Be Dragons* a "happy" book, but it is. His observations and *obiter dicta* are crafted, keen and frequently funny. They save the book from the slightest shadow of tediousness and self-absorption. He is not afraid to boast of his accomplish-ments, personal or professional, romantic or scribal, but does so with insouciance and charm. He has enjoyed his ride, is bemusedly dazzled by his success, has savoured his talents, clearly loves writing, and values the wiles and strata-gems that gave him entry where others (*Hic Sunt Dracones*) feared to tread.

He has a style that can work these various effects and responses. It can dispense an anecdote, sketch a character in a mini-essay, turn lyrical at moments of reflection or nos-talgia, and is by turns pungent and relaxed, bare for story, barbed for impact. The many, many books, the editorships and articles, have sharpened a considerable talent. He has the instinct of a gossip wedded to the mind of a true chron-icler: one who sees the arc of an age through the multitude of its particulars and personalities.

And, finally, he writes against the profound echo of what, as a child, he glimpsed and his parents felt and fled: the horror of the Second World War, and the catastrophe of the Holocaust. I have said he is cheerful, and my guess is that this is the cheerfulness of someone who has seen all that is the worst of us, felt some of it in his own Jewish legacy from those dark times, and determined there were only two faces with which to stare back at the world: an angry one or a determinedly embracing one.

He chose the latter, obviously. He is both a student of the world and—in one of his own terms—a jester. The world here is mainly, as I have said, ours, Canada. He has done a fine job of seeing a consequential part of it, has fashioned some of the very tools others in his trade now deploy. He has inflected the public record of this country, and he has lived a mixed, charming, various, replete life. He has known everyone who is anyone and passed on the highlights of that ranging acquaintance to his readers.

He has earned his cheerfulness. *Here Be Dragons* is a much more than worthy picture of ourselves, and a work of genuine wit and insight.

MICHAËLLE SHINES BY DEFAULT | October 1, 2005

I hope it's not awkward to bring this up, but the office of the governor general is a ceremonial post.

It's useful to remember this, if for no other reason than to scatter the cloud of incense hanging over the installation of Michaëlle Jean this week. The jaded cynics of the national press corps went into full rhapsody mode, with reviews of her speech that whizzed past being merely complimentary and only halted at reverential because, I suppose, there was no higher place to go.

The Globe and Mail's John Ibbitson came as close to producing a swoon in print as, outside the delicate prose of the romance novelists, it is possible to do. Of Ms. Jean he wrote, "She is the becoming Canada," a tribute made more plangent by being set off against the "old faces [and] old men" of those who hold real office in this country, one of whom—old face notwithstanding—actually appointed her.

Over at *The National Post*, the remorseless logician Andrew Coyne, who a few weeks back greeted the appointment of Ms. Jean with as blistering a denunciation as I can recall, started his piece with a surrender notice. "You are my Commander-in-Chief" was the least fervent whisper of his *billet-doux*.

All that was missing from some of the commentary was a burst of the "Hallelujah Chorus." Lawrence Martin, in *The Globe* on Thursday, essentially positioned Ms. Jean, so late of two citizenships, as a new Joan of Arc of federalism.

Her arrival on the scene would topple the separatist dream, "turning the André Boisclairs of the world into ghosts." (At the time of this writing, in October 2005, Mr. Boisclair was considered the rising star of separatism. He became leader of the Parti Québécois in 2005, but resigned in 2007 when the PQ came third in the provincial election.) Her speech, according to Mr. Martin, buried all the controversies that attended her appointment, even the one with her dressmaker. It's a rare speech that quiets the Haberdashery Wars.

This is the kind of unleashed adulation that is normally on display only in the backyard of MuchMusic when Jessica Simpson or Shania Twain pay a visit to the teenagers, and recalls nothing in the political world so much as the ancient transports of Trudeaumania.

And, lest it be forgotten in the sunrise glow of Michaëlle Jean's installation, every major speech she gives from now on, she will give as a figurehead. The voice will be hers. The words will be those of the prime minister who has dictated them. It is called the Speech from the Throne only in deference to the chair she occupies. Neither the chair nor its occupant bears blame for the prose.

Some of the response to our new governor general is easy to account for. She has immense and genuine charm. She is attractive and intelligent. As a good friend of mine from Newfoundland once said of another impressive woman—and this is a high compliment—"There are no flies on her, and if there are, they're paying rent."

Another reason is simple contrast. The real, as opposed to ceremonial, leadership of this country is woebegone and mediocre. There is something very saddening in the recollection, during the leaders' debate in the last election, of just how many in the press and the public thought that the separatist leader Gilles Duceppe was the best performer.

Mr. Duceppe is no Cicero; that he could be thought to have outshone Paul Martin, Stephen Harper and Jack Layton speaks more to the dreariness of their presentations than to the sparkle of his.

The citizens of this country have a very lively and enduring suspicion that it is one of the most favoured and fortunate nations on the Earth. But they will have to stagger their brains to remember an occasion within the past twenty years or so when any of our national leaders gave some memorable and convincing articulation of why it should be considered so.

The new governor general's speech was astonishing not in its content. In fact, in terms of one of its major themes—that the time of the "two solitudes" is past—it was seriously off-key and anachronistic. To dismiss the concept of two solitudes would have been a great line in a speech by a governor general thirty years ago. But the concept, like the phrase, is a pure museum piece.

So it wasn't the speech itself. It was the spectacle of someone at the level of national leadership at least attempting, finally, to give voice to the worth of the country, and doing so with some confidence and conviction, that dazzled spectators and commentators alike.

In the week of David Dingwall, the year of Gomery and sponsorship, the decade of no real opposition politics, even one note of something that spoke to themes larger that "gotcha" politics, partisan frenzy and the daily horrors of Question Period took on an aura of substance and nobility by default.

Make no mistake: Her Excellency gave a good speech. But it was made so much better by all the other speeches that our real leaders have not given.

THE COMPLETE SOLDIER | April 14, 2008

Rick Hillier is more popular than Avril Lavigne. But let's forget popularity, General Hillier owns a far less vaporous distinction. He is probably the most respected public figure in all the country.

It's easy to be liked when nothing's going on, and no big deal to be respected when things are calm and easy. General Hillier's standing with the Canadian public comes, however, from his service as the head of Canada's military, at a time when it is actively engaged in a still unresolved conflict, suffering the inevitable losses of real combat, in a war that claims far from universal support here in Canada. He has had what is arguably the most difficult and painful job—though for a true military man being a soldier is more of a vocation—of anyone in Canada, but from one coast to the other, from the north to the south, General Rick Hillier has earned almost universal respect and admiration.

The accomplishments of his tenure have a lot to do with this. He hauled the Canadian military out of the cellar of public opinion and from the bottom of every government's list of real priorities. Within the military and without, he refurbished its morale, bolstered its prestige. Other professions in this country are well esteemed. Soldiers are honoured.

Canada's regard for its soldiers used to be manifested almost exclusively on Remembrance Day and other ceremonial occasions. General Hillier brought that regard to every day of the living calendar. He re-cemented the connection between the military and the Canadian public. A Canadian soldier today, therefore, man or woman, in army, navy or air force, walks a little prouder, smiles a little wider, because of that strengthened connection.

General Hillier is smart, straight and knows what he wants. He works like a dog. The modern military man has to know the battlefield and warfare, but he has to be equally skilled in politics, the media, the inside arts of Parliament Hill and the twilight combats of the bureaucracy.

General Hillier has the whole package. He is distinctly unchoked by political correctness, and he could offer master classes to politicians (and journalists, too) in the almost abandoned art of saying what you mean and meaning what you say. His deepest gift, I think, was knowing what his real job was; as he's put it often, his first responsibility was to the men and women of Canada's military. He said he was working for them and their families, and they believed him. It was no pose.

Which brings me to the central characteristic of our now-departing general. He inspired trust, and people, in and out of the military, genuinely looked up to him. The

question his leaving might pose is why, in all the other public fields, and in politics, which is leadership, too, there are
not more like him. General Hillier is as large as he is—and
this is not said to his detraction—because leadership in
other areas of public life is so flat, feeble and mediocre.
Some politicians are said to have feared or envied him. They
would have feared and envied less had they tried to be bigger themselves. We can leave that for now. This is General
Hillier's moment.

I think we can all be very pleased that we have had a
public servant—for that, finally, is what a general most fundamentally is—who has elevated the service he led, and
renewed the spirits and esteem of the Canadian military,
and the spirit of esteem in which we hold them.

General Hillier is a rarity: a person in public service
who excites distinct respect and an almost populist
regard. It's interesting that—as one might say, "of all
people"—Auditor-General Sheila Fraser is another
public-servant hero—not of General Hillier's proportions, but an outstanding figure nonetheless.

CELEBRITY

LET US EXCORI8 LIVE 8 | June 25, 2005

In the realm of celebrity, Marshall McLuhan's otherwise rather naked aphorism has some application: The medium *is* the message. Britney Spears is a celebrity because she is a celebrity. Paris Hilton, Madonna—these are the great vessels of the vacant idea of our times. Famous for being famous. The essence of celebrity is to maintain celebrity. Celebrities "do" things (sing badly, act poorly, dress strangely or not at all, talk rudely, smuggle dead raccoons onto talk shows), not for the sake of these things themselves, but as "hooks" to keep the cameras trained on them, to feed their gluttonous narcissism.

Fame is not an accomplishment; it is a need. So it is an axiom that what a celebrity does always has a primary reference to his or her celebrity, and is connected only secondarily, and at a distant remove, to the actual thing done. For reference, contemplate, as we did last week, poor Sean Penn putting together his own *Coles Notes* on the Iranian elections.

For more current reference, let us turn to the so-called Live 8, the "world" concert taking place in several venues on the day of the G8 summit in Scotland. Behind this sing-along are no lesser eminences than the chicly ubiquitous Bono and the one-time singer from the Boomtown Rats, the now-ennobled Bob Geldof.

It's an internationalist soiree, a kind of postmillennial reprise of the Band Aid and Live Aid concerts Sir Bob, when he was just Mr. Bob, put on some twenty years ago for the relief of famine in Ethiopia, and which gave the world the Dickensian treacle of "Do They Know It's Christmas?" and accumulated close to $100 million in aid for Africa.

This time around, Bono and Sir Bob are aiming for something rather different. These two have extended their celebrity by straddling the world of pop music and the high conference altitudes of Davos and the G8 summits.

Bono, in particular, has become something of a self-appointed, free-floating superstar-as-ambassador. He has long since won Paul Martin as a buddy, and is on a first-name basis with the leadership in dozens of countries.

Sir Bob seems a more moody, brittle sort than Bono, as evidenced this week by a lecture he gave to Bono's buddy, Paul: that if Canada wasn't going to live up to its commitment of 0.7 per cent of GNP to foreign aid, then he, Mr. Martin, shouldn't come to the G8 summit at all.

I don't know, precisely, when the alumnus of the Boomtown Rats (and composer of "The Chains of Pain" and "My Birthday Suit") was put in charge of the guest list at the G8, and, I suspect surprisingly, neither does the hectoring ("Too Late God") Sir Bob. It strikes me as impertinence swaddled in righteousness. It's probably a punk thing.

What do they think this scattered concert is supposed, really, to do? What link do a bunch of celebrities singing passé songs—in Barrie or Paris—have to do with the politics or the development of Africa? Inevitably, the feeble and hoary answer will come back that the concerts "raise awareness." Awareness of what? Awareness of Bob Geldof and Bono, mainly.

For that matter, how exactly does one sing "for" a country? And what possible connection does this live singing, or Céline Dion offering her anorexic nimbus via satellite from Las Vegas to a giant screen in Barrie, have with the meeting of the leaders of the G8 nations in Scotland?

Tens of thousands of people jam Highway 401 to head up to Barrie to attend a summer concert that has "8" in its title, co-hosted by the roadkill comic Tom Green. What happens after the last chord is sounded? Does Zimbabwe cease its infernal turmoils? Does the protracted slaughter in Darfur shut down for the night? Does the World Bank dismantle itself, the UN find a purpose, and the myriad aid agencies of the planet suddenly find a moral force that, pre-singalong, was out of their grasp?

Of course not. *Entertainment Tonight* and its grisly clones go mad with coverage and "exclusives"; the glossy magazines, *The View* and assorted megaphones of the celebrity set tell us who was wearing what, who stayed where and who did what with whom.

But, in the end, it will be just one more self-absorbed, pretentious, hollow celebrity shtick, another moment for ex–punk stars and rock maestros in decline to strut before the world's lights and cameras for a moment more.

Celebrity will seek more celebrity, and when the hits start to fade, celebrity will discover a cause. That's all Live 8 is, and that is all it and its successors will ever be. The pop-star missionary is a contradiction in terms. As well as a furious irony.

And Paul, you go to that summit, regardless of what the rude Mr. Geldof has to say.

Well, that really worked. All the yodelling and speechifying up in Barrie, Ontario put an end to the world's woes, and as the slogan of the day promised, poverty is now history. Thank God for Bono and Dan Aykroyd. I hope people kept the colourful wristbands. A relic of the Live 8 concert is an *Entertainment Tonight*'s version of a splinter of the true cross.

Were poverty ever to return, and I can't really see that, I'm sure someone somewhere has a CD of the concert and can haul it out to exorcise world misery all over again. I think what we really need now, however, is another, all-new concert to save us from global warming and peanut allergies. And we'll need different wristbands too. Each new apocalypse averted by rock stars should have its own wristband. Hand-me-downs are for losers.

A SAINT SORELY TAXED | October 17, 2006

It's nice to see that Madonna has come down from her neon cross—a Las Vegas–looking crucifixion of the emphatically Material Girl was part of the safe shock of her recent tour. After all, if you can't blaspheme Christianity these days, what can you blaspheme?

Now she's descended on Africa, following the trendy, spangled footsteps of Brad and Angelina and other monstrously rich celebrities who have turned Africa and its misery into their own publicity-fat conscience theme park. They should start a foundation: good deeds that make it to *Entertainment Tonight*, adoptions that land you the cover of *People* magazine.

Madonna, her entourage, her private jet and Guy Ritchie have plucked one African baby from an orphanage, and the world is all a-twitter at another celebrity good deed. The story is almost big enough to drown out the news that U2, the rock band, has moved some of its assets from its native Ireland to the Netherlands. The

Netherlands has a very favourable tax rate, even better than Ireland, which for artists is already a tax haven of unimaginable indulgence.

U2 is, of course, Bono's band, Bono, the greatest scold of rich governments on the face of the earth. Bono was the man who nagged Paul Martin in public for Canada's not giving enough for African debt relief, but then, Bono—friend of Bill Clinton, consort of the princes of the world, World Economic Forum attendee, gazillionaire—nags everyone about Africa. He even read the riot act of liberal outrage to his own government because the Irish government, like Canada, was slack on debt relief for Africa. Uriah Heap with groupies.

Bono and his multimillionaire bandmates have hauled their songwriting business out of Ireland because Ireland has modestly upped the tax levy on artists making over half a million a year. So he wants Ireland to give more of its taxes to help poor Africa, but he, Bono, wants to pay less in taxes to Ireland. I'd call him a whited sepulchre, except that's a biblical reference, and Madonna would probably claim copyright.

Bono did not hesitate, at a concert here last year around election time, to tag Paul Martin, his friend, for not living up to his pledge to increase Canada's foreign aid. Bono said he was crushed. Well, I guess the "Make Poverty History" front-man has less trouble with inconsistency and hypocrisy when it's his bank account and those of his bandmates that actually take the hit. Yet Bono's been shining his rock-star celebrity halo so assiduously in public that you'd think he was a cross between Mother Theresa and Cardinal Léger.

This guy has been lecturing whole continents for decades—he's the self-declared pope of poverty—about Africa, but now hauls part of his empire from his home country to Amsterdam. Lecture us no more, Mr. Bono. A tax haven is not a pulpit. Amsterdam is not an African village. However, all is not lost. Maybe Bono will adopt someone. Let us pray—let us *all* pray—it's Madonna. They deserve each other.

EGO WARRIORS | July 14, 2007

The reviews are in concerning last weekend's eco-sanctimony staged by global warming's Nostradamus, Al Gore, and most of them aren't pretty. It was, according to the advance hype—and the hype for this event matched anything Hollywood revs up for Johnny Depp in a bandana or a new Jessica Simpson big-screen onslaught—going to command an audience in excess of two billion.

There is nothing original in rounding up a beaker full of rock stars and movie celebrities, faded songsters and a rapper or two to variously strum, gyrate and posture for a *cause du jour*. We have had "We Are the World" and Live Aid, Willie Nelson doing his minstrel bit for the American farmer, and last year's care-a-palooza, the Make Poverty History jamboree, which didn't.

NBC devoted three hours of prime time to last Saturday's effort, which trawled a measly 2.7 million viewers, a number that would be embarrassing for a home-cooking show or a rerun of *Three's Company*. Not even such A-list, world-dominating entertainers as Madonna and Shakira, assisted by those cleavage climatologists the Pussycat Dolls, could lure the torpid and the unaware, in any numbers, to the home screen. Nor could Snoop Dogg (the bard of "Nuthin' but a 'G' Thang"), appearing on stage in Hamburg (Hamburg? Who knew?) jolt the singalong into a zone of even mild, credible buzz.

What happened?

I suppose the spectacle of the world's most wasteful people, rock-star plutocrats with their cribs and bling, caravans of trailer trucks and 100,000-watt amplifiers, taking a day out of their wealth-stuffed lives to preach to the less well off of the world on the moral importance of consuming less "to save the planet" set the hypocrisy bar so high that it put too great a strain on the digestion of ordinary people. In the wicked words of one rock star who declined to climb aboard the bandwagon, "Private jets for climate change."

Unless outfitted with a cast-iron stomach—and I mean a real one—how could anybody endure Madonna of the Nine Mansions wrapping herself in the ascetics of the eco-movement? Hyper-indulgent, super-pampered, colossally wealthy, manically consumerist entertainment celebrities preaching restraint to others: Live Earth was a weird and monstrous journey to a whole new dimension of live irony. Come back, Uriah Heep. All is forgiven.

Not even the professional environmentalists could stay their gorge at Madonna's participation. They gave the world the news that the Material Girl owns shares in the most politically incorrect enterprises, such as Alcoa, the American aluminum giant, the Ford Motor Company and Weyerhaeuser, which—gasp!—chops trees for money.

Then there was the sheer, deep folly of it all. What has Shakira, or her hips, got to offer on the question of the world's weather over the next hundred years? But Shakira is Robert Oppenheimer on steroids compared with Geri Halliwell of the long-forgotten fluff band the Spice Girls—"Yo, I'll tell you what I want, what I really, really want, etc., etc., etc., etc."

Geri Halliwell, Snoop Dogg, Shakira, Madonna and the Pussycat arborists are an unlikely think tank (maybe a think tank top?) on global warming or anything else. They are career publicists of themselves, artists in the merchandising of fluff and ego.

But beyond the obvious hypocrisy, beyond the saccharine, Mickey Rooneyesque "let's put on a show" conceit of the Live Earth dud-spectacular, I think something rather deeper and, perhaps grimly encouraging, accounts for its failure.

The public has just gotten tired of "stars." These luminescent bodies are now in much the same leaky boat as most politicians because, by trying to wed themselves to some aspects of politics to strengthen or underwrite their highly capitalist careers, they are seen as manipulative in precisely the same cynical way politicians are. Entertainers are, primarily, politicians of their own careers.

They don't have the "cred" they used to have. They have been exposed as shills for themselves before anything else. And so it's not the elephantine "carbon footprint" of Madonna or the big bands that turned people away from Live Earth. It's the growing perception that all the strutting icons up there on all those stages are playing a game, just as the politicians play a game, and for very much the same self-serving, egoistic reasons.

It's an *Animal Farm* moment for our time: "The creatures outside looked from pig to man, and from man to pig, and from pig to man again; but already it was impossible to say which was which."

Now it's impossible to say which are the stars and which are the politicians. Madonna and Gore—can you spot the difference?

Al Gore is still talking, but I think his moment too— as politician who morphed into the less demanding though more remunerative role of celebrity—is either passing or passed. Al doesn't generate the "vibe" anymore. Celebrity is rocket fuel—it is very high-octane stuff—but for all but the most skillful or lucky it's only good for a short, fast rise. Al will still trot—or private jet—the world, and play John the Baptist for the coming global warming Armageddon. He's still good for a walk-on at an awards show—Snoop Dogg presents, Lindsay Lohan is in the wings—and a head-liner at some conference of the perpetually and pro-fessionally worrying class. The Nobel Prize was his apogee, and even that moment didn't have the feel of real, class-A achievement. Is it because the Nobel itself is a decaying gold star? Or is it because there was something just a little too neat, maybe compen-satory, about awarding the world's bluest blue ribbon to the man who lost—dare we write the name—to the "witless" George W. Bush?

THERE'S SOMETHING ABOUT CASSANDRA | November 1, 2008

Where is Cameron Diaz? Haven't seen—and, worse, haven't heard from—her in so long a while. Has she been disappeared? Is she in Guantanamo, the Bush-Cheney gulag for dissident celebrities?

A little more than four years ago, on a panel boasting the finest minds the world has known since the days of ancient Athens, when Socrates was tutoring Plato, Ms. Diaz was offering advice on the coming election between George Bush and John Kerry.

The setting was the daily edification we all know and love as *The Oprah Winfrey Show*. The grand empath, her Oprahness, had designed a program to stir the youth of America to vote, and crowded onto the couch (besides Ms. Diaz) an almost frightening constellation of intelligence and prestige.

There was Sean Combs, a putty artist of nomenclature, whom you may know as Puff Daddy, P. Diddy, Puffy, Diddy, Daddy Piff or Diddy Puff. The backup intellects for the occasion, doo-woppers for Mr. Diddy's famous Vote or Die campaign, were Christina Aguilera and Drew Barrymore.

Think of it as a symphony of mind.

It was the sylphlike Ms. Diaz who most lucidly framed the choice between George (Neanderthal, Halliburton, frat boy, Karl Rove puppet, tool of Big Oil, IQ of a lug wrench) Bush and John (elegant) Kerry. She issued a warning to the timid and vacant minds of young America, especially to the female half of that monstrous demographic: "If you think rape should be legal, then don't vote!"

And lest that wouldn't hold their attention—the young of America are notoriously detached—the delectable Cassandra who had transfixed the world in *There's Something About Mary* further cautioned that they "could lose the right to their bodies." Which would be inconvenient.

America didn't listen that day—at least, young America didn't. George (amoeba, cretin, theocrat, warmonger) Bush defeated John (sweet) Kerry, rape has been legal in that despoiled country for four years, and millions of young women have had to get government permission to use their bodies for anything—getting out of bed, going to a global warming protest, dropping by Starbucks or attending the MTV Awards (where a body is an absolute must—although there's a cover charge on the brain).

We haven't heard from Ms. Diaz this cycle, which is such a shame. Maybe she's just tired. Or taken up macramé. Speaking Bluetooth to power can drain the old soul. But America is nothing if not the country of renewal. If one oracle vanishes, another leaps from the self-help rack at Barnes and Noble, or from the back pages of the better fashion magazines.

The Cameron Diaz of the 2008 election—and, need I say, supporter of Barack (cool, mesmeric, "thrill up my leg," hope, change, new dawn, better dawn, dawn all day) Obama is Erica Jong. Ms. Jong wrote a book called *Fear of Flying*, which is to literature what *Charlie's Angels* is to theology.

But Ms. Jong is, make no mistake about it, a seer and guru of Diaz-like dimensions. She hangs about with an almost equally illustrious crowd, numbering such geopolitical high foreheads as Jane (Hanoi, exercise videos, Ted Turner) Fonda and Naomi (Al Gore's "earth tones" clothing consultant, author of *The Treehouse*) Wolf as among her fellow thinkers.

Ms. Jong, and God bless her courage, issued a warning this week—via the Italian press, where the Apocalypse (not surprisingly) has its own feature page—that should Barack Obama lose the election on Tuesday, "blood will run in the streets." Fearful that that was a tad ambiguous, she—this was the novelist in her breaking out—referenced America's founding trauma.

"If Obama loses, it will spark the second American Civil War." There you have it. Vote for Barack Obama, or Gettysburg will have a sequel, and poor Ken Burns will have to do that damn series all over again. The stakes are high. You betcha. (And, oh yes, Jane Fonda's having "back pains" just thinking about this. Which probably means she should stop thinking with her back, but I digress.)

Well, we all know what happened when America ignored Cameron Diaz four years ago. Global warming, Katrina, stock-market meltdown and, of course, that rape thing. The question is, will Americans similarly ignore the prescience of the artist who gave the world the concept of a "zipless fuck"?

I cannot think it will. America will not a second time be heedless. There will not be blood on the streets. No second Civil War. And America, and Barack Obama, will have no one to thank for it but Erica Jong, and the immortal slogan: Save Jane's Back—Vote Obama. Intellect will out: John McCain and Sarah Palin are toast.

In my books, this is right up there with Cameron Diaz. Sigh.

Among the many blessings, uncounted till this very moment, of the election of Barack Obama to the American presidency, are the reduction in Jane Fonda's "back pains" and the averting of the second American Civil War. I do not know which of this two history will choose to merit the superior wreath in Obama's civil crown. For, insomuch as he has stayed a scene of civil slaughter—at least according to Erica Jong and the illuminati of *The View*—he must be regarded as a true American hero. But to have assuaged the ravages wrought by years of producing exercise videos (Jane Fonda was the spandex queen of losing weight by televised exhibition) in which she so aerobically starred, to have reduced Jane Fonda's back pain, is an accomplishment from which Clio may stagger back in bewildered amazement. The goddess of History probably has no scale in which to enter achievement of this magnitude.

And good news for Cameron Diaz—Bush is gone and rape is, once more, illegal. Making statements of pathetic ignorance is, however, as legal as ever.

CARTOON CRISIS

UNDER THE COVER OF FAITH | February 11, 2006

The casual understanding of what is being called the cartoon crisis is fairly straightforward. A Danish newspaper published twelve cartoons that depicted the Prophet Mohammed. Two in particular stood out: one featured the Prophet wearing a "bomb" turban, the other featured him on a cloud meeting three suicide bombers arriving (we presume) in Paradise with the line, "Stop, stop, we ran out of virgins!"

The cartoons, measured by a secular, Western yardstick, were not exceptional. A few were mere stylized representations. The pictures were not ferocious caricatures—compared with the ferocious U.K. Cartoon of the Year of Ariel Sharon eating Palestinian babies, they were timid and innocuous.

By the standards of a moderate religious sensibility, they were irreverent. By the standards of Muslim sensibility, they were beyond question blasphemous and insulting. The cartoons' blasphemy does not hang on what many are calling the absolute prohibition against any picturing of the Prophet. The question of whether the Prophet may be represented in images or art is, I gather, not as determinatively settled as a lot of news accounts casually suggest. They are blasphemous because in Islam, as in fact in many or all the world's main religions, mocking, deriding or disrespectfully or perversely invoking the deity is a definition of blasphemy.

Portions of the West may have forgotten what blasphemy is. The entertainment industry, with reference to Christianity in particular, seems never to have either known or cared. A picture of Kanye West wearing a crown of thorns, on the cover of *Rolling Stone*, is a blasphemy. The infamously celebrated *Piss Christ*—a crucifix in a jar of urine—is blasphemous even to my lapsed sensibility. And, of course, there's Madonna's career.

The Danish cartoons were published in September 2005 in Denmark, but the uproar over them—the simultaneous protests, riots and embassy-burnings they are said to have sparked—only reached a peak now, five months later. Most people reading the news may have wondered why there was such a gap between the publication and the outrage. And why, amid so many other quarrels between the West and the Muslim world, these twelve cartoons were capable of stirring such violent passions.

Part of the answer, and it seems to me an important point to underscore, is that it is not just the original twelve cartoons, but at least three others—all more offensive than any of the originals. One shows the Prophet with a pig's snout, one features bestiality, another pedophilia.

These three were included in a "dossier" compiled by an imam in Denmark who took a tour of Muslim countries, showing them to state and religious leaders. Since that tour, he has been interviewed on Danish television about the additions, and one of the more insulting images has been shown to have been doctored.

We are not free to subtract this element from an account of the outrage. If there has been manipulation in the Muslim world of this story, and additionally, if more corrosive images have been deliberately added to the originals, corrosive images designed by their greater graphic and scatological detail to make outrage all but inescapable, then it is not just a story about twelve cartoons about Mohammed published in a Danish newspaper. It may be a bigger story about quite cynical and duplicitous manipulation, founded on a kernel of reality, then amplified with more explosive material and fed into the context of suspicion, friction and misunderstanding between the West and the Muslim world.

If some Muslims are reacting to more than the pictures in a Danish newspaper, if they are reacting to strategically gathered, supplementary pictures of unqualified venom and uncompromising insult, placed before the Muslim world by the Danish imam, then the calls for apology from Western authorities are both premature and incomplete.

A story that looked like a spontaneous combustion between Western free speech and Muslim religiosity may contain more sly politics and subtle incitement than most headlines acknowledged. The Danish cartoonists may have supplied an occasion for much mischief, but the deeper mischief, it may turn out, was not their cartoons, but the supplemented dossier, the more gruesome and insulting representations associating their Prophet with truly unspeakable circumstances.

There is very much to be said about the contest, or friction, between the foundational democratic principle of free speech and the absolutes of religious belief.

I am far from convinced, however, that in this "cartoon debate" one faction has not attempted to rig the facts and—in part—achieve political goals under the cover of faith. If that is so, there's a blasphemy all will agree on.

In the multitude of articles and Internet postings about the cartoon crisis, from the moment riots ensued and some of the cartoonists found their lives in jeopardy, it remains very surprising that the point made above, of how the crisis was managed, and in particular of how the three additional more-scurrilous-by-far drawings were inserted into the original twelve, is so rarely mentioned.

If there was genuine "rage" in what is too loosely called the Muslim world that rage was stimulated more by the fake inserts than the original cartoons. And they were inserted by those who first wanted to foment outrage, and who acted subsequently as spokespersons for the "Muslim community."

There was manipulation of the data, as the scientists say, interference with the actual occasion for the event. Parts of this crisis were in this sense a fraud. Why this point is not emphasized escapes me. Almost equally puzzling is why—with the original cartoons easily accessible on the Internet—they have not universally been judged as being, by the standards of modern caricature, as infinitely innocuous and bland. Certainly, not riot or fatwa material.

THE CASE OF SALMAN RUSHDIE IS FRESH AGAIN | February 24, 2006

Everyone will recall that when Salman Rushdie published *The Satanic Verses*, which contained what has been described as an irreverent depiction of the Prophet Mohammed, he became the object of a death sentence.

No less a figure than the spiritual leader of Iran, Ayatollah Ruhollah Khomeini, issued a fatwa requiring Mr. Rushdie's execution, and the execution of all who had been involved in publishing the book, and called upon all "zealous Muslims" to pursue this grim end. This was not just a piece of token bluster on the Ayatollah's part. It might be useful to recall the language of the edict: "In the name of God Almighty. There is only one God, to whom we shall all return. I would like to inform all intrepid Muslims in the world that the author of the book entitled *The Satanic Verses,* which has been compiled, printed, and published in opposition to Islam, the Prophet, and the Koran, as well as those publishers who were aware of its contents, have been sentenced to death. I call on all zealous Muslims to execute them quickly, wherever they find them, so that no one will dare insult the Islamic sanctities. Whoever is killed on this path will be regarded as a martyr, God willing. In addition, anyone who has access to the author of the book, but does not possess the power to execute him, should refer him to the people so that he may be punished for his actions." It may also be useful to remember that, although Mr. Rushdie went into hiding and was under armed guard for years and has (so far) survived, others were not so fortunate. There were riotous protests in India, Pakistan and Egypt that caused several deaths, and Mr. Rushdie's Norwegian publisher, William Nygaard, barely survived an assassination attempt.

Nothing in the modern culture of the West prepares us to comprehend the notion that a person can and should be sentenced to death for what that person writes, or that treats the publication of a novel, however poorly written, as, in itself, a capital crime.

Everything written, if it has anything in it, will offend someone, and if the mere taking of offence were to amount to a licence to kill the offender, well, the world would be sadly underpopulated of novelists, columnists, bloggers and the writers of editorials.

The publication of twelve cartoons in a Danish newspaper has triggered an even greater firestorm in portions of the Muslim world. There have been bomb threats against the newspaper; on Thursday, in Gaza, masked gunmen threatened to kidnap European citizens and to target European offices; protesters in Pakistan took to chanting "Death to France" and "Death to Denmark," and, on an official level, there have been calls from several governments in the Arab world to shut down the "offending" newspaper and fire its editor.

The connection with the Rushdie case is clear. Whole swaths—not all, be it noted—of the Muslim world believe that if their religious sensibilities are offended, they have both the right and the duty to threaten violence and death to those they choose to regard as offenders. They demand retraction and apology and trail their demands with threats of kidnapping and death.

Furthermore, they insist that their values and their codes apply outside their own religion and their own countries. The insolence of such demands is astonishing. Considering the treatment that the press in some of these countries accord Christians and Jews—a recent mini-series on the Protocols of the Elders of Zion aired in Lebanon and Egypt, the frequent anti-Semitic editorial cartoons in major newspapers—it is levitatingly hypocritical, as well.

It is worth noting that, however offensive the cartoons of the Prophet may have been, they cannot be as offensive as the many real suicide bombings that have been executed in the Prophet's name. If portions of the Muslim world want to protest about a real offence against their religion, they might radically take to the streets in great masses to condemn what fanatics do in the name of their religion.

All this is occurring in the wake of yet another searing illustration of the clash between fundamentalist Islam and Europe: the murder of Dutch filmmaker Theo van Gogh, who was killed in 2004 by a Dutch Muslim extremist angered by the filmmaker's depictions of Islam.

Artists, writers and the press in Western democracies have the right to create and write what they please. And so they must. It is why we are democratic. And no fundamentalism, of religion or any other variety, should be given the slightest leverage over that right.

It is not one of the many refreshments of irony that whenever, here in the West, we hear of some desperately out-of-date school board, or some "backwoods" librarian ruling a progressive book on sexuality "unsuitable" for certain age groups, or there is "resistance" to some of the more graphic "lifestyle guides," all hell, so to speak, breaks out from the artistic and social activist camps. Prophecies of "theocracy rampant" rend the tormented skies, Hollywood types lend their plastic credibility to a fundraiser against censorship. But a filmmaker gets stabbed to death in Holland, or Hirsi Ali wanders the world hedged with bodyguards, or innocuous cartoonists are under death sentence—all instances of a blatant real-time theocratic view of the world—and the silence of the progressives is deafening. Someone should make a movie about it.

COMING TO A HUMAN RIGHTS COMMISSION NEAR YOU |
January 26, 2008

Our esteemed human rights commissions are so busy these days, it worries me. The number of these gimlet-eyed scrutineers is, after all, finite.

There is, therefore, only a limited store of intellectual energy and moral fervour for them to call upon. In a brutish world, righteousness is not inexhaustible; virtue, like oil, has its peak moments and, with their current agenda, Canada's HRCs may run out of fuel.

Alberta's human rights commission, one of the keenest, a noble avatar of those old censor boards that used to guard public libraries from "steamy" literature and "brazen" language, is trying to contain—I think that is the only proper verb here—Ezra Levant.

Mr. Levant has, as the jargon expresses it, "gone before" the commission to answer for the putative crime, offence, tastelessness of his (now-defunct) magazine's, the *Western Standard*, publication of the Mohammed cartoons. But even the sturdiest tribunal can summon forces too large for it to manage. And even the deepest probing commissioner, alert as a tuning fork to the harmonies of political correctness, should have quailed before the thought of putting Ezra Levant under state-mandated interrogation.

His initial hearing is an Internet hit. He videotaped it, you see, and, against the urgings of the commission, placed in on the World Wide Web.

His performance, a marathon aria to free speech, looks to outpace even Jessica Alba beach footage as a web draw. More than 400,000 visitors have YouTubed Mr. Levant (a Daniel, I say, a Daniel come to judgment on Canadian free speech!). He is as a tidal wave breaking against a lone and solitary craft.

So, Alberta's HRC is, to put it timidly, busy with Ezra Levant. And now, three others have had the courage, folly, zeal, or, if you wish, the zealously courageous foolishness, to take on *Maclean's* magazine and Mark Steyn. The martyrs in question are, respectively, the Ontario, B.C. and federal HRCs. It's a busy time in the world of magazine censorship—and a bull market for the litigious and offended. John Donne comes to mind: "Lawyers find out still litigious men, whom quarrels move," and, if you are both, well, Canada is ripe with HRCs that want your business.

The question is, of course, does an HRC, or even a pack of them, really want to take on an institution as beloved as *Maclean's?* Next only to the Eaton's catalogue of sacred memory, *Maclean's* is a talisman of the Canadian way, it is Tim Hortons in print. For more than a century, *Maclean's* has stimulated minds, its back copies have intellectualized many a dental crisis; rolled up, it has been the fly swatter of choice for thousands. Approach *Maclean's* at your peril.

But, in addition, do they really want—after Ezra's example, mind you—to call Mark Steyn, the Victoria Falls ("The Smoke That Thunders") of prolific columnists, into one of their styleless chambers to "explain himself"? If Mr. Levant contains multitudes, how to describe Mr. Steyn? He is a prodigy of immense resource and industry. Compared to him, Trollope was a slacker, Dickens a wastrel, and Proust a miniaturist. He inundates. Books, columns, blogs and obiter dicta in a thousand venues—if Mr. Steyn goes before one or all of these commissions, he will be firing off columns between questions. He'll write a column on a question while it is being asked. I urge our guardians to consider their own interests: stay a while before essaying this profitless and useless venture.

A *Maclean's*/Steyn confrontation, in tandem with the prairie whirlwind we all know as Levant rampant—this is too much at one time for the meticulous and tidy tribunals that alone are our guardians against every stray thought that might fracture our fabulously delicate Canadian sensibilities. While they are preoccupied with Steyn-Levant;

overwhelmed, exhausted and undone by Steyn-Levant; battered, borne-down on and befuddled by Steyn-Levant; who will watch out . . . for us?

Who will there be to read before we read, and tell us what is proper for us? Who will there be to edit the editors, to copy check the copy checkers? Who will shield our vulnerable law students, and who will tend to the commission's most industrious serial complainant? There is one person so eggshell brittle that he has drummed up a fierce amount of business for the HRCs. Is so loyal a customer now to be ignored because the Steyn-Levant tsunami is about to rumble mercilessly on shore?

Mostly I fear that, if the HRCs are tied up, Canadians will be reading, unguided, what they choose to read, deciding for themselves what they like and what they don't, discarding a book or passing it to a friend, liking a column or cursing one, lit only by the light of their own reason.

The horror! Before we know it, we'll have an unstoppable epidemic of free speech, free thought and freedom of the press. And, surely, no one wants that. Otherwise, why would we have human rights commissions?

Canada's human rights commissions are a blight and an absolute contradiction in terms. They are not about "human rights." They are censor boards, vehicles of activist politics masquerading as "judicial" tribunals. They are riven with an unspoken agenda, procedureless and grotesquely unfair, and structurally biased against anyone who falls under their determined gaze. They are an offence against Canadian democracy. (See also the section beginning on page 252.)

It has been very pleasing to see how vigorous has been the resistance to the notion that Canadians, in their exercise of the right to free speech, free thought and a free press, have to genuflect to the rulings of provincial or federal human rights commissions. It is less pleasing that it has not been even more vigorous. Two people, both of them highlighted in the piece above, have been the most durable and worthy champions of real freedom of speech, and the most durable and worthy opponents of the commission commissars: Ezra Levant and Mark Steyn.

Ezra Levant has shown the fortitude of a lion and the tenacity of a bulldog in his contest against the state's bureaucratic infringement of democracy's most fundamental concept. It is too bad that because Mr. Levant is self-identified as a conservative his efforts are seen or painted as a partisan campaign. Though to be fair, many from a part of the political spectrum Mr. Levant would never visit have had the wideness of mind to support him. He has waged a costly and I am certain an emotionally draining war, and he has waged it on first principles. He deserves great respect for this.

Mark Steyn, as I took care to note, is relentless in this cause. And he is right, which is even more important. His "visibility" gave a charge to the campaign against Section 13, and his appearances before the B.C. Commission, on TVOntario, and subsequently before a committee of the Ontario legislature, gave energy and style to the cause. It does not matter what Mark Steyn's politics are: on this issue he is defending a concept that enables the idea of politics. The two of them deserve an Order of Canada citation for their work, and a generous country would throw in a good party for the both of them after the award as well.

OBAMA RISING

Mention John Kennedy and most people will quickly recall the famous line, "Ask not what your country can do for you; ask what you can do for your country." I am not sure why this is so.

To begin with, the line was not his own. It is commonly ascribed to his courtly speechwriter, Ted Sorensen. But even were it really Mr. Kennedy's, it is still difficult to see why it clots the pages of every modern quotation book and is so often invoked as a touchstone of public eloquence.

It is clumsy, for one thing. "Ask not what your country can do for you" is a very odd sequence in modern English. You don't run into a lot of "ask nots" these days. "Ask not" is an idiom of a time long gone; it has the feel of the overtly poetic about it, the fake suede of greeting-card prose.

The best we can say of Kennedy/Sorensen is that at least they were trying. Mr. Kennedy was still alert to the rapidly thinning air of a quite ancient tradition: one that understood that public utterance, especially on ceremonial occasions, should strive for elevation, elegance and dignity. Mr. Kennedy may have been the last major leader in the West to carry that ambition. In his case, it probably survived because he was a leader who grew up under the long shadow of Winston Churchill, one of history's great word-smiths, a man to whom leadership was inseparable from the ability to fashion speech, to draw from words something of their elemental power to bind and inspire.

The energy with which Mr. Churchill composed his illustrious speeches is common knowledge. So, also, is the care he gave to his studiously offhand or "spontaneous" remarks, jibes and witticisms. One of those same witticisms tells us so: "I'm just preparing my impromptu remarks." Mr. Churchill represents the end of that great tradition, which is at least as old as the great Latin and Greek orators.

Abraham Lincoln is perhaps his only superior, for his oratory had a lyric and affecting quality that Mr. Churchill's did not. Mr. Churchill could stir: he was a master of the sonorous and martial mode. Mr. Lincoln could move: much of his language had the subtlety and strange power we associate more with poetry than the platform. Mr. Lincoln was quiet and deep. Mr. Churchill reached for the accents of defiance and glory—as he said himself, to "give the lion's roar."

The volumes of Brian Mulroney and Jean Chrétien are

now competing in our nation's bookstores, but we shall not be going to them to savour or resavour favoured passages from some of their most memorable speeches. That's because there aren't any, which is not as dismissive as it sounds. It may still be possible for leaders to write and give great speeches—Vaclav Havel certainly tried during his tenure—but it is getting more difficult with each advancing year. There was no evidence, for instance, of any exertion toward eloquence in this week's Throne Speech, whose entire elegance was contained in the person who read it.

We are in the culture of the sound bite. We remember of Mr. Mulroney his onslaught against John Turner ("You had a choice, sir . . ."), just as of Mr. Chrétien we recall a telling and petty riposte ("For me, pepper, I put it on my plate.") Considering the great number of debates in which these two participated, the number of state occasions during which they spoke, this is a pathetic harvest.

The premiers fare no better. Dalton McGuinty, Jacques Parizeau or Ralph Klein, to take but three large names, may all be remembered in time, but they will not cheat oblivion because they crowded the public mind with imperishable speech.

It is not, by any means, all their fault. Mr. Churchill spoke in an age, despite its horrors, more confident of its public men, and during a time when politics itself still retained some association with noble practice. He could speak the largest of words—such as "honour" and "country"—and make appeals to the glory of his people, and neither those words nor appeals sounded hollow in his mouth.

Today, the large words have shrunk, and even in their shrunken stature do not fall obligingly from lips that have had them "poll-tested" and "focus-grouped" beforehand. Even in the many debates we have had on Afghanistan, I cannot recall any sentiment expressed touched with the fineness and depth of that most honourable undertaking.

From Lincoln's day to ours, soapbox to satellite, the means of communication have proliferated. Yet, not even Google will search up a more affecting and noble tribute than a few words spoken at Gettysburg nearly a century and a half ago.

Modern words can blanket the whole world in an instant, and that is as long as most of them will endure. They steal from light nothing but its speed.

It is, to my taste anyway, one of the most interesting questions associated with Barack Obama's ascendancy into American politics: whether Mr. Obama's almost single-handed revival of the set speech marks something of a return to what many had thought—in this text-messaging, TV-saturated, electronic age—was the utterly defunct practice of stage oratory.

Marshall McLuhan and other masters of vague speculation thought that TV (the Internet had not yet been spawned) had killed the speech. My intuition suggests quite otherwise. The speech, and the ancient unkillable art of demagoguery which is its malign offspring, may find new vigour, and deeper application in the wild regions of twenty-first-century communication. Words are older than the many BlackBerrys and text-messages that maul them, and far more potent.

ONLY WORDS | February 23, 2008

> "I gotta use words when I talk to you."
> —T.S. Eliot, *Sweeney Agonistes*

The marathon battle between Hillary Clinton and Barack Obama for the Democratic presidential nomination is already one of the great political dramas of our time.

More than any other element, more than money, organization or endorsements, what has carried Mr. Obama from relative obscurity and being a hundred-to-one shot at surviving even a month in the primaries to celebrity and front-runner status is his ability to speak on a platform. He is the front-runner over . . . Hillary Clinton!

He has overtaken a household-name candidate who began with every advantage: heaps of money; a set of professionals second to none; a husband regarded as the best natural politician of his generation; and the expectation of most seasoned observers in the press and elsewhere that the nomination was hers.

This was a lot to displace on the strength of one's vocal cords.

The phrase we hear most often describing Mr. Obama's performance is that he connects. And he does. He has reduced the frenetic Chris Matthews of MSNBC, a veteran of the rough game of politics, to exclaim, live on air during an Obama speech, "My, I felt this thrill going up my leg. I mean, I don't have that too often."

I note, only incidentally, how glad we are that he doesn't.

Facing what seem to be Mr. Obama's near-invincible platform skills, Hillary and her camp have adopted a peculiar line of attack. Mr. Obama, she says, is just using words really well, or he's just making really eloquent speeches, or he has great rhetorical gifts. This is extremely strange, for what is a political campaign except an exercise in verbal persuasion? How is it a vice to be good at the essential task?

In a bathetic pronouncement on this theme, she offered this anecdote: People come up to her and say, "You're so specific . . . Why don't you just come and, you know, really just give us one of those great rhetorical flourishes and then, you know, get everybody all whooped up?" This is so tone-deaf it should be in its own one-quotation anthology.

She implies, of course, that she could be a cross between Elmer Gantry and Winston Churchill any time she chooses, and that only her virtuous addiction to "being specific" holds her back from getting everyone "whooped up."

She observes that Mr. Obama offers "only words," while she offers "real solutions." This is perplexing. How does she, or any politician, retail solutions, real or otherwise, to an audience except through the medium of those despised words? Her criticism of Mr. Obama, a politician, for his acknowledged skill as a speaker is akin to criticizing Wayne Gretzky for his skill in scoring goals. Good hockey players score goals; politicians, the good ones, talk and make speeches very well.

The other bizarre aspect of Ms. Clinton's protestation is the attempt to imply that her (relative) inarticulateness is actually a screen concealing greater competence. It's offered, in fact, almost as proof. This is parallel to some hapless goalie trying to persuade a coach that letting all those pucks pass through the net is, actually, an emblem of greater hockey skill than his opposite number who, you know, actually stops them.

Finally, and this point is very true for the United States in particular, to suggest that skill and finesse with language, some sympathy with the evocative and poetical nature of public utterance, is a flaw, is hostile to the legendary example of some of America's greatest political heroes, is to ignore or deflate what Abraham Lincoln achieved through words, bypass dozens of others from Patrick Henry to William Jennings Bryan to Roosevelt with his fireside chats and Ronald Reagan's inspired ease with anecdote and humour.

Ms. Clinton, whether she knows it or not, is repudiating the very medium of her trade. A care in the choice of words signals a corresponding respect for the ideas those words embody. A politician that cannot handle language is intrinsically handicapped in his or her capacity. It is George Bush's one undeniable, and central, weakness as president.

Hillary Clinton is now, of course, Barack Obama's secretary of state. The woman who mocked Mr. Obama's judgment and "unpreparedness" for office with the devastating "3 a.m. phone call" ads during the primary season is now his principal legatee in dealing with the very type of crises which might precipitate just such calls. The world will rest the better knowing that if Obama is wakened at 3 a.m., Hillary will be called five minutes later.

CANADA COULD LEARN FROM OBAMA | February 19, 2008

Remember the great mess of Florida in 2000? Al Gore wins popular vote, Bush wins electoral college, and then the recounts and lawsuits, the dimpled ballots and hanging chads, the furiously bespectacled scrutineers peering though

Sherlock Holmes–like magnifying glasses at mutilated ballots, trying to determine the "intent" of the ghostly voter.

Some people said American politics would never get over it.

And here we are today, with a new star ascendant in the American primaries, a wave of young and new voters trooping off to their state contests, all for a black man, a novice senator, whose middle name is "Hussein" and then, for good measure, whose last name is a perfect rhyme for America's arch-terrorist arch-enemy.

Everything was against the Obama explosion. He was virtually unknown a year ago, and was staring down the long, steel barrel of the most formidable munition in U.S. politics: the great howitzer known as the Clinton machine. He wasn't so much a candidate as an ornamental distraction. And here we are today, with the first serious black candidate for president ringing up victory after victory, and the Clintons, Hillary and her Exocet husband, are now outfitting their only Alamo for a very last stand in Texas and Ohio.

The American electorate is "turned on" to politics in a way that even the most dewy-eyed optimist in Florida 2000 would not have dared to dream.

Why? In one sense, the answer's simple. Obama, or the Obama candidacy, is out of the mould. He's not tiredly or nakedly partisan. He's not looking over at his opponents, whether Democrats or even Republicans, as if they're running a branch office of Satan or are "enemies of the state."

He suggests that politics is not a game played between teams who "own" the game.

All that tedious, empty and inane Bush-hatred, which followed years of visceral contempt for "slick" Willie; the mutual, almost clinical, rages members of one party have for the members of the other—that's what most of U.S. politics has been: a psychodrama of the hyperpartisans.

Obama, so far, I say again, suggests that something less corrosive, something larger than animosity for the other guy, and something other than the incestuous righteousness of pure partisanship, is the vehicle of politics. His "hope" is just another word for taking politics away from the viciousness of raw ambition and egotistical scrambling as its fundamental drives.

We could learn a bit in Canadian politics from his campaign.

Our politicians should look south, look at the phenomenon of Obama, and, if they are determined to inflict another essentially repetitive election on us this spring, throw away their rote scripts, talking points, wedge issues and prefabricated attacks, all the tired tactics and tired practices of the tired old game, and try something new. Speak their minds, abandon the trumped-up warfare, and—heresy of heresies—think a little less of winning, and a little more of making their politics as large as the country they profess to serve.

It is surely the case that Canadian politics picked up nothing of the charm of the early Obama example. We didn't have a spring election; our torment was deferred till the fall, followed by one of the most hyperpartisan explosions even seen. Prime Minister Harper's attempt to cut political funding was followed by the great coalition showdown that attempted to sit Stéphane Dion in the prime minister's chair. It was a spectacle of rage, cunning and confusion rarely, if ever, seen before. Canadian politics every day erodes what tiny pockets of esteem still exist for its conduct. The Obama example, emphatically, didn't "catch."

SHE CAME TO PRAISE HIM | March 8, 2008

There is an echo of Shakespearean archetypes in the American contest, with Barack Obama as an apprentice Prospero uncertainly testing his mesmerizing powers against the sleepless ambition of Hillary Clinton, a twenty-first-century—kinder, gentler, but still remorseless—Lady Macbeth. I can hear Hillary, fully in character, declaiming to her troops, "But screw your courage to the sticking-place, and we'll not fail." The Clinton machine showed Tuesday night why it holds such esteem in the cold and calculating hearts of those who follow politics as a profession. Here was Obama coming off a sweep of eleven states in a row, finally brought to ground with a real thumping from Hillary in Ohio and Rhode Island, and beaten as well in the wide, wild state of Texas.

Bill Clinton, uproarious, spotlight-craving, ungovernable Bill, had been tucked away into lesser corners of her campaign. Bill, it was early discovered, had to be administered to the voters of the Democratic primaries in measured doses. His early appearances raised the unsettling spectre of a dual presidency and reawakened images, best forgotten, of the man's own term in the White House.

Containing Bill, as the tactic was so delightfully called, was the first step toward Hillary's re-emergence. The second was to reach for whatever was not nailed down and throw it at Obama. This was formally announced as the "kitchen sink" strategy, a homely metaphor to convey an all-out assault, maximum bombardment on every issue and flaw of Obama or his campaign, from his punchlines to his past or present associations.

I don't know if Mrs. Clinton has a cat these days. There used to be one called Socks. If there is a Socks II, it most likely will be found lying flat, bruised and lifeless on Obama's doorstep, its last moments on Earth spent as a projectile at the Hillary counterattack. In desperate times, ammo is ammo, even when it purrs.

Next, the Oprah-canonized candidate of charismatic uplift was hauled down from his hitherto-untroubled flight in the sunny altitudes of Hope and Change by a press shamed by Hillary herself into properly questioning him. In Obama's words, after Ohio and Texas, she "played the ref." He said he didn't think the press would fall for it. Poor, naive Obama.

Most telling for Canadian spectators, Clinton hit him on his NAFTA statements, accusing him of retailing a hard line to Ohio voters and then having some minion run to Canadian diplomats to signal us that it was just noise from a stump speech.

Could such things be? Could the freshest, most inspiring presence in U.S. politics since John F. Kennedy be warbling of the New Jerusalem while on the campaign platform and practising the Old Washington shuffle—politics as it always has been—while off? *Eek!* I say, and I mean it.

Her campaign ratcheted up the rhetoric. Bob Shrum, Democratic consultant par excellence, wailed: "You've got a right-wing government in Canada that is trying to help the Republicans and is out there actively interfering in this campaign." It was as good as a play, as we say back home. The NAFTA story, whatever its dubious provenance, was rocket fuel for Hillary in Ohio and, moreover, was the pebble that hit the windshield of Obama's "untouchability." After NAFTAgate, as inevitably and drearily it was named, the American press went after the Illinois senator on his Chicago connections, and the late-night talk shows—the real agents of opinion in American journalism—started dealing with Hillary with something resembling kindness.

It's all lining up for a grand collision within the Democratic Party. Both camps have supporters that by now have invested their full being into the causes of their candidates. This is not a typical campaign. With the first woman and the first black candidate as champions they see in their respective campaigns the chance to "make history." One has to lose.

If the Clinton campaign, with all its guile and toughness, does indeed halt the rise of Obama, then surely it cannot escape a penalty for forestalling the arrival of America's first black president. Nor, given the intensity with which some of Hillary's supporters look at the prospect of the first woman in the White House, can I see how Barack Obama will escape a like response for impeding her ascension. Identity or cultural politics have very brittle edges. And the Democratic campaign, whether by design or not, has become a contest between the immensely charged and emotive themes of race and gender.

Half of the hopes of this most vivid campaign are bound to be disappointed.

Neither Prospero's magic nor Lady Macbeth's steel resolve can avert a painful fracture.

A DREAM DIVIDED | August 30, 2008

Abraham Lincoln knew the power of biblical quotation. He was a public figure during a time when recourse to scriptural reference by political leaders was neither as contentious nor as rare as it is today. One of Lincoln's most famous orations, for example, is known by a phrase he borrowed from the gospel of Matthew: "A house divided against itself cannot stand."

As I watched Barack Obama on Thursday night, on stage in front of a set designed to suggest the Lincoln Memorial in Washington, a variant of that compelling maxim insistently came to mind: A speech divided against itself cannot persuade.

Mr. Obama's speech was at war with its setting. His campaign had picked the site (a massive outdoor arena) and set the stage for one type of speech, and their candidate (almost entirely) gave another. There was a second tension or contradiction within this speech as well, possibly even larger and more consequential than the first. The speech was to be given by the first black candidate for president on the forty-fifth anniversary of Martin Luther King's incomparably eloquent "I have a dream" speech. Yet, when Mr. Obama—whose achievement may reasonably be seen as a living realization of Dr. King's prophetic words—took to the stage, he left all direct linkage to the anniversary, all allusion to Dr. King and his words, to a coda, to a few paragraphs at the end of an otherwise fairly stock political speech. Until those few concluding paragraphs, Obama's presentation could have been delivered—and this is a cruel measure of the opportunities missed or declined—by Joe Biden, the campaign's designated hit man.

Dr. King's speech, we remember, was given to a massive audience in front of the Lincoln Memorial and carried on television as well. King was wise enough to realize that addressing a huge audience in the shadow of the statue to the Great Emancipator called for a style of address, a nobility of statement, that "belonged" to the occasion and its setting. Mr. Obama, for all his wonderful rhetorical instincts, in his first speech as the Democrats' officially nominated presidential candidate, missed or declined the parallel connections available to him.

In other words, his speech lacked decorum. It was at odds with—in fact, beneath—its occasion (the King anniversary) and its grand setting. I found this very strange.

Mr. Obama's candidacy is about nothing if not about his capacity to represent a plateau moment, not just in American politics but in the tormented history of America itself. There is no greater fact in the Obama candidacy than that, should he succeed, a country that began in the terrible self-contradiction of slavery for blacks—while proclaiming the equality of all men—will have awarded its ultimate office to an African American.

The Obama candidacy, in this sense, is immensely symbolic, and that is the major source of its great power. The symbolism does not have to be trumpeted by Mr. Obama

himself, nor should it be. Symbols do their own communicating. Why does anyone think that nearly 80,000 people
show up at night to hear a speech from a "politician" except
that they have an intuition that some special moment in
their country's history is unfolding, and that the Obama
candidacy is its vehicle?

He did not cause this moment. But he is its realization.
Dr. King and Lincoln, both of whose presences were meant
to be suggested by the setting and the day, were the great
historic agents, each in his own way, who moved American
history to the point where it may—finally—reconcile the
terrible contradiction of racial inequity present at the founding of a constitutionally declared egalitarian society.

But Mr. Obama's speech seemed tone-deaf to the
importance of its moment. Wisecracks about George Bush,
sniggering witticisms playing off a useless sitcom of thirty
years ago (*Eight Is Enough*), tendentious putdowns of John
McCain, stale pseudo-populism (the corporations, the oil
companies)—this kind of stuff almost stole the moment of
its overwhelming magic. Having reached the mountaintop
of which Dr. King spoke so longingly, why was Mr. Obama
so determined, rhetorically, to return to the valley?

The crowd came for history, and Mr. Obama gave them
talking points. But I said "almost." When, toward the end of
an otherwise disappointing address, Mr. Obama cued his
audience to the significance of giving this speech forty-five
years to the day of that other speech in front of the real
Lincoln Memorial, what this night meant—finally—had a

chance to breathe. And the Obama candidacy shimmered back into its peculiar and commanding magic.

Mr. Obama should be careful, however. If Americans, particularly Democrats, wanted another combat politician, Hillary Clinton would have been on the stage Thursday night. They have opted, instead, for a campaign touched with a sense of nobility. A house divided, or the dream? Which is it to be?

Obama flirts with disappointment very frequently; it's almost a signature of his political style. Here, his party had built a great showy set, set the speech for the anniversary of MLK's great "I Have a Dream" oration, and he—in the main—delivered a pedestrian speech.

On Inauguration day, with the memories of Lincoln's imperishable addresses having been stoked by Obama— like Lincoln, travelling to Washington by train—he gave another slack speech. (See "A Clichéd Dud," page 73.) I have no doubt President Obama retains the oratorical virtuosity people saw variously during the primaries— but it either vanishes, or he declines to exercise it, on precisely those occasions when it would be most decorous.

HE'S NOT GOD, BUT HE *IS* AMERICA | December 27, 2008

Time magazine has genuflected to the obvious and named Barack Obama its person of the year. Which is a good thing. *Time* can be spotty in its choices—either gruesomely correct, as when it named the Planet (incense to the Gaia crowd), or unwholesomely sycophantic, as when it stuck You (that's you, smart reader) on the cover.

Seeing Mr. Obama, I thought: *Could have been worse.* I guess the Chaise Longue will have to wait for a quieter year. But this year, the magazine couldn't have gone anywhere else. A fair portion of the American press may have jettisoned every pretense of standard reporting on Mr. Obama, hardly distinguishable in the tone of commentary from preteen girls "Oh-my-God-ing" in the presence of the latest boy band.

Time has gushed with the best of them. In November, in yet another cover story on The One, it rated Mr. Obama above the sons of kings and even, oh my, above Christ himself: "Some princes are born in palaces. Some are born in mangers. But a few are born in the imagination, out of scraps of history and hope . . ."

I shed a tear on reading that. Brought back the molasses knobs of my youth, great glucose bombs that would fell a moose with their sheer sweetness. Yet, the excesses of *Time*, and the distinct strain of pure idolatry that has infested great swaths of the North American press, don't change the consideration that Barack Obama was *the* story of 2008.

He swiped the Democratic nomination from the Clintons, who, until Mr. Obama appeared on the scene, had that trinket so much in their possession that the contest for the top spot was marked down purely as a ritual. It was Hillary's, and that was all there was to it. And then, from out of the murky backwaters of Chicago politics, came a little-known black politician with the exotic name of Barack Hussein Obama, who glided with balletic insouciance past the shark's teeth, muscle and cunning of Clinton Inc.

He should be person of the year—of the decade—just for that. But it might also be useful to hold in mind, while the hymns to The One as he approaches Inauguration Day increase in volume and fervour, that that's all he's done. His Senate record is an empty suitcase. His national achievement is—outside the nomination—precisely nil. Sarah Palin's resumé is, objectively, much more substantial.

Hillary was right when she jibed that Mr. Obama was just one speech—the address he gave to the Democratic convention that loosed John Kerry on the American electorate. Off the platform, he's a great "um-er" and "ah-er" who stumbles with a sentence in a manner that hails to mind the image of George W. Bush on one of the latter's many desperate safaris to link a cowering subject to its about-to-be mauled predicate.

If Mr. Obama were a standard politician, the empty resumé would have done him in. But this is precisely the point about Mr. Obama, that he has blasted free of that category. Recall that string of losses he endured toward the end of the eternal primary campaign. Hillary was beating him state after state after state. And, yet, it hardly seemed to matter. Any other politician would have worn that serial trouncing like a wound. Mr. Obama walked on stage after each successive loss as though he'd just woken up from a comforting nap. The composure he sometimes displays, as many have noted, is almost unearthly: he possesses a centred confidence so strong that it almost deflects reality.

The Obama persona confounds politics as we have known it for at least a generation. His person summons the wish that politics be better. There was not a little intuitive genius in founding his campaign on the most frequently abused concept in politics: hope. That there is a profound desire for improvement in the conduct of public life in America is too obvious to need statement. (The same is true in our country. Oh Lord, how true.)

On some days, U.S. politics appears to be a frightful compound of graft, mismanagement, incompetence, cronyism, sexual misconduct, mediocrity, avarice and feral partisanship. The people who love America fear for her, not from apprehension over her enemies, but from despair over her putative leaders.

Barack Obama, by some gift of personality, sent out a flash of inspiration that called the exiled strain of idealism back into U.S. politics. It was not so much that he made politics exciting as that he gave some warrant for the thought it could be worthy.

He is not Lincoln. He is not, despite *Time*'s saccharine innuendo, better than the guy from the manger. But he's the one who's given the process of politics a second chance in our time. Person of the year. Easily.

BARACKWATCH | January 3, 2009

"It is now sixteen or seventeen years since I saw the Queen of France . . . and surely never lighted on this orb, which she hardly seemed to touch, a more delightful vision."

That's Edmund Burke reflecting on the fate of Marie Antoinette. He was, as we should say today, a fan. "I saw her just above the horizon, decorating and cheering the elevated sphere she just began to move in; glittering like the morning star, full of life, and splendour, and joy."

The prose has a touch of that Chris Matthews "thrill up my leg" quality, although of course infinitely more refined than anything produced to date, either above or below, the host of *Hardball*'s knee: "I thought 10,000 swords must have leaped from their scabbards to avenge even a look that threatened her with insult. But the age of chivalry is gone . . ."

Prophetic Burke. He was right about the age of chivalry. But the age of powdered encomium, what we would call the "puff piece," is still very much with us.

Celebrity reportage, witlessness in full genuflection to tackiness, has exploded the meanings of flattery and self-abasement. Entertainment reporters, as they deliriously regard themselves, are high-paid oxymorons. They all but lick the shoes of those they cover, and even that exemption is, I'm fairly confident, not total.

Till very recently, the worship of celebrities was more or less confined to high-gloss, low-IQ entertainment magazines and their TV equivalents. But with the advent of Barack Obama—and, I should insist, not at his prompting—it has done a worrisome crossover. In the year blessedly past, we had a column in the San Francisco *Chronicle* that makes even Burke's ode seem hesitant, ambiguous even.

The columnist wrote, gasped, thrilled, vibrated that Mr. Obama was " . . . that rare kind of attuned being who has the ability to lead us not merely to new foreign policies or health-care plans . . . but who can actually help usher in *a new way of being on the planet*, of relating and connecting and engaging with this bizarre earthly experiment. These kinds of people actually help us *evolve*." Rhapsody is too timid a word.

Mr. Obama, the column reveals, is a Lightworker, a new-age messianic superpresence. The heading over this prostration, er, column was: "Is Obama an enlightened being?" Call Steven Spielberg. E.T. is back.

There have been other descriptions of Mr. Obama during the primaries and the election that have been almost as dementedly ardent.

Normally, the press stands apart from mass adulation. Not so with Mr. Obama. A recent report in *The Washington*

Post read like a mash note from a teenager. The article had a picture of the Lightworker, shirtless, and commented: " . . . he was photographed looking like the paradigm of a new kind of presidential fitness, one geared less toward preventing heart attacks than winning swimsuit competitions." I beg to differ. Pass the defibrillator, now.

The reporter/disciple was, however, just warming up. Next, he galloped off into territory left unexplored even in the perspiration-saturated pages of chicklit: "The sun glinted off chiseled pectorals sculpted during four weightlifting sessions each week, and a body toned by regular treadmill runs and basketball games."

If this guy gives up the politics beat, there are a hundred massage parlours out there thirsty for this kind of copy. This is *The Washington Post*, remember. Has the financial crisis tipped the collective media mind into entertainment-reporting mode?

Very little of this, I repeat, is Mr. Obama's fault. (Although that famous line of his on winning the nomination as "the moment when the rise of the seas began to slow and the planet began to heal" was an unhappy toe-dip into the waters of absurd self-inflation.) But if the mainstream press offers "the sun glinted off chiselled pectorals," let's stop calling it news. This is *Baywatch* punditry.

Not worth a mention? On the contrary, there swirls around the figure or persona of Mr. Obama a set of expectations radically disconnected from rationality. He cannot possibly match the fantasies he inspires in some. It's worth wondering whether eight years of equal but opposite irrationality—the hysterically negative coverage of George W. Bush—has produced its own counter-response. Or whether that strand of new-age therapeutics, the Dr. Phil/Oprah "self-realization" claptrap, has warped U.S. politics into a kind of abysmal "healing workshop." That would certainly account for some Americans thinking they've elected a Lightworker rather than a president.

The press should be trimming these fantasies, not constructing them. But it's easier to sigh than to analyze. So on Inauguration Day, don't be surprised if you read a story that begins (alas, poor Burke), "And surely never lighted on this orb, which he hardly seemed to touch . . ."

A CLICHÉD DUD | January 24, 2009

Put him on a platform and Barack Obama can take any string of words and make them sing. He's the best speech performer of our day.

His voice has charm and power. He has an instinctive sense of the lyric and rhythmic underpinning of language, those surplus properties that impart a power beyond sense, beyond just what the words say. He has mastered the timing of public address, when to pause, when to rush a phrase, how to link gesture and stance to moments of emphasis. This is the full package.

Barack Obama could read a string of fortune cookie messages and some people would come away thinking they'd heard the Gettysburg Address.

He gave a great performance Tuesday. The speech itself, however, was a dud. So much skill operating on so lifeless a text. It was Vladimir Horowitz playing "Chopsticks." A speech that has hardly begun gives us clouds that are "gathering," storms that are "raging," a fear that is "nagging," grievances that are "petty," interests that are "narrow" and decisions that are "unpleasant" displays an alarming hospitality to cliché. Is there a dull-adjective shop in the new White House?

If they carve this one in marble, the appropriate subscript will read: Bring me your poor, your tired, your hackneyed phrases—your obvious descriptors yearning to be twee.

It contains sentences that begin as merely flat but end in perfect banality: "Now, there are some who question the scale of our ambitions, who suggest that our system cannot tolerate too many big plans." How many times have you heard that sad rhetorical turn? And where the sentence should deliver its punch, in comes the pale tepid verbal paint of "too many big plans."

There are sentences of pure fudge: "We will begin to responsibly leave Iraq to its people, and forge a hard-earned peace in Afghanistan." The first half of that sentence should have been the plainer declaration that the war against insurgent forces and al-Qaeda in Iraq has turned to success, and might have made a mention of the general, David Petraeus, who worked the change. He's why Mr. Obama can leave.

The second half is a pure skate. Mr. Obama is going to "forge a hard-earned peace in Afghanistan"? Actually, he's going to re-engage in an unfinished war with 30,000 or so new troops. Mr. Obama's words make it seem like peace is the starting point. Afghanistan may be as tough for him as Iraq was for George Bush.

Do you have a sleepy idea? Give it a platitude to curl up in. Has there ever been a chamber of commerce speech that has *not* included this sentence: "The state of the economy calls for action . . . and we will act—not only to create new jobs, but to lay a new foundation for growth." Poor old growth. Always laying that new foundation.

Mr. Obama's few ventures into vivid metaphor were not always happy or consistent: "We have tasted the bitter swill of civil war and segregation, and emerged from that dark chapter stronger and more united." The Civil War wasn't a taste of anything. Neither was segregation. Both were a full meal, one of horror, the other of dishonour to the nation's ideals. I'm not sure "swill" belongs in there at all, but it's a strange swill that half a phrase later is a "dark chapter." It should have been, in any case, dark chapters (war and segregation)—plural.

Finally, I'd like to note what isn't in this inaugural address. There is no citation of that one greater orator, whose inspiring words and assassination-amputated life reconfigured the conscience of America so that a black politician becoming its president became truly possible: Martin Luther King.

The real preface to Mr. Obama's inaugural address, the precondition of his being able to deliver it, will be found in Dr. King's immensely superior "I have a dream" speech. It is inexplicable that Dr. King, the most eloquent man America produced in the twentieth century, was not quoted directly by a president whose elevation to office should be seen as the consummation of Dr. King's martyred life's effort.

An inaugural address worthy of its occasion winds history into its every sentence. Echo and allusion, direct quotation, bind the day to the great words and deeds of all the days before it. Mr. Obama's speech would have gained both power and grace by direct citation of the unquestioned hero of the civil-rights movement.

But this week's address, sadly, was far less than its moment, and in much need of all the genuine power and grace a reference to that grand and fully eloquent man, Martin Luther King, would have given it.

The above piece inspired an extra-large bag of mail from readers, not all of it, or even most of it, I have to say, sympathizing with my reaction to President Obama's inaugural speech.

The new president's first official visit was to Canada, you will recall, his early presence no doubt reinforcing the general enthusiasm of Canadians for his style and manner. Both the prime minister and the leader of the opposition were jealous of their time with him, each hoping, I guess, to gain something by association with politics' new superstar. Mr. Ignatieff's party went so far as to beam the image of him with President Obama on one of the electronic billboards overlooking Times Square. I don't know how many votes that will harvest in say, Saskatchewan, but it is surely an illustration of the value the Liberals see in branding their leader as a friend of The One. See also "It Might Have Been," page 326.

BAD ENGLISH

NOTHING IS SACRED | July 10, 2004

We are, I hope, past the hollow fury that greeted Mel Gibson's *The Passion of the Christ*. Mr. Gibson has done well for himself—even Michael Moore must envy the box-office success of *The Passion*. Of course, here in Canada, we've had the irritant of the recent federal election to keep our minds off things godly, even those that come with previews and in Dolby sound.

Election past, I've felt some need to put the satanic thoroughly behind me, and found a welcome means in a couple of books about William Tyndale, the earliest translator of the New Testament into English. I hadn't realized till now that his work was so foundational to the great text of the King James Version, which has had the approval of centuries for its elegance, beauty and pith. Poor Tyndale got burnt at the stake for his labours.

Two books exhaust the glories of the English language: that great translation, worked by the scholars and linguists of the early seventeenth century, and the works of Shakespeare. Between them, Shakespeare and the King James set the limits of what the English language is capable of, in poetry or prose, in rhythm and cadence, in eloquence and plain speaking. It takes a nervy person to tamper with either of them.

Alas, there are always nervy people. Shakespeare has been bowdlerized, amputated, updated, and there is even a plain-language version put out for the "benefit" of college students. I read a sample in a downtown bookstore recently: "Wha' sup, Romeo?" Fortunately, there was a washroom nearby.

But the Bible, being a sacred book, possesses, one would think, more defences and stronger sanctions against vandalism by the tasteless. Alas, no. New versions of the Bible have always been with us, but with the age of therapy, feminism and the dread, clammy spectre of inclusiveness, the poor old Bible has been pillaged—they call it "updating the text"—by more Visigoths than humbled Rome. About the only qualification these modern updates bring to the art of translation is an absolute tone-deafness to the prose they set out with such reckless insolence to mutilate.

The latest torment is a translation going under the inspiring rubric *Good as New.* It is what the makers of computer commercials call user-friendly.

A few samples are all I have space for. Let us try the famous, sad episode where Peter, the chief of the apostles, denies Christ. The earlier version, familiar to Christians worldwide from the Authorized Version: "Now Peter sat without in the palace: and a damsel came unto him, saying, 'Thou also was with Jesus of Galilee.' But he denied before them all, saying, 'I know not what thou sayest.'"

What a lovely thing it is. Peter is sitting "without in the palace." A "damsel," with wonderfully antique formality, "comes unto him." She merely states that "Thou also was with Jesus of Galilee." But the bare statement is for Peter a most terrible inquiry and challenge. It angers him. His fury, a compound of cowardice, and shame at that cowardice is in the clipped "I know not what thou sayest."

Now, let's see what happens when you take the Authorized Version to the body shop and let loose the monkey mechanics of *Good as New*. (I forgot to mention: *Good as New* has updated the names. Peter is such an off-putting name. In the new dispensation he is now—I am not making this up—cue the music: *Rocky*.) "Meanwhile Rocky was still sitting in the courtyard. A woman came up to him and said: 'Haven't I seen you with Jesus, the hero from Galilee?' Rocky shook his head and said: 'I don't know what the hell you're talking about!'"

John the Baptist is renamed The Dipper, a.k.a. The Voice; Mary Magdalene is a comfy-cute Maggie. Even the Biblical execrations are defanged. For example, the perfectly good imprecation "Woe unto you, scribes and Pharisees, hypocrites!" is Simonized into some 1950s-style pseudo-slang: "Take a running jump, Holy Joes, humbugs!"

Ah, Tyndale. Burning anew with a hotter flame, I suspect, martyred by zealots of bad English.

The Archbishop of Canterbury has given his seal to this gibberish. He regards it as "fully earthed." So is compost. And he expects it to spread in "epidemic profusion." I can't quarrel with his metaphor: It won't be the first time a plague of bad taste, backed up by the two Horsepersons of Witlessness and Condescension, caught the ear of a trendy time.

I'm with Peter, er, Rocky on this one: I don't know what the hell they're talking about.

SILLY BITCHING | August 11, 2007

Samuel Johnson's preface to his landmark *Dictionary of the English Language* is the best essay in English on English. Its great, rolling sentences, superbly chosen diction, stately rhythms, and the ever-affecting cadences of its concluding paragraphs embody the Johnsonian manner at its most powerful and most penetrating.

Who has read those last paragraphs wherein Johnson surveys his mighty labour and not been startled by the sudden, sad and beguiling personalization of the preface? First, in summing up his efforts, he writes: "It may gratify curiosity to inform it, that the English Dictionary was written with little assistance of the learned, and without any patronage of the great; not in the soft obscurities of retirement, or under the shelter of academick bowers, but amidst inconvenience and distraction, in sickness and in sorrow: and it may repress the triumph of malignant criticism to observe, that if our language is not here fully displayed, I have only failed in an attempt which no human powers have hitherto completed."

And then comes the turn: "I may surely be contented without the praise of perfection, which, if I could obtain, in this gloom of solitude, what would it avail me? I have protracted my work till most of those whom I wished to please, have sunk into the grave, and success and miscarriage are empty sounds: I therefore dismiss it with frigid tranquillity, having little to fear or hope from censure or from praise."

What a great style—of person and prose both—there is in that melancholy observation that "most of those whom I wished to please, have sunk into the grave, and success and miscarriage are empty sounds," and how much it earns from the courtesy and dignity of its saying.

I owe it to the fussbudget and increasingly ridiculous city government of New York that Johnson's words ornament this column. The Michael Bloomberg city council is the very Mary Poppins of nanny government, with hardly a week going by without its trying to introduce new curbs on what people do, say, eat or inhale as they go about their daily lives.

The most recent was a motion by Brooklyn councilwoman Darlene Mealy to place a citywide ban on the word "bitch." I think she's concerned about one usage of that versatile and venerable term, the one the *Compact Oxford English Dictionary* defines rather daintily as "a woman whom one considers to be malicious or unpleasant."

This is a good thing because there are other meanings to its noun form that should surely escape the proscribing scythe of even the most prudish puritan of political correctness—its neutral designation of a female dog being the most obvious. And then there is the unlimited semantic largesse of its adjectival and verbal variants.

Bitching, meaning to complain, is surely a term without which life in New York would be impossible, New Yorkers being universally regarded as some of the most virtuosic bitchers the world has even seen, their bitching of such energy and invention that it constitutes an unheralded art form.

In fact, what the mealy-mouthed Ms. Mealy is actually doing with her vacuous motion is bitching about a word she doesn't like. That there are opprobrious and rude terms in the lexicon is something no one will deny. That there are opprobrious and rude terms that are sometimes directed, justly and unjustly, at women is an equally obvious axiom.

But are there any of us, who crawl here between earth and sky and then disappear into dust, who do not at some time, justly or unjustly, fall under a hail of harsh insults, crude epithets, blasphemous injunctions, obscene recommendations, vile descriptors and, in epic moments, whole anathemas of inspired and filthy objurgation? Bosses, friends and enemies, sons, daughters, parents and in-laws, strangers and intimates—at some time or other, any or all of these let loose upon our careless heads a string of mean and vicious words, compared to which poor feeble "bitch" is a lollipop next to a vat of acid.

But we cannot pass laws to limit the expressive range of human speech. The freedom to be harsh is the cruel side of the liberty to be graceful. We can, should and do deplore demeaning and degrading language. But its restriction belongs in the territory of manners and upbringing, not in the niggardly nannyism of city hall legislation. Besides which, it is the deepest folly even to imagine that language can be suffocated by diktat.

This is what those who have read Samuel Johnson find affirmed in words as glorious as the subject has yet to find: "to enchain syllables, and to lash the wind, are equally the undertakings of pride, unwilling to measure its desires by its strength."

THE EVIL THAT MEN DO

SAUDI HOSPITALITY | August 23, 2003

He was a torturer and a sadist (the terms do not necessarily exhaust one another). He was a mass killer. Some 300,000 people died under his barbarous rule. This is the most frequently cited tabulation, but when killing reaches into the hundreds of thousands, we must remember some amount of "rounding off" is almost always inevitable.

He was sexually lawless, very likely cannibalistic, ever suspicious and vengeful, devoid of personal grace. He despoiled Uganda, and his rule was a slander on all the promise of postcolonial government in Africa. Yet, when chased out of power, he became the recipient for the rest of his miserable life of the perplexing hospitality of the Saudi government.

Idi Amin died in a hospital in Jeddah of multiple organ failure. We can hope, I suppose, that the organs that failed were his own. He was buried in Jeddah—the current administration in Uganda having correctly decided that the country he polluted while alive should not have to bear the stain of his posthumous presence as well.

A trivial question occurs at the very beginning of any thought of the life and crimes of Idi Amin: What had this grotesque monster left undone that would have made him *persona non grata* in the kingdom of Saudi Arabia? Post-Uganda, he was reported to live in style, accompanied by his many wives and children and supported by a state pension from his hosts.

What virtue was the Saudi government answering when it gave harbour and support to a non-citizen who had wrecked a country, killed hundreds of thousands of his own people and defiled every universal canon of civilized behaviour? Merely parroting that he was a "guest" won't do.

But let us leave what it takes to be tossed out of the Hotel Saudi Arabia and visit an even more substantial question. General Amin left the Uganda he brought to tears and tatters in 1979—so, for something close to twenty-four years since then, this blot upon the human race passed his days in untroubled serenity, supplied with the all the requisites of the good life, to the apparent disinterest of those we have fashionably come to call the world community.

Why was Idi Amin given the bye?

More recent tyrants of comparably splendid depravity absorb the world's liveliest attention, call forth the alert jurists of the International Criminal Court and stir lonely judges in Spain to extraordinary reaches of indictment.

Slobodan Milosevic, once the ethnic cleanser du jour, was hauled before the UN International War Crimes Tribunal in The Hague while some of his victims were yet warm. The name of Augusto Pinochet could stir the streets of any number of capitals years after his rule and torture were history. Killers who keep their count low—the Carlos the Jackal type—remain newsworthy till the moment of their death or capture.

But here was Amin, truly a Caligula of our day, whose name and practices were a perfect synonym for all that is gruesome, wanton and cruel, wandering the rich streets of Jeddah and browsing the meat departments of its better supermarkets (perhaps nostalgic for the days when the selection was more mobile), not so much forgotten as disregarded.

How did he earn this right of disregard? Was it, I wonder, because there was a cast of ridiculousness in his public demeanour? Does a brute cease to horrify because he contains an admixture of the clown? One report tells the story that when he came to New York in 1975 to address the United Nations, he showed up at the Waldorf-Astoria with his own personal dancers, as well as live chickens. (These categories were possibly discrete.)

It is true that a taint of the ludicrous, or the simply lunatic, can put judgment at bay? But surely the fact, which I think is incontestable, that Mr. Amin was a buffoon does not erase his grander, more malign character as a butcher. Was it that he was one of a chain of reckless tyrants who have played on the stage of Africa since its emergence from colonialism, the kleptocrats and dictators who have sown misery so wide and deep in that sad land, that he "merged" with a too-common phenomenon? That in a continent that housed so many tyrants, even one so *outré* and brutal didn't stand out?

I don't think so—yet the very recent careers of Robert Mugabe and Charles Taylor are evidence that atrocious stewardship, if out of Africa, doesn't summon the moral revulsion that attaches to like behaviour almost anywhere else in the world.

What we can say is that some filter is at work, something that separates some tyrants from others and exempts them from the zeal to see them face some kind of justice that attaches to others.

That Mr. Amin should have gone quietly and unmolested to his grave, after the nightmare he visited upon Uganda, should be a scar upon the conscience of the world.

BECAUSE THEY WERE JEWS | April 6, 2004

Commenting on the bombing of a Jewish school library in Montreal yesterday, the prime minister said, "The assault was not directed against the Jewish community of Montreal, but against all Canadians."

I know what the prime minister meant by saying that. It's a noble thought, that we're all diminished by violence and hate, that an attack on any group of Canadians for whatever reason is an attack on the civil and moral code that makes us Canadians. In the abstract, the prime minister was right, but what was the name of the school that was actually bombed? Well, it's the United Talmud Torah School in Montreal.

The *Talmud Torah*. I cannot see how it is possible to get more Jewish, more quintessentially expressive of Jewishness, than in the combination of those two words that refer to the absolute foundational text and commentaries of the Jewish faith. So let's be very clear: the bombing—not a word we're used to hearing in Canada, I note in passing—was directed very particularly at the Jewish community in Montreal, at its *Jewishness*, and to walk away from its immense particularity is to diminish its very concrete outrageousness.

It wasn't a school. It was a Jewish school, and it wasn't *any* Jewish school, but the United Talmud Torah School. It was bombed because of its intimate identification with being Jewish. The second part of the crime was the note that accompanied it, which read that the bombing was prompted by the Israeli/Palestinian conflict and that more attacks were being planned.

Now, I know that there are very strong opinions on the Israeli/Palestinian conflict, and with opinions as opinions, neither I nor any other Canadian can have any real problem. But there really does seem to be a tilt, that some of those who most see themselves as critics of the Israeli side of this conflict (and please note I said *some* of those) seem to think they have some extra warrant or righteousness in how far they can go to express their detestation of Israel's policies, its government and, by extension, of Jews.

And as is the case in the bombing of the Talmud Torah library in Montreal, they also feel that tormenting and intimidating Jews anywhere is an earned licence because of where they stand on the Israeli/Palestinian conflict. So we have swastikas on Jewish homes in placid Toronto, we have the upsurge in assaults on Jews in Europe, and we have all too frequently, in demonstrations almost everywhere in the world, the placards and chants equating Israel and its government with its own demonic anti-type, the Nazism of Adolf Hitler.

We have, in effect, the Holocaust thrown in the face of the people who were its targets. I salute the prime minister for the civic nobility of what he had to say, but by attempting to generalize what happened in Montreal yesterday, he has in effect diffused its horror. It was a piece of hatred for the Jews of Montreal. It was an expression on Canadian soil of that simmering anti-Semitism that takes some camouflage, some protective colouring from asserting a solidarity with the Palestinian cause.

Anti-Semitism, springing from whatever source, is the most toxic political virus in the world. That's something we've already learned in that other school—the school where six million went to their death.

CASTRO'S USEFUL IDIOTS | August 5, 2006

Fidel Castro's parlous condition this week brought me to an online review of a film biography of him. *Fidel* was released in 2002, and it is clear early on that the reviewer, A.O. Scott, was not too impressed by filmmaker Estela Bravo's enthusiasm for her subject.

I detected a skeptical gleam, for example, in this line: "This is an exercise not in biography but in hero worship."

Nonetheless, hero worship of Fidel Castro, however perplexing, is despairingly common. Over the forty-seven years of Castro's dictatorship, whole contingents of Hollywood types have given themselves over to Castro idolatry, which—considering his regime is a one-party state solidly in the mould of every one-party state that has ever been—is odd even for the moralists of Bel Air.

But then, Castro, much like his early colleague in revolution and arms, Che Guevara, has always—bizarrely, in my view—possessed an unfathomable fashionability among the sophisticated and "right-thinking" classes. No less than our own Pierre Trudeau seemed to have harboured an affection for the Communist tyrant. It is possible, in Mr. Trudeau's case, his dalliances with the dictator answered to some private amusement, that he (Mr. Trudeau) knew how much breaking bread with Fidel annoyed the mandarins of the U.S. State Department and the Nixon White House.

However, it was always a QED too far for me to understand how the mature Mr. Trudeau's visceral and intellectual commitments to civil liberties and the primacy of the individual ever comported with, in logic or morality, toasting an island despot, a leader who had embraced the demonstrably evil creed of communism.

It is, of course, their status as icons of anti-Americanism that mainly accounts for Fidel and Che's (harsh and harsher) durability in the fashionable mind. Anti-Americanism is the plenary indulgence of all progressive thought. But let us return to the Scott review.

From it, I quote: "At one point, the American novelist Alice Walker, with sublime soft-headedness, marvels that Mr. Castro cannot dance or sing. 'It's a good thing he's got all those other good qualities,' she says."

Mr. Scott doesn't let that go entirely without remark: "This is about the harshest criticism Ms. Bravo permits, and one wonders just which good qualities Ms. Walker had in mind. The persecution of homosexuals? The silencing of political opposition? The jailing of dissidents?"

All justifiable queries, we will agree. But the line that stopped me cold was one A.O. Scott, wickedly, buried in parentheses just before these questions, and in all its glory is as follows: "(Later, she compares him to a redwood tree.)"

I think we have here a landmark moment in ecology as revelation. Novelists are the artists of our time, so we're told. They penetrate the surface, they unravel the hidden connections or speak the unheard messages of our age. Alice Walker is a novelist, and Fidel Castro reminds her of a tree. It would be interesting to hear her take on Tito. A dogwood, perhaps? So much for the art of the novel.

As I write this, the redwood, er, the Supreme One, is recovering from an operation, and his condition is a "state secret." (Maybe they're counting the rings.)

No surprise there. Dictatorships and health bulletins on the dictator are not compatible entities. (Let us not even explore the topic of dictatorships and death certificates.) In shrouding his decay or passing, Mr. Castro is merely maintaining one item of a desiccated liturgy.

But when he shuffles off this mortal coil, we should all be prepared for a full flood of kindly reminiscence and adulatory appraisal. There will be much talk of the wonderful Cuban health care system. And there will be much talk of the wonderful Cuban health care system.

Because embracing the second-most malevolent political system of the last century, and maintaining that embrace for close on four decades after its hideous innards were exposed for all the world to see—after Alexander Solzhenitsyn, after Andrei Sakharov, after the labours of Robert Conquest—must be counterbalanced by something, anything, that may be said to tend toward the humane and benign. The Cuban health care system has performed that dubious service for as long as Castro has held supreme rule in Cuba. It is a toy of an excuse.

Dictatorship is as much an insult as a horror. It is a fundamental insult to the people it rules, an insult to their dignity, to their honour and to their souls. Wrap it any way you wish—compare him to a redwood—but Mr. Castro was a dictator.

Hospitals can be named after him from here to eternity, it will never change the fact he never trusted the people he ruled to make a single real choice over who led them.

EICHMANN IN TEHRAN | December 16, 2006

Mocking the absolute misery of another human being has to be—next to deliberately and wantonly designing that misery—the lowest of human behaviours.

Mocking the misery, torment and death of six million human beings, therefore, belongs to some unspeakable category of epic depravity.

What form, what shape, would the keenest of such mockery take? Would it be to jeer publicly and laugh at the torments and death of so many, to take open delight at the nearly unimaginable pain and terror visited on so many?

To cheer the misery of millions would surely be an offence to scorch the ears of hell itself. But, if you are a Jew, I suspect that the last and perfect insult, the one that surpasses even open mockery of the Holocaust—its last cruelty, so to speak—is to say there was no Holocaust.

And yet, here we are, barely six years out of the bleak century forever stained by Adolf Hitler's near-extermination of European Jewry in the great murder factories of the concentration camps, and the president of Iran, Mahmoud Ahmadinejad, hosts a "conference" on the "myth" of the Holocaust. He assembles a clutch of "scholars" to launch an inquiry into the Holocaust, most eminent among whom is that paragon of erudition and dispassionate inquiry, a veritable Causabon-under-a-white-sheet, the former Ku Klux Klanner David Duke. Dr. Duke, as he pretentiously styles himself, may be a depleted merchant of old and expired hatreds in North America, but he's the headline guest and revered scholar at the conference in the soon-to-be-nuclear Iran.

Lesser Aristotles include Robert Faurisson, a French professor who denies the existence of the gas chambers; an Australian, Michele Renouf, who hails Mr. Ahmadinejad as a hero just for holding the conference, and another Australian, Frederick Toben, who delivered to the assembled illuminati this ferocious particular: "The number of victims at the Auschwitz concentration camp could be about 2,007." The use of "about" in that sentence is amazing.

There was also a Canadian professor, Shiraz Dossa from St. Francis Xavier University, who evidently travelled to this zoo of mountebanks unawake to the thought that a conference called to discuss the myth of the Holocaust would be a gathering dedicated to the idea of the Holocaust as a myth. When the news broke that the professor was attending this festival of blight, he lamented that the gathering was full of "hacks and lunatics" and that he wouldn't even "shake hands with most of them." One can only hope for the students of St. F.X. that Professor Dossa is not teaching either logic or holiday planning.

The target of it all, as it always is, was Israel and the Jews. For Mr. Ahmadinejad, the nearly illimitable suffering of the six million is a Jewish lie. On state television, he proclaimed: "They [the Jews] have fabricated a legend under the name Massacre of the Jews, and they hold it higher than God himself, religion itself and the prophets themselves." The same Mr. Ahmadinejad, who mocks and derides the historical Holocaust, opens this demented seminar with the clear promise of one soon to come: "The Zionist regime will be wiped out soon, the same way the Soviet Union was, and humanity will achieve freedom." He has so often proclaimed that Israel will be "wiped off the map" that the phrase hardly needs quotation marks. But note, too, how he links Israel's eradication with humanity, all humanity, "achieving freedom."

The death of Israel—i.e., the death of Jews—as millennial panacea, the removal of the one impediment to universal harmony—where have we heard this before? We are not far, not far by one inch, from the racist dogmas that found such terrible audience in 1930s Germany. The Jew now, as then, is always out of scale—in power, in insidiousness, in perniciousness to the common good of mankind.

"If somebody in their country questions God, nobody says anything," Mr. Ahmadinejad said. "But if somebody denies the myth of the massacre of Jews, the Zionist loud-speakers and the governments in the pay of Zionism will start to scream."

This is anti-Semitism's latest diabolic twist. The Holocaust was powered by the great lie of the Jewish world conspiracy, and now the Holocaust itself is another "Jewish conspiracy." Anti-Semitism as the snake that swallows its own tail. The malice here is profound. While most of the sane world looked upon this conference as deranged and hateful, and many worthy people said as much, hatred and mockery of Israel and the Jews has become so common that this outlandish gathering in Tehran this week seemed almost ordinary, predictable.

Let us recall that was Arendt's reading of Eichmann: ordinary, predictable, banal.

Ahmadinejad, however much his ravings excite the chuckles of "right thinkers" everywhere—as "not to be taken seriously," as merely a "pose" for geopolitical purposes—is not a harmless clown. The complacency with which so much of the world takes his government's acquisition of nuclear weapons approaches the status of being an absolute proof that "Never Again" was never a resolution—just a convenient slogan.

A FEROCIOUS PARABLE | January 28, 2008

A recent immigrant to Canada—Toronto, to be particular—is another in the grim chain of innocent people gunned down on this city's streets and in one horrible case, even on school property. His name was Hou Chang Mao.

What was Hou Chang Mao engaged in when some miserable waste of breath let loose the bullet that took all the rest of Mr. Hou's hopeful, honourable life away from him, and him away from his two—now wretched and terribly grieving—children? Why, the reckless new citizen was outside a fruit store on a main street in this great multicultural city, stacking oranges in a crate. It's still a truth that newcomers to this country start at the bottom, do long and dreary work, sacrifice for the next generation of their children—work hard, and play by the rules, to use the stiff phrase—and Hou Chang Mao was a model of that extremely benign and, to my mind, extremely honourable stereotype.

Mr. Hou's death is really hard to take. He had just come back from China, where he'd gone to bring his (now weeping) eighteen-year-old daughter to join him and his twenty-three-year-old (now tormented) son. What a horrific somersault for that young woman—to come to this fresh, vital, safe country, and barely here, when her father, at nothing more than stacking oranges in a crate outside a grocery store, is shot down by some menacing coward.

It should make us shudder to consider what she thinks of this country now. What a brutal twist this story puts to this man's hopes and dreams. How hard was it for him to get here in the first place? What were his visions of this country before he arrived? What had he told his children? How can they now square all that he had told them then with the image of their father dead on a Toronto sidewalk? For that matter, in some wide sense, how can we?

The next day, his son was brave enough to try to say, through a translator, a few things about this callous and empty slaughter, and the sight of him and his grieving sister trying to balance shock and grief, their visible, astonished pain at a dream turned upside down, would melt stone.

I suppose it's pointless to ask if those who execute the innocent and the harmless, who by their idiot violence create widows and orphans, ever really contemplate how perfectly selfish and egotistical they are. Their squabbles over moronic ideas of honour, or their vile and empty turf battles, or the laughable idea of "respect" that supposedly "justifies" letting bullets fly—if anybody else dies, well hey, we didn't mean to kill them.

Well, it doesn't mean much, either, to those children that their father wasn't meant to be killed. And apparently doesn't mean enough, either, yet, for some people who were there to come forward and honour the dead man with a visit to the police station and a little information.

Canada has lost a decent human being; two children in a strange land have lost an honourable and self-sacrificing father. And some fragment of the hope and sanity that this country stands for in the minds of so many who are not its citizens, but would one day like to be, has been icily chipped away, by mean people not worth the shadow of the life they ended.

In the swirl of "big" news, this isn't a big story, but Hou Chang Mao's life and death is a ferocious and sad parable whose meaning may outstay a hundred headlines. And his family deserves our respect and sympathy.

LITERATURE

IMAGE OF A POET | November 15, 2003

> The intellect of man is forced to choose perfection
> of the life or of the work.

This is W.B. Yeats's formulation, typical in its aphoristic force, the concentrated eloquence he imparts to what is, otherwise, a bare assertion. Typical also in its subject matter.

Yeats was no careless rhapsode. Writers often speak of their craft, the self-conscious, studious, disciplined portion of their calling. Craft is the careful twin of art's wild mystery. Yeats, more than most poets who have spoken of what they do, was alert from the first days of his muse that it is as much a study and a progress to write poetry, as it is a rush of inspiration, the fluttering of a visiting muse, or the unbidden speech of secret origins.

He thought very much about what he did and knew that real poetry, great achievement, was never merely "given." It was given only after an apprenticeship of toil, study, practice and time. It filled a life to "do" poetry. That, I suppose, is the burden of the couplet.

But we must never take poets at their word. Yeats is almost singular in the degree to which the "life" and the "work" are not opponents, not the counter-matter one of the other. It is nice work to find the daylight between the life of William Butler Yeats and the poetry of William Butler Yeats. Where shall we look to find the space open between them? The many poems to, or of, Maude Gonne? Where does the life stop and the poem begin in either of these? Yeats's passion, yearning, pursuit and eventual renunciation of Gonne is an electrical current in the poetry and the life. "Easter 1916"? The great matter of Ireland, the Troubles, as they have come to be called, were not a spectacle to be limned by the indifferent, fingernail-paring artist.

They were as much of Yeats's life as sexual passion. The Byzantium poems, with their strange and beautiful, hypnotic rhythms and images—not even these were "dream" poems, pieces carved out of the fantasies of some solitary. Yeats's spiritualism, his thirst for arcana and busy traffic with the nebulous concourse of the "other world," was a real pursuit for him. There was a lot of Coleridge in Yeats—the beckoning of the numinous had a reality and force more "grounded" people find difficult to understand, and many dismiss as embarrassingly ridiculous. They eminently were not ridiculous for him. Byzantium and the cluster of poems that seem fixed on the idea of art itself, art pure and changeless, came out of his insistent intercourse with that (for him) real world of mystic chatter and esoteric speculation.

If we were to take Yeats's postulated opposites, the life *or* the work, and choose to read just the one or the other, we could not do so. The life infiltrates the work; the work, the life. He who saw poetry as a vocation, who may indeed be the last Western poet to whom we can apply without an inch of irony the term bard, with its connotations of gifted authority or licence to speak "larger" than other men, saw the doing of poetry, the art, as the centre of any hope for the perfect life.

It is because one is wound so intimately, the temptation is to say so perfectly, with the other—how can we know the dancer from the dance?—that the case of Yeats is so singular an instance of the use of biography as a help to poetry. The biography of Wallace Stevens may be interesting. It may offer some clues and hints as to what went on in that strange and coloured mind. But Stevens's life, such as can be known from biography, will not unwind "The Comedian as the Letter C."

How different with Yeats. Here we need a concordance of the biographical with the literary. So, for those who think the poetry of Yeats one of the great inheritances of the century now mercifully finished, *W.B. Yeats: A Life; II: The Arch-Poet 1915–1939*, the second half of the mighty work of University of Oxford historian R.F. Foster, is welcome. It is one of the many merits of Foster's approach that he demonstrates, frequently and in specific detail, Yeats's marked awareness that he was "cutting a figure," that as a poet and an Irish citizen he deliberately composed a persona. All poets are self-aware: it is almost a definition of a poet to be so. Poets mine themselves, their emotions, their family histories. What is the poetry of Wordsworth but a lifelong excavation of certain episodes of intense personal experience, the history of his self-consciousness?

Yeats was self-aware in something of this same precocious and extravagant manner, and aware as well of how others of his time and place were aware of him. He played both to the mirror of himself and of others' opinion of him. Much of his poetry is pitched to construct what today we call his "image"—how the Irish people saw him, and would come to see him. His poetry is, to some degree, an artful biography, and seen by him as such.

Foster, for instance, gives illuminating comment on what Yeats called his "bread and butter" letter to the Swedish Academy, *The Bounty of Sweden*, which incorporated his lecture to the Academy upon receiving the Nobel Prize for Literature in 1923. It is a calculated document, intended to burnish and reinforce some of Yeats's central convictions about Irish culture and politics. Foster writes: *"The Bounty of Sweden*, taken as a whole, shows both WBY's brilliant ability to reconstruct history in terms of its meaning for himself and to place his work, and his circle, at the centre."

An earlier comment by Foster on the awarding of the Nobel, including a quotation from Yeats, underscores how deeply the poet saw, or wished others to see, his achievement, his work, as intrinsically interleaved with the achievement and history of his country: "An Irish winner of the [Nobel] prize, a year after Ireland gained its independence, had a symbolic value in the world's eyes, and he was careful to point this out: His reply to the many letters of congratulations was consistent. 'I consider that this honour has come to me less as an individual than as a representative of Irish literature, it is part of Europe's welcome to the Free State.'" In a poet of less capacity, one less intricated with the public life of his country, such an observation might seem the height of giddy, grand egotism, but the truth is simply that Yeats had the right to such a claim. His poetry cannot be detached from the theatre of early modern Irish history; it is a great part of that history's world voice.

And it achieves not a little of its power, that peculiar Yeatsian sublimity, its unmistakable public voice, from its attachment to the grand themes, the mix of honour, beauty, horror and reverence he saw playing throughout the history of his time. It is a great part of the merit of Foster's work that it traces the current, the charge which enters Yeats's poetry, to its sources, and enables those who would understand at least part of that poetry's power to realize that it springs from his passionate affiliation with the cause of Ireland.

Yeats is a peculiar mix. He can be among the most esoteric of poets—almost hermetic, a delver into mysticism and self-constructed mythologies. At the same time, he can be among the most exoteric, no more enigmatic than a newspaper headline. It is another virtue of Foster's work that he combs with diligence and acuity both realms, and marks their intersection, the flashpoint of inspiration, where they flare into lyricism or image.

"Leda and the Swan" is one of Yeats's fiercest, finest works. It is also a difficult poem, difficult because of the compression inherent in its form—so much "thought" packed into the narrow house of the sonnet. Foster's treatment of it is typical of the virtues of his book. He cites the journal of Lady Gregory, Yeats's longtime friend, patron and colleague, for a telling entry on what Yeats was thinking at the time of his first effort at the poem. The Russian Revolution woke him to the thought that "the reign of democracy is over . . . and in reaction there will be violent government from above." Lady Gregory's entry continues: "It is the thought of this force coming into the world that he is expressing in his Leda poem, not quite yet complete."

The same entry concludes with a glimpse into how the poem "occupies" him, a quick look at Yeats in the workshop: "He sat up till 30'c this morning working over it, and read it to me as complete at midday, and then half an hour later I hear him at it again." The last phrase there—the poem's complete, he's working at it again half an hour later—is a wonderful vignette.

Foster has much more on "Leda," its revisions, alterations, the hostile response from the *Catholic Bulletin*, and finally his own (Foster's) compact, insightful reading of the poem.

The treatment afforded "Leda and the Swan" can be taken as a touchstone of the book's method and manner. Diligent, thorough, unobstructed by jargon or modishness, careful with the details of both the life and any poem under consideration, measured and intelligent in its readings and criticism, this is a model approach to literary biography.

"Did that play of mine send out/ Certain men the English shot?/ Did words of mine put too great strain/ On that woman's reeling brain?" ("The Man and the Echo"). The work of Yeats occupies a brilliant space in the intersection of the private and public "meaning" of poetry. And so it is especially the case that a biography of Yeats, more than of most other poets, is part of our schooling in the poetry. It really is impossible to separate Yeats's life and work—they interpenetrate so thoroughly. This is what makes *The Arch-Poet* the wonderful work that it is. Foster is unimpaired by any other ambition or agenda, save to offer in accessible language and scholarly detail all that is useful or necessary to tune us to the poetry.

I shall take but one last example of his method. "Easter 1916," the great poem of the Irish uprising, is infallibly Yeatsian, stamped with his signature rhythms, oracular voice and saturated with the public matter of Ireland. It has also the peculiarly Yeatsian ambition of intending to condition the way its matter, the uprising, would be enrolled in future Irish history.

Is the poem private? Yes, as belonging to, as issuing only from, the particular consciousness of W.B. Yeats. Private in the manner that all poetry is private, that it is the shaped utterance of one mind, of one singularly tuned imagination. Is the poem public? Yes, both in its subject and its intent. "Easter 1916" is meant to be an influence, a force, in the shaping of Irish understanding and aspiration. It is something of an "uprising" itself. Those unfamiliar with the background to the 1916 rebellion, innocent of Yeats's complicated relationship to many of its key participants, his lifelong mission to register the essence of Ireland and its people, will find here all that is needed to read the poem in its fullness.

Not all poets deserve the determined application Foster has brought to this biography. But the poetry of Yeats is one of the great achievements of the last century, a lifework of astonishing fertility and accomplishment—it may be the last great instalment, in the high vein, of Romanticism.

It is, as well, very much a part of that history it incorporates in so many brilliant poems. The poetic imagination of W.B. Yeats has inflected the record of modern Irish history, and in a handful of poems—"Leda and the Swan," "The Second Coming," "Easter 1916" principal among them—has worked out from that particular history to catch the sombre and deadly themes of the entire murderous century just past.

Yeats is a very Irish poet, and as an Irish poet he began; but he is a great poet not only because of the insuperable verbal gifts with which he was endowed, but because he was also endowed with that last or final gift of real poetry: its ability to reach into and read our world.

Roy Foster has quite magnificently done his best to help us reach into and read W.B. Yeats. To recommend this book to others is an honour.

PAMELA ANDERSON'S OUTSTANDING OEUVRE | August 7, 2004

Pamela Anderson has published her first novel. All the news stories pointedly reference that it's her first, which means, I suppose, that she's not just visiting the form, but like the great practitioners of the past—Dickens, Balzac and Jacqueline Susann—Ms. Anderson and the muse are setting up house for the long haul.

I couldn't be happier. Literature has always cohabited with elitism, and far too shamelessly. From James Joyce to Thomas Pynchon, authors have posed as demigods, vessels of some rare and superfine genius, producing works that demanded of their readers the skills of a cryptographer and the endurance of a Clydesdale. It's high time art took a stroll on the beach.

I haven't read her novel yet—it's so fresh off the presses it's still dripping mascara—but I know that this will be a heartbreaking work of staggering exposition, as transparent as wind, as still of mind as a tranquillized sheep.

Pamela has always favoured the direct style, and being in the same room as a word processor is unlikely to have changed that. What you get is what you see. This has been the hallmark of her tradecraft from the beginning. From the Tool Time Girl on *Home Improvement*, to *Baywatch*, to *VIP*, to her studiously unartful home productions, the Anderson oeuvre has the clarity of Evian and the simplicity of lettuce.

I much look forward to Pamela's infiltration of the Booker panels and word festivals. This is a great and democratizing moment.

She hired a ghostwriter for her book (its title is *Star*), which is another piece of welcome transgressiveness. Biographies, we know, have ghostwriters. The memoirs of ex-politicians, for example, are almost always ventriloquial. But in what sense can a novelist, you may well be asking—in this case, Ms. Anderson—"write" a novel using a ghostwriter? Does she hire some buzzing brain and tell him to sit in a corner until he makes something up she likes, which then becomes merely by the force of her approval . . . hers? I certainly hope so. There's precedent from other trades. Nobody builds their own houses anymore, but you don't see the carpenter's name next to anyone's doorbell.

Besides, Pamela Anderson is a celebrity—and, as Homer (Simpson) once said of rock stars, is there nothing that celebrities can't do? It's her book because her name is on the cover. And if its story bears an uncanny, almost Siamese, resemblance to her own life, this does not mean it still isn't a novel. Was it not Oscar Wilde, another literary poseur, who first made the claim that all real art imitates life?

Nor should it be left unnoticed that what Ms. Anderson has actually done here is to have brought the novel, the form, home. The more austere guides to English fiction usually credit Samuel Richardson as being the father of the novel. You were nobody in the eighteenth century if you weren't a Richardson fan. If Oprah had been around in the 1740s—and we can only fervently wish that she had been—Richardson would have been her literary Dr. Phil.

Richardson's first book, and the progenitor of the English novel, was a steamy, lubricious potboiler about a young servant girl's attempts to resist the endless assaults upon her "virtue" by her master. The plot was built upon "the principle of procrastinated rape" that V.S. Pritchett said was the motor of most romance works. Richardson, Anderson, the principle lives on: sex sells.

And what was that novel's name? *Pamela*. The subtitle was *Virtue Rewarded*, which I suppose is the only point where this parallel may be seen to fail. Virtue, certainly in no sense in which the word could be understood in the eighteenth century, or most centuries before or after, has not been a persistent intruder in the life of the present-day heroine.

But if *Pamela* begat the novel, may not Pamela take it back?

Now, there will be some who, on learning that a novel by Pamela Anderson is about to crowd Joyce Carol Oates out of the Indigo shops—and if there is any justice in this indifferent universe, give a nudge to the stacks of Bill Clinton's *My Life*—will whiningly ask whether it's actually worth reading.

I have culled a sample of its prose from the news reports, and you will agree the answer is, ever so buoyantly, yes.

Star tells of the heroine's unsettling reaction to the changes of puberty. Her mother reassures her: "You're not dying, you're just growing up. Looks like you're finally going to get some boobs. You're becoming a woman, honey. You're blooming!" And bloom she does. Then comes a sentence that would make Flaubert weep: "Her breasts came on suddenly and tenaciously, as if trying to make up for lost time." And weep again—perhaps, if possible, even more copiously—over one that follows: "The hard bump turned out to be one of a pair of unruly and self-willed nipples."

It's the "self-willed" that does it. That's genius.

SANITY TAKES A HOLIDAY | December 11, 2004

Would there have been a *Buffy the Vampire Slayer* TV series without Bram Stoker? No. However far from his *Dracula* the campy reruns may be, the persistence of the vampire story, and the fable's elemental features—blood-parched undead, fearful only of sunlight, garlic and the crucifix (vampires, not political consultants)—owe everything to Stoker's renewal of the legend.

Stoker took the ancient myth and folk tale of the vampire and packaged it as a literary entertainment. The latter half of the nineteenth century is somewhat remarkable in the history of English fiction for the number of authors who wrote stories or created characters that tapped the properties of myth: Robert Louis Stevenson with *The Strange Case of Dr. Jekyll and Mr. Hyde*, Mary Shelley with *Frankenstein*, Arthur Conan Doyle with his immortals, Sherlock Holmes and Dr. Watson.

To the fertility and imagination of the ordinary novelist, these writers, and others, added the gift of encapsulating an archetype, of drawing in strong and vivid colours, figures who became enduring and emblematic. Most especially, they had the gift of creating characters who escape the stories they inhabit, who seem either to live on, independent of the fictions in which they were created (Sherlock Holmes), or stand for the perfect individual representation of an already-present myth or legend (Count Dracula).

Most of the writers I've named claim their standing among the immortals of fiction on the basis of a single work or character. But there is a writer of the same period who stands in creative pre-eminence to them all.

Charles Dickens is the king of English novelists. Dickens could stamp life on a character with a catchphrase or with a single paragraph of description. The Dickensian world is a thickly populated assembly of unforgettable individualities, from Mrs. (Sairy) Gamp to Fagin and Pip. Dickens's characters have an extra-fictional reality. Dickens was also the greatest of namers, the very Adam of English fiction.

The naming of "Sherlock Holmes" was not a lucky hit. Doyle worried mightily over what to call his rationalist sleuth, and only after much trial, and many unhappy attempts, settled upon his hero's now-seemingly-inevitable moniker. Doyle had a few other fine hits—Moriarty was a great find for a fiend—but his capacity was a talent, not genius.

Dickens, by contrast, was inexhaustibly clever and sure when it came to parcelling out names. *The Mystery of Edwin Drood*. The name is the novel: morbid, gloomy, eerie and grim.

Nowhere in all of Dickens are these marvellous faculties of his, building characters and finding their perfect names, more beguilingly deployed than in *A Christmas Carol*. Here, in contrast with the voluminous novels, he works in such a small space. *A Christmas Carol* is, in the Dickensian canon, a riff, a mere firecracker of a book next to the great infernos of *Bleak House* or *A Tale of Two Cities*. But the trim tale is a feast of naming. Ebenezer Scrooge, the ghosts of Christmas Past, Present and Future, Bob Cratchit, Tiny Tim, Marley's ghost—this is the character list of the Christmas season, the only figures outside the foundational gospel account of the Bethlehem story itself that designate Christmas wherever in the world it is celebrated.

Dickens linked the two stories, his and the Scriptures', with the character of Tiny Tim, whom we might call the Other Christmas Child. And it is from Tiny Tim that we receive the signature phrase of *A Christmas Carol*, when at that story's end he wishes, "God bless us, every one!"

Evidently, that benign and concordant felicitation was too much for a school in Kirkland, Washington, which banned a production of *A Christmas Carol*, partly because "God bless us, every one!" was too overtly religious.

There is something apocalyptically demented in anyone, anywhere, taking offence at *A Christmas Carol* during Christmas. Must the innocent enjoyment of thousands fall victim to the hyperactive sensibilities of one or two seasonal grinches? Why must the "injured" sensibility always trump the majority enjoyment? I'll bet schools could stage *Last Exit to Brooklyn*, or some version of *Naked Lunch*, and pass whatever is the current litmus test, but in the current mood of reflexive cringing toward designated sensibilities, *A Christmas Carol* has to go.

This is an annual insanity. From corporate bulletins to municipal parades, during each successive Christmas, every vulgarity known to man goes out under the rubric of season's greetings, but the merest echoes of the real thing, from the gospels or Charles Dickens, are filtered and discarded as being "insensitive." It is the great dumb, blind and cowardly prudery of that protracted and repressive lunacy we know as political correctness.

We will look back on these times and blush that we did not blush at how feeble and sheepish we were during its Scrooge-like and savagely petty dominion.

CLIMB EVERY MOUNT DOOM | March 19, 2005

Tolkien's *The Lord of the Rings* is inexhaustible. It's an epic recasting of the most ancient of themes, the struggle between goodness and evil, darkness and light. It is a work that has found vast welcome over time.

That most endearing ubiquity, Virginia Woolf's "common reader," has made it both bestseller and classic. Despite its length, despite Tolkien's occasional lapses into tedious exposition and overtelling detail, despite the initially indigestible mix of odd names and exotic geography and a plot that ramifies with more complexities than the sponsorship hearings, readers everywhere and of all ages have taken to the great sweep of the story and its heroic melodrama.

Harry Potter is but a clatter on the cobblestones to the great harmonies of *Lord of the Rings*. Tolkien's work is in every way deeper, broader and richer. There is an animated version, of which I've only caught fragments, but not surprisingly, it works, too. The great proof of the power of the Tolkien magic lies, of course, in the movie trilogy. It is a triumph, not of the movie's stars, but of its director.

Peter Jackson, who not a little resembles Gimli, the dwarf of the fellowship, in both temperament and facial ornament, managed the major miracle of taking the vast and complicated story from the page to the screen. Mr. Jackson took on a story that millions of readers had already imprinted on their own imaginations and dared recast it, cinematically, in his.

We will always give precedence to the original inventor. The imagination that gave birth to this fable is undoubtedly the superior one; the author has our reverence. But considering the spoilage Hollywood has worked on other great tales, the wreckage it has wrought on various classics over the years, Peter Jackson must be acknowledged as a considerable fabulist in his own right.

Over the years, Shakespeare, Jane Austen and Henry James have had their works passed through the Hollywood chop shop; *Clueless*, we are told, owes something to Jane Austen, though fortunately Jane sleeps too deeply to acknowledge the debt. *Shakespeare in Love*, with Gwyneth Paltrow flitting by in a gauzy nightgown igniting the Bard's muse, seemed to me to invite the curse that tradition tells us Shakespeare wrote for his grave: "Good friend, for Jesu's sake forbear/ To dig the dust enclosed here;/ Blest be the man who spares these stones,/ And curst be he that moves my bones." Shakespeare's bones are his words. But not to worry. He'll survive. Hollywood is ephemeral, Shakespeare immortal. He has survived the obscurantism and sectarian zealotry that have reigned in the most fashionable quarters of Shakespeare studies for the past quarter century. The childish rages against dead white European males and all their works, the ludicrous declarations of the Death of the Author, the more zany "transgressive" approaches to the corpus of English literary masterpieces: all have had their weary, jargon-jewelled day. They are gone, or fading. Willie lives. Poststructuralism, where is thy sting-a-ling-a-ling?

Peter Jackson's triumph is the more impressive for being the exception to Hollywood's mostly vacuous, sometimes grotesque rereadings of classic works and classic writers. Just as a side note, when I saw some years ago what Jane Fonda did to the life of America's one genius misanthrope, Ambrose Bierce, in the hideously sentimentalized *The Old Gringo*—if I may borrow a phrase, tears were not enough. I hope he (bitter Bierce) gets her, in the afterlife he didn't believe in.

Now Tolkien's work is about to face the supreme threat. *Lord of the Rings* is scheduled to open *as a musical*, in Toronto, next February. I think of the musical as literature's own Mount Doom. Is it possible that the melancholy, heroic, extravagantly fantastic and pseudo-mythical *Lord* can survive the costumery, camp and brittleness that are endemic to the musical? Will Gandalf rap? Will the hobbits wear tights? And will there be the almost inevitable overlay of treacly melodies, freight-train-volume arias for the star diva ("Don't Cry for Me, Mordor" doesn't leap off the larynx, thank God) and all the other awful signatures of the Rice-Webber world?

We can but hope. If anything can survive this transition, it's the Tolkien story and the Tolkien world. And remember, too, that by February of next year we'll have come out of the Gomery Commission. So a story of prancing orcs, menacing outriders, dark forces summoned by a hidden lord, and a truly mystifying quest about truth and power, will already be familiar to most Canadians. As well as the idea that all this is just a song and dance to begin with.

THIS IS THE LIFE | February 21, 2009

To write the Life of him who excelled all mankind in writing the lives of others, and who, whether we consider his extraordinary endowments, or his various works, has been equalled by few in any age, is an arduous, and may be reckoned in me a presumptuous task.

Many will immediately recognize that citation, such has been the enduring popularity and fame of the work these words begin. They constitute the first sentence of the text of James Boswell's *Life of Samuel Johnson* which, while it was not the first biography of Johnson (other intimates and acquaintances stole the lead) has been considered by all but eccentrics the best and most engaging, and considered by an almost equal number to be among the very best of all biographies, literary or otherwise, ever written.

Boswell's words, placed very plainly at the start of his biography (as we should say "upfront") describe a quite real dilemma. The dilemma, by a curious irony, as I hope to show later, was greatly compounded for all others who followed Boswell, by Boswell's own work.

The problem is there in the opening phrase: "To write the Life of him who excelled all mankind in writing the lives of others." Students and devotees of Samuel Johnson, of whom the number is many and blessed, will already know that Boswell is not puffing here, not overstating the challenge of his undertaking.

It is easy to understand the force of Boswell's apprehension. He's following a form Johnson pioneered, and in addition he's setting his prose alongside Samuel Johnson's. Those are the anxieties contained in the phrase about writing ". . . the Life of him who excelled all others . . ." and plainly confessed as "arduous" and possibly "presumptuous."

However, what Boswell's phrase does not extend to, or passes by, was the deeper challenge that faced him, and all who have followed him—for there have been many, many biographies of Johnson. Johnson's whole *oeuvre* is in varying degrees *auto*biographical.

Everywhere in Johnson's multifarious output, even in the *Dictionary* (see: patron, oats) Johnson is unwinding the story of himself. Boswell knew that it was not just that in undertaking Johnson's life he was competing with a literary giant who had set the standard for writing the "lives of others" but in great measure he was competing at a much more essential level: competing with Johnson himself in the writing of Johnson's life.

The point holds for all biographers since. Anyone who writes a life of Johnson competes with Johnson. But, and what a but it is, that same anyone is competing with the one man who knew him better than any other, had a stenographer's grasp of the very idiom of his conversation, and who for nearly twenty years was so much an intimate as to be a "secret sharer" of the great man's moods and manners, his great undertakings, his social life, his depressions and confessions. He is competing with the most vivid biography of the most vivid literary figure that English literature possesses.

Surprisingly this has not daunted periodic retellings of Johnson's life, right up to this present day. But these considerations do place a frame around our evaluations of any life of Johnson other than Boswell's. They must do something other than Boswell. Perhaps they will offer something of a Johnson *vade mecum*, a convenient and fluent digest of the salient facts and episodes of his life, together with an appreciation of the major works. They may "reset" Johnson for our time, as I think Walter Jackson Bate did a generation ago in his *Samuel Johnson*. Or they may set as their purpose, purely to introduce Johnson to those who have not fallen under his influence, serve as appetizer, as it were, to Boswell's incomparable narrative.

It is on these grounds that I approach the two new lives, occasioned by the 300th anniversary of Johnson's birth: *Samuel Johnson: A Biography*, by Peter Martin; and Jeffrey Meyers's *Samuel Johnson: The Struggle*.

I can recommend them both for providing a clear unrolling of Johnson's early personal history, for filling that one partial void in Boswell's opus. His school days, the picture of his father the bookseller, his early and tumultuous brief stay at Oxford, some early flirtations—both books give a fine account of this relatively neglected period. They are similarly fine in giving something of the flavour of the gritty London of the period when Johnson, as a young man, went to seek his fortune and make his name. Readers of Johnson's own *Life of Savage* (the ill-favoured bastard, persecuted friend and fellow poet, who was Johnson's companion during the early bleak, hungry days in the great capital) will have already tasted some of that flavour but both Martin and Meyers capture its tone and texture, and are particularly good in retailing just how difficult, and precarious, was Johnson's effort to break into the jobbery of a writer's life.

We appreciate something of Johnson's quite ferocious determination from their pages. They both put into fine relief how often the young Johnson's pride was at war with his wish to succeed. It was a mark of his flinty character than never deserted him. Johnson's relationship with booksellers alternated between testy courtship and fits of vehement defiance.

They are both good too in moving through the progress of Johnson's career. The notice given to *London* by Pope (mentioned above), his gradual acquisition of reputation, the epochal delegation of booksellers to commission him for the great *Dictionary* his undertaking of the *Rambler* essays, the completion of the *Dictionary*, academic acknowledgement from Oxford University in the form of an honorary degree; the story is well told, quotations from Boswell and Johnson are frequent and judicious, the anecdotes (familiar to some) are enlivening, and a picture of the fierce, complicated, manically eccentric genius emerges that will provoke both admiration and wonder.

How strange a man Samuel Johnson was. His physical deformities (I do not think the term too strong) from childhood tormented him. His (once acquired) intense Christianity haunted him all his life with a sense of something close to his own worthlessness, and with a *timor mortis*, fear of death, that was almost medieval in its morbidity. He castigated himself for sloth, irresolution, and idleness yet was—look at any good library shelf—a prodigy of laborious achievement.

He was the most generous, or perhaps better, most charitable of men. He housed six poor souls in his own lodgings for most of his life. [There's an example of a "response" to homelessness.] Yet he was alive to slights, perceived and real, with a sensitivity that is still painful to read about. He could be furious and a bully in conversation, yet always alive to the real needs of others. He rescued authors from debt, visited friends in prison, and ghosted material for fellow "hacks" to boost their fortune or gird their esteem.

This is but part of the picture of Samuel Johnson, and both these new books are dutiful in presenting it anew. There is much more of course. And if there are readers who have not yet taken Johnson into their personal library, who have not made themselves familiar with the great essays, the *Lives*, or the poems and of course the *Dictionary*, then either of these books is better than serviceable. Yet, I recur to my opening thoughts, there is still, and always, Boswell. It is in Boswell that Johnson, despite the critical hail that has fallen on his head from Macaulay's vituperate essay to the present day, that Johnson really lives.

The presence of Boswell has driven every subsequent biography to do something new. Scholarship has added much that is worth the telling. And English criticism still engages, has always engaged, with the many ardent judgements on taste, poetry, prosody, the act of writing, that run through the entire corpus of Johnson's writing. Early in the last century T.S. Eliot wrestled with Johnson, as did somewhat later, F.R. Leavis, and closer to our own day the wonderful Harold Bloom sends almost as many "hosannas" Johnson's way, as he does to his idol Shakespeare.

In these two most recent efforts what may be new is the concentration on the very personal, the attempt to render what Johnson thought, felt (or, speculatively) experienced in his relations with Tetty, his wife, his dalliances—if that they may be called—with the various women he met throughout his life, and most particularly his long relationship with Hester Thrale, the wife of his (informal) patron, the beerseller Henry Thrale.

In Martin's book there is far too much of a speculative knowingness. We are told what we cannot know—what Johnson "must have felt": how "his pride would not have borne it." The psychologizing is wearying. It extends to Tetty's son Jervis, imagined as viewing Johnson's courtship of her mother and recoiling from it: "At eighteen he was old enough to see the overtures of this strange looking interloper only seven years older than he as a humiliation and a grotesque absurdity." What a pudding this whole sentence is. It is, at the kindest, novelistically toned speculation.

Meyer has made the bigger splash however with rumi-
nations on a possible sadomasochistic relationship between
Hester Thrale and Johnson, speculations on whippings and
handcuffs, all of which have very much an *au courant* air
about them, and should do something to lift *Samuel
Johnson: A Struggle* on to the tonier afternoon TV therapy
gropes.

I do not think there's a need to tease an interest in
Samuel Johnson. If we merely sample his own writings we
will quickly sense the extraordinary individual behind
them. For there's enough of Johnson in Johnson's own
writings to whet the appetite to read him. That will moti-
vate most people to wish to read further.

And that, lest we forget, is—finally—the largest merit
of any biography of him, even Boswell's, the reading of
Johnson's writings. He is a writer of at times unsurpassed
exactitude and analysis. Read the essay on Shakespeare.
He has an almost unsurpassed mastery of architecturally
structured sentences, immense symmetries of phrase and
rhythm, that roll with an eloquence almost departed from
the English language. *Rasselas* is a dull story told in brilliant, beautiful sentences. His feel for words, his grasp of
the multiple levels of each particular word's meaning,
rivals the range of Milton's prose or Macaulay's.

Read the great Preface to the *English Dictionary*. He is
greatly underestimated for his cleverness and humour, and
not sufficiently regarded as one of the most affecting writers
in the language. His words on hearing of David Garrick's

death, how it "eclipsed the gaiety of nations" are both profound and beautiful.

We do not need stray speculation, knowingness, or exotic sexual gossip to lead us to Johnson. But perhaps when one is, as every biographer of Johnson must be, in competition with Boswell, something "new" must be tried. What was not new in both these books works very well. And it was like a light on every page when Johnson himself was quoted. And that is the essential allure of the both of them. Psychologizing and sexual speculation aside, whatever brings a new reader to that unmistakable voice and emphatic, animated, inspired prose is a good thing. Which is of course what that first and still best recorder of the magnificent life of Samuel Johnson, James Boswell, accomplished, with such inimitable brilliance, so long ago.

DOGGEREL OF WAR | October 15, 2005

I have been reading some poems on the Iraq war by this year's Nobel Prize winner, Harold Pinter. They are called poems only by courtesy of how they look in print. Any talented fifteen-year-old could write as well. They are short, blunt, angry and perfectly pleased with themselves. The following excerpt will give a little of their flavour. It's from a poem of 14 lines called "The Special Relationship":

The bombs go off
The legs go off
The heads go off
The arms go off . . .
The dead are dust
A man bows down before another man
And sucks his lust.

Others are rougher, use the almost obligatory raw language that accompanies protest these days, and convey a fierce zeal against America and George Bush.

I can very easily see that if someone shares Mr. Pinter's view of that war, then reading Mr. Pinter's poems will produce a delightful sensation—but not the delightful sensation that accompanies genuine poetry. It is, rather, the sensation of being confirmed in a view already held.

Mr. Pinter's verse operates as an endorsement to feelings and attitudes already fully developed in those readers who·agree with him. It is not exploratory. As such, the works are much closer in category to slogans than poems. I am not saying that they should be condemned for that reason. The people who vehemently oppose the Iraq war, and who despise Mr. Bush and much of present-day America, have every right to be pleased when a famous playwright confects odd pieces of near-doggerel that echo their anger and are packaged as verse.

But I do not think they should be confused with

poetry, nor are they, even on the most elastic and forgiving understanding, even near relations to literature.

It is worth noting that, before winning the Nobel this week, Mr. Pinter had achieved another distinction for his war poems. He won the Wilfred Owen Poetry Award, which is, I think, unfortunate. For Wilfred Owen was a real poet—and if Mr. Pinter's winning of that award does nothing else, if it points people to that somewhat neglected genius of pity and poetry, why, then it is a very wonderful thing indeed.

Owen, unlike Mr. Pinter, struggles upward toward his subject. One may almost see him craving to find the unique set of words, the singular rhythms and images, which alone can attempt to communicate the desolation, horror and pity of his vast subject.

It is worth anyone's while to go to one of Owen's most familiar poems, the inevitably anthologized "Anthem for Doomed Youth," and see how the tenderness of Owen's language actually intensifies the horror of what he is recording.

> *What candles may be held to speed them all?*
> *Not in the hands of boys, but in their eyes*
> *Shall shine the holy glimmers of good-byes.*
> *The pallor of girls' brows shall be their pall;*
> *Their flowers the tenderness of patient minds,*
> *And each slow dusk a drawing-down of blinds.*

These lines, for all their lushness, are a miracle of the lyric form.

Here, by contrast, is Pinter:

Here they go again
The Yanks in their armoured parade
Chanting their ballads of joy
As they gallop across the big world...

The difference, I think, is clear and simple. Harold Pinter is performing politics. Wilfred Owen is writing poetry.

The idea has been about for some time now that writers, in particular, have some special authority, which endows them with a finer moral insight than the general run of people.

Of course, this isn't true. Writers are as stupid and as smart, as craven and brave, no more and no less, than any other set of people. W.B. Yeats was occasionally silly, Ezra Pound could be an intellectual monster, Owen was, as I have said, a genius of pity, and Wallace Stevens, when he wasn't writing poetry, was much like any other insurance agent.

So, when you hear that an eminent poet is "against the war"—or "for it," for that matter (though, given the tide of fashionable opinion, the latter is less likely)—all you have heard is an opinion of no greater depth or authority than your own, or the doctor's, or the video jockey's.

And if the writer expresses that opinion in language that is not clearly, deeply thought and creatively deployed, then you may also take it that it is not the writer, as a writer, you are hearing from, but, more accurately, the writer taking a holiday from his muse for the less demanding exertions of politics.

Which is eminently the case with Mr. Pinter's poems. I can only hope it is not for them, but for his plays—which constitute what there is of Harold Pinter's craft—that he won the Nobel.

Poets, writers, musicians and actors very foolishly lay claim to an authority, a moral acuity, on issues of the day they simply do not have. The word "artist" is self-applied these days with a promiscuity that has all but emptied its meaning. I think of that European fraud who packaged his own defecation in tin cans and sold the "product" to the Saatchi Gallery. There are mountebanks by the hundreds who call themselves artists. And then there are too those pop stars—Avril Lavigne, Snoop Dogg, Madonna—who lovingly take the term that used to belong to Beethoven and da Vinci and trowel it on themselves. The opinions of such "artists" are in no way superior to those of the meanest bank clerk. No offence, really, to bank clerks. T.S. Eliot was a bank clerk.

WAR ON TERROR

THEY KILL BECAUSE THEY CAN | July 9, 2005

The organized and premeditated slaughter of innocents is the very signature of terror. In the post–9/11 world, there has been Bali. There has been Madrid. And, two days ago, there was London.

As I write, the death count is around fifty, the number of injured approaches a thousand.

Responsibility for the slaughter and mayhem has not been definitely assigned, but most serious analysis converges on al-Qaeda or one of its European tentacles. The London attack surely bears all the vile stigmata of al-Qaeda's previous slaughters: pre-planning and co-ordination, a series of explosions within a short time at highly vulnerable sites (the London subway and transport system during morning rush hour) and, above all, great moral carelessness over the "targets." Al-Qaeda demonstrated in New York on that September morning nearly four years ago that it likes to harvest as many as possible in its murderous schemes. It was but happenstance that the towers were not full, and that a "mere" 2,749 were erased from the book of life, rather than fifty thousand.

Fifty thousand dead wouldn't have stirred a feather on the conscience of Osama bin Laden and his fanatics, presuming that conscience is a faculty or a concept either he or his followers acknowledge or possess.

The attack on London coincided with the meeting of the G8 leaders. Whatever one's opinion of the efficacy of these summits, and whatever one's belief in the professions of intent of the leaders who attend them, both the summits and the leaders occupy a moral universe. They are built around ideas of moral aspiration. They pay homage—whether realized in action or not—to humanitarian ideals. Whatever the shortcomings of individual leaders, and however tormented their progress toward the goals they almost ritually set themselves, these leaders very clearly stand in the sunshine of human political activity.

Terrorists, on the other, dark, hand, have declared the perfect opposite. Death to all outside their own warped mania is all their intent. The terrorist would see the world in ruins, and mutter some perverted hosanna over the spectacle of millions dead, if a ruined world, or millions dead, served his grim and fanatical idea of purpose.

London this week, in a strange and possibly heartless way, tells me we're still lucky. Lucky only in the chilling sense that the dead hearts of Mr. bin Laden and his likes have not yet found the means, or had the opportunity, to deal a blow on the scale that all of us must by now know they would wish to deal.

There is no moral reserve in terrorism. If they could have concluded the lives of all Londoners on Thursday morning, they would have done so.

Fifty, 2,749 or many millions—the totals of the dead, and the totals of the ruptured lives of those who are left to mourn those dead, are as nothing to the terrorist, except that the terrorist always prefers the larger figure.

Terrorism is the awful hybrid of nihilism and fanaticism. It has within its seed something akin to the moral squalor of the Hitlerian period, where lives outside the golden bloodstock of the pure Aryan were as nothing—were seen as second-rate, or brutish, or verminous. Hitler's was a racist ideology in the purest distillate the world had, to that time, seen. Modern terrorism, if such is possible, may be even more bleak.

The terrorism we are only beginning to comprehend may, for the moment, wear the cloak of a certain religiosity, cover itself with the language and rhetoric of militant Islam. But why should anyone accept Mr. bin Laden's twisted pieties, his rage against the "infidels and Jews" as anything but (for him) a convenient rationalization? He who murders will not tremble at a lie. What really moves him, or his like, despite the ritual jihadi rhetoric is not yet ours to know.

I suspect it all has less to do with "religious" motives, however base and primitive those be, than they profess. The demonic arrogance of these self-styled leaders is its own motivation. Their mere whim to whip the world to bloodlust and despair betrays the emptiness of no real cause at all. I suspect the religious overlay is a kind of the-atricalism. Nihilism. This is a key component of terrorism, a greater emptiness than normal people are possibly able to contemplate.

They act because, so far, they can. They kill, because that is what they do. And they will continue to do so unless they are stopped. The ability and the wish to take innocent lives, on a vast scale, is off the moral and intel-lectual radar of most human beings. We have not taken the measure of modern terrorism because it is so far out-side our moral spectrum; the spectrum of those without a vestige of conscience is alien to our sensibility as it is to our understanding.

London this week, New York and Washington nearly four years ago, were by no means the full blossoms of modern terrorism. Just the infant rattle of a terrible idea yet to unfold in its full and horrible realization, and there-fore a practice that has emphatically to be stopped.

FANATICAL MINDS DEFY LOGIC | July 23, 2005

Two terror attacks in two weeks. It's Londoners who are having the really rough summer. A revealing feature of Thursday's "rerun" came from the fact that the rucksack bombs didn't explode—only the detonators fired. Early speculation built on this failure to suggest that the attack might have been the work of "amateurs."

Here we are, but five years into the great new millennium, and terrorism has become so familiar, so pervasive, that it can accommodate a couple of categories: typical terrorism—i.e., done by professionals—and the copycat or "incompetent" variety, the work of amateurs.

It was interesting, too, during the early hours of this speculation, that this kind of talk seemed so normal. None of the pundits betrayed the slightest surprise that terrorism might have "migrated" from purely professional nihilists or committed jihadist fundamentalists to a second tier of free-lancers, publicity seekers or copycats.

Such talk showed how habituated we have become to the pervasive and diffuse sense that it can happen any-where, at any time. We all know what "it" is. And when bombs go off, whether in the London subways—as was really the case this month—or in Paris, Washington, Montreal or Toronto, as may well be the case next time, we will all be shocked by the carnage, but not surprised by the event.

We will be shocked because carnage visited on inno-cent people, from whatever motive, will always shock those who have remained within the circle of civilized humanity. But we will not be surprised because, since the mass slaughter of September 11, the Western world has been on notice that its citizens are targets in an amorphous, conspiratorial campaign that flies under the accommodating banner of Islamic fundamentalism.

We are similarly on notice that the self-appointed leaders of al-Qaeda and its franchises follow a logic of their own choosing. Whether that logic may be divined with any degree of fidelity from what they actually proclaim as their goals and motives, or whether (apart from the malignant delight they take in the deeds themselves) they have anything that conforms to rational and understandable goals, are wide-open questions.

What we do know is that the logic of fanatics is a specialized product; it does not ape or mime the logic of ordinary people. Efforts to "understand" the terrorists are efforts to bring the calculus and standards of responsible minds as instruments to map their opposites: irresponsible minds that do not acknowledge standards of any kind.

The rhetorical questions that have saturated a thousand news stories since the first London bombings—How could young, homegrown British subjects from Leeds take up the suicide bombing of fellow citizens?—illustrate this point.

People are agape with perplexity that "their own" have ventured mass slaughter of their fellows. These were not "imports" on some desperate mission, sent by the international outlaws of terrorism. These were men, born and bred in Britain, of families who, from all accounts, cherished all that Britain, as a democratic multicultural state, offered them. They were nice. They were friendly.

They did, some of them, good works.

All such questioning is beside the point. The only "under-standing" of a terrorist deed is the deed itself. Attempts to find some formulaic shortcut to understanding them—it's the plight of the Palestinians, it's Tony Blair's joining in the armed deposition of Saddam Hussein, it's American policy in the Middle East—are rote, puzzled stutterings in the face of something, fundamentally inexplicable.

Terrorism will not be understood out of existence. It must instead be challenged, guarded against, and to the degree that arms and intelligence, and the co-operation of nations, will allow, it must be utterly incapacitated. The only logic that fanaticism allows is the expansion of its power to kill. The only logic that will defeat it is force.

Following the second London bombing, it was Australia's John Howard, not Tony Blair, who best sketched the failings of looking for "cause and effect" to explain terror: "We lose sight of the challenge we have if we allow ourselves to see these attacks in the context of particular circumstances rather than the abuse, through a perverted ideology, of people and their murder."

I wrote after the first London bombings that the British were lucky the dead and wounded were so few—few only in the context of an appetite for destruction that, should it find the means, would be boundless. London was, by that under-standing, even luckier this week.

But luck is thin and fleeting. We temporize with terror-ism when we look for root causes. The attacks will continue until they are stopped. Terrorists will inflict misery with exponential fury when they can. On the one question that counts, the sentence so many are appalled to hear applies: George Bush was right: it *is* a war.

WHAT WE ARE FIGHTING FOR | May 23, 2006

After last week's Commons vote, I wonder how many people are much clearer in their understanding of our mission in Afghanistan. We have made commitments to Afghanistan. We were part of the operation that rid that country of the Taliban government and pursued al-Qaeda after 9/11. We did that, not only as an ally of the United States after the attack on the Twin Towers and the Pentagon, but also because there were Canadians killed in those attacks. Canada agreed that eliminating a government that had sheltered and nursed the terrorist organization that committed the atrocity of 9/11 was both right and in our own self-interest, that not pursuing the Taliban and al-Qaeda would only leave Afghanistan as a potential site of similar designs in the future.

That mission had UN approval, was composed of a concert of forces, of which our country's was one. But protection against future terrorism meant more than just displacing the Taliban government. It meant offering, insofar as an international force could offer, the citizens of Afghanistan the opportunity to build a new kind of government, one elected, one less hospitable to hijacking by sinister forces and more open to the basic civil liberties that people in the democracies take for granted. It was to assist in that effort that Canadian troops remained.

It is not possible merely to wish benevolent government on a nation whose history, both recent and of old, has been a field of war, invasion and lawlessness. So, our troops remained deployed to (a) guarantee a measure of security while Afghanistan citizens went about the first steps to democracy and the extension of basic rights, (b) assist in building the essential elements—schools, a justice system, infrastructure, roads—that any society must have, and (c) offer humanitarian assistance where possible.

Four years after the Taliban were deposed, even after Afghanistan made the first steps to building a democracy, that country is still under threat from forces, both Taliban and others, who do not wish to see that result and who are on a campaign to demoralize Afghans, destabilize their government, intimidate their citizens and drive from Afghanistan all those who are assisting its democratic growth.

Those forces must be fought. The first principle of establishing a representative government in Afghanistan is to fight those who would deny it: the Taliban, remnants of al-Qaeda and the so-called insurgents. There is no other way that the secondary parts of the mission, the more benign or peacekeeping operations, can be performed.

So, we are at war. We are at war because we acknowledge our own interest in Afghanistan and because, as Canadians, we see the value of extending, if we can, some measure of liberty and democracy to a people who have not tasted those virtues. The campaign in Afghanistan can be seen as harmonious with the liberation efforts that Canadian forces, to their honour, were associated with in the far more enormous campaigns of the First and Second World Wars. That, as I see it, is the rationale of our mission in Afghanistan. To the extent that a majority of Canadians accept these goals and fully appreciate and understand them, the mission will have the kind of support outside Parliament that is necessary to maintain it.

Achieving that appreciation and understanding will take far more, however, than the very mixed effort in Parliament last week.

THE REAL TRUTH | July 15, 2006

I was never an *X-Files* fan. Agents Mulder and Scully grimly walked through hundreds of episodes, wearily tearing away at the flimsy curtain the rest of us call "reality," whispering of cover-ups, UFOs, secret agencies within secret agencies, and powerful forces "out there," and I was happy to have missed almost every one of them.

Moody and Sullen, as one bright parodist renamed them, were knights errant of the paranormal and the paranoid. Though relentlessly grey, brooding and portentous,

The X-Files made a sweet pitch to adolescent minds (of all ages) with its signature motto: "The Truth Is Out There." Capital letters mandatory. (It's not philosophy unless it's in capital letters.)

The X-Files was fast food for the conspiracy gluttons, the intellectually lazy who relish the frisson of some exotic theory of "hidden others" who have arranged the world, and all that happens in it, in dark code: *they* with their laboratories and computers, *they* with their power and money, *they* with their secret societies (think *The Da Vinci Code*), run everything. In other words, the world is a puppet show run by dark and hidden adepts of power and politics, and only a few—the conspiracy-mongers—have peeped behind the occluding screen.

The assassination of John F. Kennedy, now nearly forty years on, has spawned a literature of suspicion and conjecture of intimidating bulk and mass. The "grassy knoll" and the "second gunman" have inspired more plots than the entire membership of the International Association of Crime Writers. It's a law of this kind of thinking: the further from the event under scrutiny, the more mountainous the unhinged speculation surrounding it.

Except—except for September 11, 2001. I would have thought that the horrors of that day, the magnitude of the attacks, the immense coverage of the actual crashes into the towers, the even more immense coverage in the days after, had evacuated September 11 of all mystery and speculation. We know that day too well.

We swiftly learned the identities of all nineteen hijackers. We saw, in (alas) real time, the buildings collapse; we saw the heroic efforts of firefighters and police in New York; we have since read and heard of the numerous cellphone conversations before the brave passengers of Flight 93 tried to wrest control of the doomed jet from the hijackers. We have even seen the video of Osama bin Laden wherein he gloatingly narrates the success of his mission, takes pride in his drear accomplishment.

What else is there, the reasonable mind pleads to ask? But no. The questioning of 9/11 is a full-blown industry on the Internet. The buildings didn't collapse because two fuel-loaded jets crashed into them; a missile, not another jet, hit the Pentagon; Flight 93 was brought down with a missile—the fantasies spin on. Books have been written telling the "real truth" of that day.

One truly bizarre, or comic, online posting conducts an experiment (with pictures) using rabbit wire, a concrete cinder block and a container of kerosene to "prove" the steel pillars of the twin towers would not have melted in the fires that followed the crash. Engineers who visited this site have left jibbering and in tears.

Bush was behind 9/11. The Israelis were behind 9/11. Bush and the Israelis and a neo-con cabal were behind 9/11. Osama didn't do it. Thousands of people engineered a controlled demolition of the towers; the hijacked jets crashing into them were no more than an elaborate version of the street magician's "bait and switch."

I cannot comprehend what tilt of mind refuses the tidal wave of tragic facts about that horrible day in favour of near-lunatic and unmoored speculation. The answer must be that the hatred of U.S. President George Bush has, among the most strident of those who despise him, reached incandescent proportions and has merged with that strain of freewheeling paranoia that is an undercurrent of much of our modern times. Hating Mr. Bush ferociously, and believing so firmly that the truth is always "Out There" (never in front of your face), has produced a monstrous fable of conspiracy, cover-up, sinister motivations of an all-controlling apparatus that has abused the world and engaged in two wars (Iraq and Afghanistan), all for some agenda that works for the benefit of (who else?) Israel and the Jews.

The 9/11 conspiracy theories—whether those who peddle them are aware of it or not—trail in the spurious and repulsive wake of that arch-conspiracy, the demented Protocols of the Elders of Zion. One would have thought the last century had got us past that delirious and hate-nourished fantasy-hoax.

GREAT AND GOOD

POWER BASED ON FAITH, NOT ARMS | April 9, 2005

The mighty of the Earth—presidents, kings, queens and diplomats—were drawn to Rome this week. For a few days, it seemed the ancient capital was reliving the days of its early power and glory, when it was the heart of the greatest empire of its day, and when the coronation or the death of an emperor summoned the potentates of all the then known world.

That spectacle in ancient days was the requisite homage exerted by earthly dominion, the obsequious response of vassal states and client rulers to a great imperial machine.

Imperial Rome, the Rome of the Caesars, was mighty and disciplined. Obeisance was the necessary coin of satellites and satraps to the overwhelming predominance of manifest power.

It is almost chilling that, nearly two thousand years after Augustus, after all that has changed over that vast time, this same city should, even for a few days, become again the

epicentre of the world's focus, and that the highest representatives of the world's more powerful and wealthy nations,
together with those of some of the world's weakest and
most miserable, have been drawn almost irresistibly once
more to that venerable capital.

For reasons vastly different, however. John Paul II was
no Augustus Caesar. The insolent taunt of murderous
Stalin, which was recalled so many times in the past seven
days—How many divisions does the Pope command?—was
its own answer. Of power, in the sense Stalin used the word
and abused its exercise, John Paul II had none. Yet where is
wretched Stalin now, for all his legions? Darkening the
darker pages of history, remembered as a monster.

So it was not power, not the leverage of a great military,
or that other power of great wealth to which the world so
frequently offers obliging genuflection, that summoned
those kings, queens and presidents. The death of a pope,
even a great one, does not shatter alliances, rearrange the
pieces on the chessboard—those days, too, are long past.

The leaders of almost the entire world (China being the
churlish exception, but then, China is still yoked to decayed
communism) presented themselves because they had
watched and seen, over two and a half decades, that this
pontiff presented himself in a uniquely special way to all the
world. They had seen that a man holding the highest office
of what very many regard as an anachronistic institution—
and representing what very many equally regard as an out-
moded idea, ethos and practice, that of religion—exercised

a sublime ability to move and enter into the spirit of millions and millions of people.

In the great fury of this modern secular age, in a world freighted with injustice, shadowed by terrorism and frantic with the thirst for speed, novelty and distraction, Pope John Paul II, by the example of his person and by the immensity of his ability to communicate, was the singular example of a kind of integrity that most had thought had long since vanished.

Egoless, direct, transparent, resolute—there are a host of personal attributes of this remarkable man—he reached into millions of hearts of every condition and faith, and into the hearts of many agnostics and even atheists as well.

It is not a phenomenon that will be unriddled—unless, of course, the world is prepared to understand it on his terms, on the terms of his faith in Christ and on his understanding of faith itself. That, for those outside the circle of Catholicism, is almost certainly a bridge too far, especially in our corner of the world, in the tumultuously secular West. A culture that offers intellectual hospitality to the chatterings of Dr. Phil and the romps of *Desperate Housewives* doesn't have the stamina to pursue the idea of faith and its agency.

But the record is there. Before the advent of this man, the world was living nightmarishly the terrible equilibrium of the Cold War and the ever-present anxiety of a nuclear holocaust. Suddenly (in retrospect, it seems almost overnight), beginning in Poland, Russian communism was gone, and a score of countries and their citizens unshackled from totalitarian tyranny. The massive structure of a great anti-religious dispensation collapsed and vanished.

And all of was this traceable, in part it is true, but also inescapably, to the presence of this one figure, whose only force—besides those delightfully caparisoned Swiss Guards—was unadorned belief.

The operation of the intangible on the tangible, of the pulses of the spirit on the reality of the world, is the dynamic of faith. John Paul II radiated a faith so plain and deep that it shattered what was, at bottom, simply false and cruel.

Which is why, during this week, Rome is again for a time the centre of the world. Why millions have stood in line merely to pass this pope one last time, and why the mighty and the powerful find it irresistible not to acknowledge, by their presence, that a marvel has been among us.

John Paul's passing vibrates unfailing with the passing of Alexander Solzhenitsyn—another voice of steel and courage. Some centuries hence, when they call up the biblical phrase "there were giants . . . in those days," it won't be Dr. Phil or the slutry of *Desperate Housewives* being evoked.

SOLZHENITSYN'S STATURE | August 9, 2008

The death of Alexander Solzhenitsyn was the passing of a human-rights giant. There are few individuals, writers or otherwise, who even approach his stature as an opponent of repression and tyranny. Solzhenitsyn belongs to a very select set of people whose courage and example lit the darkness of the century just past, among whom are Nelson Mandela, Martin Luther King and Gandhi.

Here in the contemporary West, the phrase "speaking truth to power" all too often drops from the lips of some self-regarding protester, the ravings of 9/11 "truthers," or a Hollywood B-lister taking on "Big Oil." Michael Moore was, I believe, hailed as speaking truth to power when he "took on" the world's easiest and favourite target, George Bush, and played to the tuxedoed Amen corner at the Cannes Film Festival. That the film he made was mendacious, that its thesis was a guaranteed applause line, that there was not a one-in-a-billion chance he would "suffer" from making *Fahrenheit 9/11*, shows how empty, how deflated, the application of that once so potent phrase has become. Speaking mush to millions is more like it.

How different the life and example of Solzhenitsyn, though even juxtaposing the commercial propagandist Moore and the Soviet hero makes me cringe—mosquitoes and eagles don't belong on the same page. A few references to Stalin in a letter (one a description of the tyrant as "the whiskered one") was enough to have the army hero

Solzhenitsyn sentenced to eight years and internal exile for life. There was a "human-rights" violation. A Soviet soldier makes a few wisecracks in a letter and gets sent off to the horrors and deprivations of the Stalinist labour camps.

We in the West don't know of such things. For all the inanities, incompetence and disappointments of our politics, and however much on our worst and most cynical days we deplore their glide into artful contests between barely disguised twins (Democrat–Republican, Liberal–Conservative, who can tell the difference?), we have been so secured from the true horrors of unfettered state power that we barely understand how good we actually have it.

We can bash away at our leaders, mock our MPs, late-night comics can ridicule a president, citizens can charge into committee rooms, newspapers can excoriate a policy or a minister, not only with abandon but without the slightest fear that anything of any real consequence will happen to us. Modern democracy is so very obliging to protest that protest has become routine.

Our protests, our sallies against government or authority, are free in two senses: we may perform them when we wish—no one will stop us—and they carry no penalty, no cost. For those who have not done so, a little reading of Alexander Solzhenitsyn is a magnificent assist to sharpening our awareness of how extraordinarily exceptional such a state of affairs actually is.

The Gulag Archipelago is both a monumental encyclopedia of Stalinist repression and one of the greatest writerly acts of memorialization ever achieved. It is also the most sustained indictment of a monstrous, heartless and lying regime ever written. It is an anatomy of totalitarianism written by a single individual, toward whom its force and enmity had already been turned. Solzhenitsyn was to be but dust under tyranny's wheel, but a great heart and greater courage, allied to a superhuman sense of utter conscience, turned the tables.

There are many elements, many events, that combined to end the nightmare of Soviet communism, inaugurated by Vladimir Lenin in 1917, to end the regime in which human rights were a fiction and a mockery, cruelty was policy and absolute power the only real doctrine. But the decision of Alexander Solzhenitsyn to write what he knew, to organize and structure his account (the writer's gift) to produce maximum effect, and to release it to the world regardless of the consequences to himself (some of which he had already and so bitterly tasted), was surely the *sine qua non* of real truth speaking to real power. Without Alexander Solzhenitsyn, without *The Gulag Archipelago*, the great tyranny might still endure.

Doubtless, he wrote the *Gulag*, as he said himself so many times, primarily to give voice to those who suffered and to put the lie to the regime built upon lies. But to those of us here in the West who have been spared, by providence or luck, the hell that all tyranny introduces to its citizens, it has compelling relevance as well. For one, it will deeply remind us of the importance of human rights, and remind us, too, of what is really meant by that now tattered and trivialized phrase, when insults in some comedy store are allowed to be wrapped in its devalued banner and Canadian bureaucrats debate whether washing or not washing one's hands in a fast-food outlet is a "violation" of them.

With Alexander Solzhenitsyn's passing, the world is less one hero.

If Solzhenitsyn's passing had no other virtue than to remind the world of what a truly independent mind and independent person looks like, and what power the example of both contains, it was not a mournful occasion. It's a stock comment on Solzhenitsyn that he was a hero to conservatives when he was seen as just, or only, a critic of communism and then less a pet of liberals when he scathingly rebuked the West for its gluttonous materialism and mindless amusements.

What he, most emphatically, was not was a shrivelled, manic, closed-minded hack of any "side." He was not, in other words, a partisan.

OUT OF HIS TREE | May 6, 2006

I read this week that Keith Richards had fallen out of a palm tree. It was reassuring. Good old Keith, I thought, still rockin' through life, still with a cigarette locked, maybe even welded, between his lips, on tour with Sir (Struts-a-lot) Jagger—no knighthood for Keith—and still finding time to get up a palm tree somewhere so he could fall out of it.

Things happen around, or to, or with, Keith Richards that don't happen to the whole boring galaxy of super-celebrities, and they always have. There's not a self-respecting palm tree in the world that would drop Paul McCartney, for example.

Keith wasn't badly hurt, I understand. Updates mentioned a concussion—how could they tell?—and there was some early talk of an operation to drain blood from his head, which wouldn't have been a novelty to Keith. In a way, that's what he does for a living.

Apparently, however, that won't be necessary after all. I'm glad they didn't have to bore. Certain crania should be left unmined.

Some people say Keith Richards hasn't aged well. What they mean, of course, is that, in the great conga line of Botoxed, breast-sculpted, personal-trainered, South Beach–dieting, yoga-pretzeled, old age–phobic, health-and-youth delusionists whose nipped and tucked faces gargoyle out at us from the front covers of the celebrity magazines, Keith Richards refuses to hop in sequence.

What they mean when they say he hasn't aged well is that he has actually aged, while they, chained to vanity and self-delusion, have tried to put surgery and silicone between them and mortality. They've made the fool's bargain. That bell will toll, and toll for them, and a hundred face peels won't mute the summons.

The wild, abandoned years have washed over Keith Richards, and he's welcomed every splash, and welcomed, too, every line and dent that hard days and long nights have graven into that iconic, laughing face.

I like him because he's *not* healthy. While others are sucking extract of seaweed to cleanse their colons, he's outside—probably up a palm tree having a smoke.

Every time he walks by some deluxe spa—where the already super-pampered are toning their muscles, or ripping their abs, or taming their wattles, or smelling their way to "wellness" (seriously, is aromatherapy a joke?)—he must have to cross himself to ward off the folly within.

I like him because he knows who he is. When the preening front man Mick Jagger strutted, where Sir Elton and Sir Paul and Sir Bob Geldof had pranced before him, into the meretricious embrace of the British honours system and accepted a knighthood, it was plain man Keith who was the real rock star that day.

"I don't want to step out onstage with someone wearing a coronet and sporting the old ermine," Keith told the British music magazine *Uncut* in an expletive-rich interview. "I told Mick it's a paltry honour. . . . It's not what the Stones is about, is it?"

Ah, to have heard the expletives. But "paltry," you'll agree, is perfect.

I like him, too, because he seems to be cause-phobic.

No chance of Keith Richards showing up in PEI or Newfoundland someday, shading himself under the blimpish canopy of Pamela Anderson's hyperinflations, to plead the cause of seals and chimps. No chance of him showing up wearing a Kabbalah trinket to "raise our consciousness" of the declining pitch of the howler monkey, or whatever happens to be the cause of the week, in a *tête-à-tête* with the Chairman of the Bored, Larry King.

I liked it, too, when he declined the worldwide exhibition of the super-famous and the super-rich when they gave of their glamorous time to Make Poverty History. He asked the right questions and made the right remarks. To *Uncut* magazine, he said: "I mean, who's this gratifying, and where are the Africans? Where was their say?" Referring to the pressure on him to participate, he said, "Oh yeah, all the Sirs had a bash, believe me."

"All the Sirs had a bash." There's a T-shirt slogan worth a million "I care" wristbands. All the Sirs, the Dorian Grays of geriatric rock, are caricatures of themselves. Flocking to the palace for tea, lapped in ermine (bash no seals!), gushing their goodwill for the world's poor—then back to their castles to check on their gold.

So, it is good to hear that Keith Richards is still falling out of trees. He may be the only one in the whole parade of what we deliriously call rock icons who still keeps some honest sense of abandon—which is the heart of music, rock and roll or otherwise—and who doesn't worship his own battered image. The rest of them are plutocrats and poseurs.

But Keith Richards is in a palm tree all by himself (or, as the case may be, just beneath one).

Ah, Keith! the only real god in the whole vanity-sodden pantheon. Up another tree, Keith, smoke another cigarette, and fall as often as you damn well please. A hundred Madonnas doesn't add up to one-tenth of a Keith Richards. (See also "Cars Are Smokers, Too" on page 201.)

THE PLEASURES OF SMOKING

MONEY TO BURN | May 31, 2003

It's ancient history—possibly before the *Cheers* era, definitely before *Friends*—but there was a time, and it lasted for a long while, when Kraft Dinner was seventeen cents a package. And cigarettes were forty cents for a deck of twenty. Kraft Dinner and smokes for little more than half a buck. If we'd had good weather, and of course we didn't— I summon these reveries from long-ago Newfoundland—it would have been paradise. A good, fat, fresh codfish could be had from the boat for a dime—but, tearful with remembered joy, I digress.

Those times are no more. Cigarettes now are almost as expensive as a similar volume of platinum, and of the two (Kraft Dinner, Export "A"), I am not certain which is more acceptable to smoke. Kraft Dinner may now be bought at certain convenience stores in the city of Toronto for a princely $1.50, a price nearly nine times the earlier one.

Kraft Dinner, however, has maintained its cachet. Packaged pasta has prevailed, where nicotine and its sibling tars, so rancorously and at such cost to the Canadian social fabric, have—alas—gone the way of anathema.

In fact, Kraft Dinner revolves in that all-but-unobtainable orbit of the Tim Hortons doughnut and the A&W Teen Burger. It is one of that great trinity of quick digestibles that have been enrolled as genuine Canadian cultural icons. Hamburgers, macaroni and doughnuts—Canada, this is your nation.

In passing, I must note that it is my personal view that the Kraft Dinner we get nowadays, despite the urgent assurances on the package, is not the "classic" of old. The pasta is smaller, and the powdered cheddar in a sack (which, when blended with butter and milk, is used to pave over the macaroni), is less thick, less intimate with the little elbows than it used to be. A definite fall-off, in my view.

I've summoned these reveries, not out of cloying nostalgia or in obedience to the dread mantra that hails everything from "the good old days" as infallibly superior to an ever-specious present. Not at all. Rather, it was all the talk of pot on Parliament Hill, all that murky doublespeak of "decriminalizing," while insisting pot was still illegal. The weary contortions of the Liberals trying to look really liberal—going soft on weed is the very amaranth of liberalism—while not surrendering their equally precious commitment to the nation's health, and of course the well-being of the children.

Put reefer and Parliament in the same sentence, and linguistic contortions cannot be far behind. Nor did the hypocrisy of a government that has been fundamentalist on one mode of inhaling seeking to add parliamentary respectability to another mode—at least equally obnoxious, twice as smelly and real hell on the carpet. What really focused my attention during the pot debate, if focus may be allowed on such a topic, wasn't the justice side of the argument, but its health corollary. It was the announcement by Health Minister Anne McLellan that her department was allocating $245 million—please stare at that figure—to advertise the dangers of smoking the pot that her colleagues were, by implication, proclaiming innocuous.

There was a time when a million dollars was thought to be an immense amount of money. But here is a government, on one of its off days, proposing as a sidebar, as a mere sputtering afterthought, to toss $245 million—two hundred and forty-five!!! Nearly a quarter of a billion—to blunt the portended impact of some of its own most progressive legislation.

When did money cease to mean anything? When did expenditures of hundreds of millions of dollars, merely to deflect the impact of another government program, become so insanely trivial that the amount at stake barely crawled into some newscasts? When did they, meaning the politicians *or* the citizenry, become so numb, dare I say narcotized, to such vast expenditures?

Was it the estimated price of almost a billion dollars—

one thousand million—to construct a useless list of the country's firearms? Was it the other billion dollars that went sluicing through Human Resources and Development Canada? The rhetorical question that screams to be asked is, What are they smoking?

I forebear to explore beyond to ask the other blatant question: Does anyone, anyone at all, anywhere, believe that money spent by the government in pursuit of "public-service messaging" ever rattled the opinion of anyone whose sentience was greater than a stone's?

Hear that sound? It's a quarter of a billion dollars whistling its way to nullity. And so I thought of the long-ago days when even seventeen cents could supply nourishment and comfort, and those ever-so-long-ago days when a pittance was really a pittance, instead of, as now, a stack of bullion that once would make Croesus drool.

A JOINT IS A SMOKE | Novemeber 27, 2004

Social pressure accounts for the decline of smoking. It is surely not the risible Health Canada public-service messages, or the extravagantly inane scare pictures on cigarette packs, that have worked.

These latter are wildly over the top. There's one picture of a carious mouth, a portrait of such dental horror that it must have been lifted from some mummy comic book.

If two-year-olds were ardent smokers, this campaign would have its perfect audience. Mix it up with a health-service warning from the tooth fairy and there wouldn't be a two-year-old lighting up anywhere.

No, it isn't the official stuff that cut down on the tobacco habit. It's the frown of acquaintances, the increasing chill that ever-so-superior non-smokers send out to the last wastrel of their set who dares to take out the Player's Light pack. It's really very simple. Social opprobrium is the scourge that reforms. The only thing stronger than nicotine is the fear of friends' disapproval.

Alas, reform is never a straight line. Just when it might be thought the art of inhaling was going the way of the hula hoop and the dodo, we have a report this week that there is something of a renaissance of pot smoking. Hemp is hip again.

Since 1994, the number of people smoking pot in this country has doubled. Even more impressive, a key component of the population—the very element most government campaigns are most urgent about "saving," namely the young—has taken to pot with a vengeance. The same study also revealed that almost 30 per cent of 15- to 17-year-olds and 47 per cent of 18- and 19-year-olds used marijuana in the past year.

It went further, reporting—and I'm really glad to hear it—that "It's easier to get marijuana on a school ground today than it is to get alcohol or cigarettes."

(Just as a footnote here, I can't remember when it was

ever particularly easy to get booze on a playground, but then, I grew up in circumscribed and difficult times. The Most Holy Rosary Parish School of Placentia Bay, Newfoundland, had few supplements to the basic curriculum, and tots of vodka or rum during recess were most definitely not among them. It might have helped. There were problems in trigonometry that definitely needed some form of remedial lubrication.)

I think what we're seeing here is another illustration of that wonderful irony that goes under the rubric of the Law of Unintended Consequences. Peer pressure and remorseless rudeness (driving smokers out of doors) has whittled away at the cohort that looked to tobacco for a friendly lift during each day's many mortifications. But vague signals of approval toward marijuana as an alternate solace, its much-hyped value as a "medicinal" tool (remember the tired line from every party, "I only drink for medicinal purposes") and the official moves to decriminalize pot have worked to celebrate the mellowing weed.

No one is going to frown at a pot smoker. She may be mollifying a pain. She is certainly not to be branded as a slave to Big Tobacco. And just look at her teeth: they're perfect. No mummy's curse has scarred that mouth. And the young, bless their adventurous and experimenting hearts, know more than any others what is hip and what is not. Cigarettes are so passé. Besides, they offer no real mood change.

Come to think of it, this may be the real appeal of marijuana. As well as the comforts of addiction, a joint offers a bland, smooth, edgeless few moments in a turbulent world. It puts a soft blanket over transient anxieties, suspends the critical judgment and enhances, beyond all measure of their intrinsic worth, the reception of some truly awful songs.

It is impossible to understand the popularity of some ancient bands and singers—the Mamas and the Papas, the Grateful Dead, Joan Baez (eech), Peter, Paul and Mary—without allowing for considerable numbing of the brain and a benign stupor that buried their dreadful lyrics beneath the radar of any self-regarding consciousness. The entire fame and popularity of Bob Dylan is only explicable on a similar subtraction of critical response.

I suppose the question that remains to be faced is whether the switch from one form of cigarette to another—pot is mainly smoked, and while RJ Reynolds may not be rolling them, joints *are* cigarettes—is a good thing. Do we have the same alarms about the second-hand waft from a doobie as we do from the less-noxious Export "A"? Are we to worry about the "passive relaxation" effect?

These are deep questions. They require meditation. Wind chimes, an old Cheech and Chong soundtrack, a few doobies and Health Canada beside us in the wilderness—we'll figure them out.

GREAT NEWS OUT OF VANCOUVER | September 29, 2007

The Cinderella City is about to enact one of the most comprehensive, ferocious, detailed and high-minded anti-smoking bylaws this side of Alpha Centauri. I am really glad to see this.

It's been well known for decades now that Vancouver is one of the world's most beautiful cities, and further that it has resolved every major social and political problem known to man or metropolis. The Downtown Eastside, old-timers will recall, was cleaned up decades ago, and is now a most splendid housing-estate cum park, with a mix of citizens of every income and colour and culture—a true model to the world. Thanks to the forward-looking city governors of previous years, and their generous support of science and research into waste disposal, Vancouver's garbage now evaporates, harmlessly, into the wide air as soon as it is placed on the streets. Garbage trucks can now only be found in the city's famous network of museums.

Finally, where every other city in North America is a stifling box of car-packed gridlock and toxic exhaust, there hasn't been a traffic jam in Vancouver since—let me see—about 1975, I think. The great monorails, the uncluttered bridges, the zillion bike lanes and the brisk, courteous efficiency of the city's drivers as they zip, unimpeded, in their tidy little hybrids in and out of the downtown are the envy of every other municipal government on the continent. Shangri-La, thy new name is Vancouver.

So I'm glad the city council of that marvellous city by the mountains and the sea has finally gone to the mat, so to speak, on the last social scourge and only outstanding civic problem the city has.

Are the city's proposed anti-smoking bylaws thorough, you ask? Let me put it this way: It's just too bad there isn't a Nobel Prize for Zeal, because, were there one, the civic fathers and mothers of Vancouver would be booking flights to Oslo even as I type their praises. The only failure in the bylaws, as I read the accounts of them, is that smokers are—not yet anyway—required to carry a handbell and sound their approach when they enter municipal boundaries

I especially like the bylaw for transient smokers. If a taxi is passing through Vancouver, neither the passenger nor driver may smoke—even if agreeable to both parties, and even if the taxi is licensed by another civic authority. This could be fine-tuned, though. Both the cab and its passenger could be defumigated at the city's boundaries—it would be a pity to fustify an impeccable city.

Sidewalks, public buildings, bars, restaurants—well, you know they covered them. No smoking "within six metres of any entryway, window or air intake." If you want to light up in Vancouver now, by my calculations the only legal spot would probably be on the median line of a major highway, or at the end of a long diving board extended from an apartment window.

But this is Vancouver. So let there be no surprise, as it approaches the sublime apogee of utter civic perfectibility, that it was mindful—that even here, in addressing its last plague—it had to consider its dues to multiculturalism, plurality and tolerance for all.

Vancouver *will* allow hookah parlours. That's "hookah," in case you stumbled. There are, I read, three hookah parlours, which offer their glass bowls and water pipes to some of the city's newer citizens.

According to the World Health Organization, "a typical one-hour session of hookah smoking exposes the user to 100 to 200 times the volume of smoke inhaled from a single cigarette." Now, any trivial inconsistency that nitpicking libertarians, or the live-and-let-live extremists, might have with this is more than trumped by the consideration that an hour on the hookah will combat "the depression common for newcomers" to the city. And if toking an hour on the hookah with two hundred times the volume of smoke from a single cigarette chases away the newcomer blues, well, hook up the hookah, toke away, I say.

Another petty glitch I spotted in a *Vancouver Sun* article suggests that "the one foggy point in the new bylaw was whether it will apply to crack cocaine and crystal meth smoking." Picky, picky, picky. Crack cocaine and crystal meth? Bubblegum addictions. I'm sure the city council will get around to crack cocaine and crystal meth smoking when, and only when, they've reined in the jelly-bean rings on city playgrounds.

So, it's a perfect set of bylaws. Accommodation for hookahs, a little ambiguity on the toy drugs of crack and meth, but a steel fence of regulation—even for those just passing through—on the only problem left in the city that is the only unflawed diamond in a zirconian world: damned cigarette smoking.

Three cheers to Vancouver and its Committee for Public Safety. Now, I gottah gettah hookah.

REPUTATIONS

THE BUSH PARADOX | January 31, 2004

There's a paradox at the centre of the terrific animus toward George W. Bush. For his detractors, and they are legion and intense, the man is a cipher, a mere stand-in, for the real powers in the White House. A puppet of the functioning minds and stronger personalities of Donald Rumsfeld, Dick Cheney, Karl Rove and the outer ring of advisers such as Paul Wolfowitz and Richard Perle.

He is simultaneously thought of as a bumbling preppy, an arrested-development delinquent, the prototypical frat-boy party animal, the kind of middle-aged man who thinks John Belushi's *Animal House* is the only real film made in the last thirty years and whose idea of reading is a Tom Clancy novel—or, on less challenging days, the latest issue of *Guns & Ammo* magazine.

The indictment is scathing and thorough. George W. is an automaton of Pooh-sized mentality ("a bear of very little brain") with the attention span of a slow-witted gnat, the introspective capacity of a starlet and the mental agility of a stale Fig Newton.

His enemies scarcely credit him with doing his own breathing, and would comment that, if he *is* breathing on his own, he is surely not conscious of his doing so. He lucked into the presidency on the strength of his father's name, a private fortune that was made for him by his friends, and the sheer, eerie incompetence of the Al Gore campaign. There was nothing, absolutely nothing, that George W. Bush, on his own merits or as a consequence of his own actions, contributed to the effort that landed him in the White House and placed in his late-adolescent hands the exercise of the greatest power that this Earth has ever known.

That is the short and polite version—but such is the character of George W. Bush in the minds of millions and millions of people who actively detest him, among them some millions of his fellow-citizens.

Mr. Bush, in the account of his despisers, is a nullity, a nothing, a creature so limited in the resources of his person, his competence, his presence, that he is almost a non-being. Why, how does such a nothing stimulate so commanding an intensity and range of visceral loathing? The distaste for Mr. Bush is not a casual dismissal; it is passionate.

He inspires a sharpness of revulsion that people usually reserve for more personal antipathies: the bitterness of hostility following the reversal or despoliation of a cherished intimacy. If this Texan is such a perfect nobody, why does anyone care?

It is not because he is president, though that is usually the rationalization put forward: that, because he is president, and therefore has such power to do so many evil, stupid things, it is not only right to detest him, it is an obligation.

No, this line of reasoning is a kind of after-scaffolding for an emotion that has little to do with reason at all. Mr. Bush is loathed, first, in his own right—as a pickup-driving, nicknaming, inarticulate and haughty George Dubya. That he should be president just adds rocket boosters to the initial hate.

If he is, as a person, so innocuous, so unfinished and essentially trivial, what drives the anger and contempt of so many people? Part of an answer might be that, for those outside America, for whom anti-Americanism is professional or ideological, the projection of the person inhabiting the White House as little less than a fool and a stooge adds an extra fillip of insult and contempt to their career animosity.

For those within America who are fervidly anti-Bush, the same characterization offers them a proportionately larger and higher image of themselves. They are bigger because "Bush" is so small. Michael Moore, ludicrous, pompous and banal all at once, stands so much taller, morally and intellectually, when set against that dim caricature occupying the White House. The people who hate George Bush have a great deal of their own self-esteem invested in maintaining the idea of that upstart, vacuous, Texan dummy in the Oval Office.

By the reading of his enemies, George Bush does not have the personal force, the sustenance of character, to generate the enormous field of contempt and enmity with which he is surrounded. A vacuum doesn't inspire hate.

By contrast, Bill Clinton—quicksilver Bill, the man of a thousand reflexes, intellectual, at home equally at the most highbrow symposium or riffing on a Hollywood stage—has a personality as large and volatile as some weather systems. But it's Mr. Bush, the nullity, the man empty of personality, who charges millions with the most profound and negative emotions. The response is all out of proportion to its stimulus. It is irrational.

The Bush paradox is the central fact in world politics today. It has one equally curious rider. The world's real villain, Osama bin Laden, very largely gets, by contrast, an emotional bye.

FROM BRIAN'S LIPS TO PETER'S MICROPHONE | September 17, 2005

Some are indifferent to high office, and some few seek it merely on a whim.

There are others for whom ambition has all the force of a carnal mania.

The drive for power is manifold. It can exist purely for its own sake—to be the one person who's in charge, to be at the top of the heap—for the delicious thrill of outstripping everyone else. For others, power exists but as an instrument for doing things, to work great change for a common good. This set, alas, is a small one, but politics earns whatever good name it may claim because these few exist.

And then there are those who burn their life's energy, marshal all their cunning and intelligence to achieve acclaim, because they *need* to. They need the office. It fulfills them. And there is no set of whom we should be more wary. The politician who seeks to erase a sense of personal inadequacy by a scuttle up the ladders of power is undergoing a kind of therapy by means of the ballot box.

People sense this dynamic. Was there ever, in modern times, a more needful politician than Richard Nixon? There were many things that were enigmatic about Nixon, but his need for the office of the presidency, his compulsion to achieve that rare summit and, from its eminence, look back and down in scorn and triumph at what he called his "enemies," is not among them.

I am reminded of a counter-example from our country: Robert Stanfield, the best friend modern Canadian politics has ever had. Mainly for the example, both of character and actions, of the public man who is not compelled to seek office, who is not the silent slave of his own ambition. Stanfield once had a chance to topple the Trudeau government, and declined to do so—an act of grace in an arena largely unmarked by graciousness, and a moment of great personal discipline and self-denial.

Stanfield and Nixon probably represent the extremes of

the range. Most of those who seek office operate from a medley of motives on a line stretched between utter compulsion and total disinterest. Brian Mulroney is up there, shivering closer to Nixon than to Stanfield. This is not said to abuse him. Mr. Mulroney was a Grand Canyon of openness compared to the Watergate exile, and infinitely less cloistered—genuinely cheerful and sociable, where Nixon was saturnine and solitary. Where they meet is in the need to excel, to find in the occupancy of high office overwhelming approval and distinction. From the hail of observations made by Mr. Mulroney, now tumbling onto the front pages of the nation's newspapers from Peter Newman's taped tell-all, it appears that, for Mr. Mulroney, distinction is not just a matter of having been prime minister—it's being better and smarter and shrewder than everyone else who was on the scene with him or just before him.

Vegematics have fewer blades than a telephone call from Brian Mulroney. Pierre Trudeau, Lucien Bouchard, Kim Campbell, Clyde Wells—they are all diced and sliced with an energy and thoroughness that, in some cases, is actually painful to read—and, in some cases, is inaccurate and malicious as well. Clyde Wells, for example, may have many flaws of character, but to select as his damning deficiency that he is unprincipled turns the man completely upside down. Principle is Clyde Wells's oxygen.

Kim Campbell did mess up her campaign, but the great tsunami that washed over the Tory party, and left poor Jean Charest and Elsie Wayne alone on the beach after the vote, had been set roiling by the anger Mr. Mulroney stirred before he left office. Mr. Mulroney prefers not to see that some of his setbacks, and some of the abiding dislike some Canadians still carry toward him, were stimulated in part by his own actions and his own character.

But the desire to be the tallest tree in the forest is not an excuse or a reason for taking a chainsaw to every other tree. He is not content with having been elected prime minister—twice. Others must be diminished, so that he stands taller. At least that's the message of the tapes.

But the tapes, raw and unedited, are at the very best problematic. They are in the idiom of private conversation—hence their unfettered flow and pungency. Mr. Mulroney may have signed off on them, but they retain the flavour of a person talking to a confidant. They are true in the sense that he says what he says, but taking the private manner and loosing it raw between two book covers adds a force and an impact that doesn't properly belong to them. They have been transposed from one medium to another. They have been translated from a sphere of assumed intimacy to the public record. And this amplifies the negatives for Mr. Mulroney in a way that is not fair to him.

The Secret Tapes was the first blow to Brian Mulroney's attempt to resuscitate his post–prime ministerial reputation. On the principle that time heals all wounds, Mr. Mulroney had, as much as a former prime minister can, stayed away from the front pages and headlines following the near-total immolation of the Tories after (and largely the consequence of) his two terms as leader. He may also have been investing in the dubious wisdom of that other folk axiom that absence makes the heart grow fonder.

Publication of *The Secret Tapes* stripped both those ancient Kleenex of whatever truth they had. Mr. Mulroney's "rehabilitation" was stayed ere it could begin. Then came the cash-in-paper-bags story, and the return of Airbus and the Ancient Mariner: Karlheinz Schreiber. Poor Brian. He is the Rodney Dangerfield of Canadian politics.

ADRIENNE CLARKSON PRESENTS | September 23, 2006

> But what are kings, when regiment is gone,
> But perfect shadows in a sunshine day?

The quotation is from Christopher Marlowe, and the word "regiment," on which it turns, here carries a meaning of "authority," "sway," "rule" and, quite possibly, something close to our modern terms "status" and "prestige." Regiment in this context is a constellation of all of these meanings.

The authority of a real king was always a fasces of tangible power—command over life and death, the control of armies, unquestioned rule—and the invisible but equally mighty influences of dread and reverence.

It's no news that kings (or queens) aren't what they used to be. Their regiment has decayed and vanished. Modern-day royals, most emphatically the set at Buckingham Palace with which Canada has historical and constitutional associations, exist in a twilight of anachronistic significance, tabloid-feeding celebrity and lower-rank pop-star acclaim.

All of which may be disappointing to those who struggle to hold the monarchy in esteem, and may be poignant, too, but none of it is news to the least-engaged consciousness. It raises the question now, more forcefully than at any other period, about our "ties" to the monarchy, of the value of those ties, particularly the utility and prestige of the one office in our country still bearing the imprimatur of its royal origins: the governor general.

The case for the governor general is what I take to be the burden of Adrienne Clarkson's *Heart Matters*. It is a memoir of Clarkson's interesting and distinguished life. It is a divided book. Its earlier pages are, at times, an affecting recounting of her family's progress from difficult beginnings and wartime peril, their arrival in Canada, her growing up, the complex, painful, yet always affectionate relationship with her mother, her pride in her father, and his pride in her.

But from the moment the book takes up her adult career, from the days of CBC's *Take 30* all the way through to *Adrienne Clarkson Presents* (to my mind, a real foreshadowing of how she saw herself in the governor general's office), the book takes on a drier, brisker tone. We depart from subdued recollection and memoir to more bristling justification and defence.

In the old days of luxuriant titles, this section of *Heart Matters* might have carried the scroll, *An Apology for the Office of the Governor General of Canada and My Contributions to It, Together with Some Observations on the Worth of Politicians, the Male of the Species, the Conduct of Some Others in Lesser Office, and a Return of Fire to the Last Prime Minister But One, Mr. Paul Martin, for His Imperfect Treatment of the GG.*

Clarkson thinks very highly of the office of governor general, an opinion that any reading of *Heart Matters* will confirm is not entirely unhinged from the fact that she held it. She seems to believe that this last echo of Canada's colonial beginnings under the imperial flag has a merit and vitality crucial to the understanding, perhaps even the survival, of the glorious experiment we call Canada. This is a high-voltage estimation of what is at best a decorative, expensive, ceremonial survival.

In the twenty-first century, royalty has been decanted of all its mystique, seriousness and point. Insofar as the office of the GG is presumed to be a surrogate representation of the "real thing" in Great Britain, of what possible value can it be? The British royals have become vessels of the most ordinary clay, and set an almost alpine standard of dysfunction, vulgarity, selfishness and self-absorption. All regiment is gone. So the office of GG is only a second-hand, down-market edition of something that has lost its function and place. We have the shadow of the tattered shadow.

Clarkson romanticizes both the life and function of Rideau Hall, and seems to think its pious protocols and dusty duties are of real power, that the advice of a GG to a prime minister, or where a cabinet should be sworn in, are matters on which the edifice of the modern state may depend.

All hymns, I suppose, however boring, are lovely if you're the bishop of the cathedral in which they are sung. And a five-year stint at the top of the social order—one area in which the charisma of royal surrogacy still has cogency—must be a very pleasant interlude. Rideau Hall is still an address to conjure with, and the position of governor general has the considerable charm of being the cynosure of a continuous garden party. The governor general gets to open Parliament, drive around in a barouche, host literati and distribute medals, meet the interesting of foreign nations and take first rank at every occasion of national ceremony.

There is not one of these duties or recreations that would be diminished one whit, jot or tittle, were it to be performed or exercised by a ceremonial head of state who owed nothing to the Crown and its by now very mixed traditions.

Heart Matters offers some not encouraging illustrations of Clarkson's judgment. The first is that there is a *Heart*

Matters at all. So much of the book's argument stands on the importance of certain traditions and codes that adhere to the office of governor general—from the vital secrecy imposed on those invited to hold the office until the invitation is confirmed, to the necessity of swearing in cabinet officers at Rideau Hall and the propriety of consultations by a given prime minister with the GG herself—that it is a shock that Clarkson has violated the deepest sanction of them all. She has turned publicist while the viceregal cushions are still warm from her imprint.

Does not discretion adhere to the office so late venerated and vacated? Nannies to Donald Trump may write tell-alls in the age of faux-celebrity (and I think they should be encouraged to do so). I applaud "personal assistants" to tyrannous and mouth-breathing rock stars who launch rockets of steamy prose at the bottoms they so recently, ravenously kissed. Politicians who have been "passed over" by their leaders may strike deadly blows in return. But Her Excellency? Why such haste to ventilate?

We now know how highly she thinks of Jean Chrétien and his wife, Aline, and begrudge her none of that obliging warmth. But the gratitude describes a self-serving loop. Chrétien appointed her, and it would be a rude doyenne of Rideau Hall indeed who did not see the wisdom of the man who set her there. I wonder, now that an ex–governor general has set the illustrious example, how long we shall have to wait for the aides, valets, caterers and assorted functionaries of Rideau Hall to oil up their laptops and give us the view from below the stairs of the Clarkson–Ralston Saul era.

The loyalty to Chrétien wanders into something like an outright attack on his successor. It is evident that Clarkson does not like Paul Martin, and I am wondering why all of Canada should know this now. She obviously sees Martin, and those who assisted him, as tacky and vulgar. They want a different venue for their swearing-in. Clarkson will have none of it. And when the GG's wishes prevail over the elected prime minister's, some of these rude rubes show up at Rideau Hall . . . in sneakers and T-shirts. Egad.

Clarkson has great confidence in herself as an observer. This may be a byproduct of her time as a journalist. I am not sure that confidence is buttressed by a passage in which she speaks of her ability to see the large view of things "in the way that Tolstoy saw the whole field in describing the Battle of Borodino in *War and Peace*." This passage comes at the tail end of an account of the great PR difficulties that surrounded the expensive and crowded "circumpolar junket" of the GG and thirty-five or so Canadian worthies. Whatever may have been at stake in that ruckus, I feel it's less in the territory of Tolstoy than of P.G. Wodehouse.

I find my faith in her judgment further estranged by the near-risible certitude of a few of her observations on politicians and men. She adverts at one point to the clotted speculations of Carl Jung, and I feared for a paragraph of two we were on a Ferris wheel of outdated misogyny.

If Clarkson believes what she thinks she understands from this Jungian mush, I fear for us all—men, I mean. Apparently, she does. "My personal view is that the world of politics is like this because it is a male world, with male values—the worship of triumphalism, contempt for weakness, and distrust of compassion. All of these are male feelings and attributes . . ." There goes half the country. This isn't the world of politics, or the world of journalism, or commerce, or science. It's a five-cent version of adolescent feminism.

It might have been useful to have something a little closer to reality and experience, some reflections on politics and journalism, the showbiz quotient of both, and what advantages those who know the media give and take from each other. What did Chrétien receive from Clarkson? Among other gifts, her celebrity. Canadian celebrity may be low-voltage compared to its U.S. archetype, but there is some virtue for the politician who can call upon someone already known to Canadians.

Clarkson, however, emphatically says, "I despise the idea of celebrity." Coming from one of our most famous people, this is a curious turn. I may offer it as a personal axiom that people do not choose television for a career because they wish to consolidate their anonymity. Before she became GG, Adrienne Clarkson was a very big name. She was almost as famous as Don Cherry.

As governor general, she refused to give autographs because "I could not see giving a movie-star kind of quality to an office that should inspire respect." I fear she freighted the office with a more austere conception of its dignity than it can bear. Authors give autographs, yet literature staggers on.

And the "movie-star quality" of the GG's office may be the only real lever to extending its decaying impact in a media age. Clarkson's successor, Michaëlle Jean, is going to be a powerful presence simply by virtue of the fact that her innate "star quality" now has a stage on which to exert itself.

Finally, *Heart Matters* itself will not suffer at the bookstores because it is something of a tell-all written by a celebrity who occupied the nation's highest constitutional office.

Heart Matters is, as I have said, a divided affair. The portion of it that is family and personal memoir has considerable charm. It shows those qualities of confidence, application, ambition, intelligence and familial affection that established Adrienne Clarkson as a successful broadcaster and made her a national presence admired by many.

Its other half, dealing with the significance of Rideau Hall as a fulcrum for national enlightenment, with its laboured esteem for the prime minister who awarded her with placement within its gilded walls and her aggressive broadsides against the less enlightened one who succeeded him, is a disappointment and a contradiction.

PAUL MARTIN FIGHTS ON | November 1, 2008

It is a rather too-perfect illustration of the no-longer-novel concept of the memoir as politics by other means. Paul Martin's *Hell or High Water: My Life In and Out of Politics* is almost certainly quite the last instalment of the Chrétien–Martin wars, that decade-long internal struggle for mastery of the Liberal Party.

Mr. Martin and his loyalists ultimately prevailed in that struggle. The proud and rancorous Jean Chrétien was more or less forced, finally, to give Paul Martin his turn. The victory was a pyrrhic one, however, an almost classic illustration of a battle that so wearies the forces of a nominal victor as to turn to ashes at the very moment of ostensible triumph.

The Liberal Party is still reeling from the effects of that clash, some of whose indirect fallout was the surprising rise of Stéphane Dion to its leadership. Even the Liberals' dismal showing in the recent election arises from the divisions and loss of coherence suffered by the party as a result of that protracted and bitter feud.

The Martin–Chrétien fight was something of a Trojan War for the Liberal Party. If Paul Martin has a story to tell, it is surely this: how, from within the party, and while serving as the highest-profile finance minister Canada has even seen, he executed the longest-running coup against a successful three-term prime minister who was himself one of the most aggressive and canny politicians ever to hold that high office.

I would have liked to have seen much more than the clipped and almost rote summary *Hell and High Water* offers of that long, ardent campaign. What a yarn it must be. How did a relatively freshman MP, albeit, as son of Paul Martin Sr., one of distinguished political lineage, effectively bring the control of the party's apparatus under his hands? How, under the Argus gaze and jealous watch of Mr. Chrétien, did he work the slow and detailed magic of his coup? Recollect that when Mr. Chrétien finally yielded, such worthies as Brian Tobin, John Manley and Allan Rock, none of them frail egos or shy of ambition, simply whimpered away from contesting the leadership contest that resulted. Such was the near-total control of the party machinery Martin, and what, in this book, he so endearingly calls his team, had achieved.

What was it like, on a daily basis, to endure the tense equilibrium between Chrétien and Martin? *Hell or High Water* gives a few anecdotes of climatic moments when an absolute break was impending: Martin's top aides insisting he cancel a speech to introduce one by Chrétien is a typical bland example. But even these few have been the stuff of the informed gossip of Parliament Hill for years. And what Martin does tell—naturally, I suppose, since it is his memoir—works mainly to smooth the presentation of himself, and cast Chrétien and his team as angry, petty or paranoid.

He glides past all this drama, Chrétien growling and breathing fire from his lair, while Martin and his minions (cellphone ninjas) unravel his authority piece by piece. He and his team are portrayed in soft lights—everyone Martin works with is incredibly dedicated, brilliant, puts in super-human hours or is charged with their leader's vision of Canada. They are merely "preparing" for the day when Chrétien steps down. It could be a high school soap opera, not the intense, ill-tempered civil war that consumed the best energies of Canada's "natural governing party" for a decade.

But this is not the book's deepest reticence. The one big question is: How did it all fall apart so quickly? How did the man who was so artful on the reach for the top prove so clumsy in staying there? Martin as finance minister, Martin as leader-in-waiting, was projected as the man who would amass huge majorities, extend the Liberal Party into regions of Canada where it had been a toxic presence. He was a wider, more generous-minded public man than those who typically tread ambition's path, the leader with a humanist vision and the embodiment of a kind of natural ease and decency that was almost prototypically Canadian.

It will not do simply to record the mischiefs and petty revenges Chrétien designed for his successor, to point to the sponsorship scandal as poison in the well from which no one could recover, as providing anything close to a full account-ing of what went wrong. Nor, in Martin's second election, does the retelling of RCMP Commissioner Giuliano Zaccardelli's brutal, and almost certainly deliberate, inter-vention (the income trust leak) explain in any full sense why the lustre had so terribly decayed, or why watching the latter months of his term as prime minister was, even to non-partisans, very close to painful. The dour, "frightening" Stephen Harper, an infant in national politics, replaced him, a near giant. How did that happen?

All prime ministers are struck by political storms, all leaders are tested under fire. Something was missing in Paul Martin, whom the nation had viewed as Chrétien without the nasty edge, with a wider vision and a defter touch—so that, ambition satisfied, he suffered the painful disintegration that he did, his reputation transmuted so quickly into the cruel name bestowed by *The Economist:* Mr. Dithers.

The levers of power in his hands, what scattered his focus? Having built an agenda remarkable in range and detail—on international affairs, aboriginal issues, medicare, humanitarian intervention—why was its communication so dismal?

Mr. Martin goes nowhere near really answering these central questions. *Hell or High Water* is repair work for a reputation—renovation, not revelation. Its prose is bland, far more the catalogues and clichés of a party platform than a book of genuine personal scrutiny. He may be out of office, but he is not out of politics. Paul Martin is still campaigning.

Finally, on more personal grounds, this could have been an immensely affecting story. How hard must it have been for him, to fulfill a dream so intimately bound up with the story of his own father (elbowed aside by the arrival of that frolicsome novelty, Trudeau), and then to see it vaporize in the few months he unsteadily managed to hang on to power.

Longer than Kim Campbell and Joe Clark, but it was not merely to best the fruit-fly duration of those tenures that Mr. Martin endured the long climb to feel the "cherry knock against [his] lips" and see it drawn away again.

It would be hard telling to go to the core on these matters, but it is a real regret that he has not done so. I regard him as possessing, in a manner far more subtle than we see in most high public figures, special qualities of decency, honour and a true, deep fealty to the country he admires beyond all others. It was the glimpse of those qualities, even when he was embroiled in the long wait for the keys to 24 Sussex, that caught the admiration, and fired the expectation, of so many Canadians. I even think it true that many Canadians felt genuinely sorry that he did not really find his way, translate his dream, once he achieved power. I wish *Hell or High Water* had found the courage and the candour to unfold the real stories.

There is a lot more to Paul Martin, and a lot more to his singular career, than this too-quick apologia, this last dance with Jean Chrétien, permits us to see.

ART

EROS BY ANY OTHER NAME | June 28, 2003

Now, here's a mouthful: *Public Sex, Art, and Democracy.*

It's the title of a play that has opened in a Vancouver art gallery. The climax of the play—in the classical, theatrical understanding of the word as well as in its more mundane sexual connotation—is a "Lewinsky." Prior to the play's performance, one of its organizers alerted the world that it would feature live oral sex—a first in Canada, so it is claimed.

On stage, I mean. Or so I surely hope.

It was also claimed that the performance—the play itself, and the performance within the performance—would be art. I presume that's why it was getting its first run in an art gallery: to send the right signal. Much as if one stumbled across two oral sex actors in, say, Stanley Park, you might conclude they were engaged in landscape architecture. Conversely however, if the orally incontinent were caught bobbing for apples in the back seat of a parked car, the mind would not float automatically to Rembrandt or his peers in the great artistic tradition of the West. You'd probably mutter, unappreciative boor that you are, something like "Couldn't you wait till you got home?"

But if two sufficiently randyfied actors, artists, performers—it's difficult to settle on the right word here—go to it in an art gallery (to the left of the soapstone carving there, and just before you get to our exhibition of Peruvian shawls), I think a cue is being given that the viewer hasn't been transported to some wet T-shirt festival, but is actually watching something artistic.

Now, I'm all with King Lear on this: "Let copulation thrive." But I don't know—two people naked, busy about each other; throw in a hammock, a monkey with a bullwhip, and a crate of 10W30 crank oil, and it might even be called a party. But in this case, it's Vancouver, and furthermore it's an art gallery in Vancouver, and with that combination, all definitions are up for grabs.

Art appreciation, like sex, can be ticklish. Of course, the high question is: Is copulation, or any of its delightful approximations, variants, and surrogates, "art" because the "artists" charge admission to watch? We had that kind of "art" for years in New York's Times Square and every low-rent entertainment district in North America for years—twenty-five cents a peep.

And what of the patrons? Are they "connoisseurs?" As in, "I like the way he's fondling her back, it's a 'quotation' from Tommy Lee's early work in the famous home video with Pamela, and I think I recognize some of the foreplay from the *Debbie Does* oeuvre." Or are they just your garden-variety skanky voyeurs, albeit sipping Chablis?

Is it art just because it's not in the bedroom or at the local motel? Is sex art when, by the ancient tenets of real estate, it exploits "location, location, location?" If one were to smoke in an art gallery, would you be having a cigarette or making a statement?

Subtle stuff, I know. But remember the full title of this exhibition: *Public Sex, Art, and Democracy*. The art bit I can kind of understand. But democracy? How did the voters get hauled into this grope? Is there a stage backdrop of Tiananmen Square on which the hungry amorists cast their eager silhouettes?

On television, I caught the spokesman I referred to earlier, obviously dazed by the stress of rehearsals, saying the performance was "about" expression, and going on to make the truly lunatic observation that our society was "erotophobic."

Erotophobic? Western society of the last fifty years, erotophobic! There are not enough exclamation marks in this universe to convey the extremity of my recoil from a statement so reality-impaired.

Eroto*mania* is the condition of our times, not erotophobia. Every pulse of pop culture is sexual. Every square inch of public space breathes sex. Television, movies, music, advertisements, lifestyle—sex drives every atom of Western culture in the modern world. From *Charlie's Angels: Full*

Throttle back to *Oh! Calcutta!* and the sixties. This generation discovered sex. Philip Larkin wrote a poem about it.

So: if one of the reasons piously offered up for Vancouver's latest "artwork" is to free the Western polity from the chains of its own prudery, I say, look about you. If you think this is a society starved of sex, and afraid of it, you have been living on a desert island. Swim ashore, lad. Have a gin and tonic, and catch the latest Viagra pitch from Bob Dole.

I have the low suspicion, actually, that the "play" in question is just sex in a public place, and all this chatter about "art and democracy" is the latest tacky styling of the emperor's new clothes.

Erotophobic! Look out the window, man. Caligula would blush.

MEDIOCRITY AND MISCHIEF | December 1, 2007

I expect that most people in the country have heard or read by now the short, dim story of Thorarinn Jonsson, a student at the Ontario College of Art and Design. This is the young man who, propelled by the muse of Conceptual Art, placed a fake bomb at the entrance to the Royal Ontario Museum. He pasted a message on his "installation," the fake bomb, saying it was not a bomb. It seems to me he missed a turn in this fascinating dialectic, because a real genius would also have posted another message on the first message saying, "This is not a real message." But who's perfect?

He chose a really unfortunate time to lay his alarming creation near the doors of one of Toronto's most famous public buildings. I realize this thought might suggest there *is* a fortunate time to place fake bombs on public thoroughfares and in front of landmark buildings, but, having no background in conceptual art, I really lack the mental machinery to "contextualize" all this. For that matter, I don't even understand how you can contextualize a bomb, fake or not—bombs, real or spurious, not being text to begin with.

It was unfortunate in this particular case, because this was an evening for the ROM to put on a gala to raise money for the Canadian Foundation for AIDS Research. The young Picasso of the fake pipe bomb then left a voice-mail message on a randomly selected phone at the museum that must have immensely cheered the sad soul of whoever first heard it: "Listen, there's no bomb by the entrance to the museum."

Then—oh Lord, he's fertile—this Duchamp of detonation posted a video on YouTube showing a young woman walking through the ROM before a bomb—apparently—explodes. This provocative and scary posting was, as they say in art circles, to help "facilitate discussion." And in the high-minded discussion that followed, it was opined that the entire sequence—the placing of the bomb, the gnomic phone message, the note pinned to the package—was meant to illustrate, wait for it, the hoary cliché that has adorned every feverish, moronic installation that the avant-garde has ever inflicted on a patient and weary world. It was meant to illustrate "the banality of day-to-day life."

Well, of course it was. I know that every time I stumble over a facsimile of a bomb when wandering into Union Station or going through some airport terminal, the first thing that pops into my head is: "Oh, Lord. The deep banality of life. I'd forgotten. Witless me."

As these events unfolded, the less artistically receptive portion of Toronto—people who actually have a life that extends beyond a project of telling everyone else how banal theirs is—reacted with a shameful display of sanity and caution. The police were summoned. Traffic was shut down. The ROM was evacuated, its patrons unwilling to take the note on the bomb that said it was not a bomb in the aesthetic spirit in which it was so clearly intended.

I expect that, to some of the luminaries at the Ontario College of Art and Design, these thoughts will be looked at as very Philistine—or, even worse, bourgeois—responses, but it is not to be expected that people soaked in the banality of day-to-day life vibrate to the same strings as those who have given themselves over to the mistress muse of Conceptual Art. This is the same school, one recalls, that gave the world Jesse Power, who, along with some other artistes, produced a film—"performance art," they chose to label it—featuring the torture and killing of a cat.

Dead cats and fake bombs. Oh, for the bohemian life.

It is hard to know what to say with any real seriousness about this whole monumentally stupid and essentially arrogant tale. Except, perhaps, that it is yet one more wearying illustration of how utterly empty, in some cases, the very words "art" and "artist" have become. Remember the "crack in the floor" of the Tate Gallery in London recently—the crack in the floor was the piece of art. Or how about this even more recent example executed during a "green party" of "four male Viennese conceptual artists who wore high heels and buckets on their heads but no pants, and who spent the evening building a plywood structure over the bewildered guests' heads"? *The New York Times* story continues: "And then the Gelitin members, along with three Icelandic artists, also men, . . . took the buckets off their heads and urinated—with dead-eye accuracy . . .—into one another's pails."

Some dare call it art.

We have burned away excellence and mastery as the only fit criteria for real artistic performance, and crowded the world with the petty, foolish projects of poseurs and imposters.

Conceptual art, it would seem, is a passport for mediocrity and mischief.

THE ENVIRONMENT

A CARING HEART | March 20, 2004

My first thought is that it was a couple of playful environmentalists' premature April Fool's joke. On Thursday, like a lot of others I suspect, I was very taken with *The Globe*'s front-page photos.

More precisely, I was very taken by one of them: the picture of the golden eagle. Most birds are lovely to look at. Eagles are noble.

I suppose that, in these careful and enlightened times, to say that one animal is "noble" and others are not is a mortal sin against the grim egalitarianism that is the first principle of the keener consciences of our age. This principle holds that, while we may register differences, as between people or animals, to rate those differences—and, accordingly, to say of this person or that animal that one is superior to another—is a dreadful moral failure. In fact, in the rarer altitudes of ecological enlightenment, it is a fatal offence even to draw a line between human and animal.

This toad and that nuclear physicist, this slug and that classical pianist, they are both, in all that is of consequence, one. He who unpacks the quark is as one with the belcher of the bogs; she who unravels Liszt in all his tormenting keyboard velocities is no more than that still, wet blob on the underbough.

To speak or think otherwise is "species-ist," one of these new and arid Orwellian coinages by which the true believers castigate and categorize the morally underdeveloped of our kind.

It is all bosh, of course. People do not travel thousands of miles and book passage on expensive tour boats to look at halibut. They do to look at whales. Whales are more impressive than halibut. This might not be nice if you are a halibut, and is probably quite a nick in the self-esteem of that unassuming and, happily, quite delicious fish, but alas, it is so.

This ranking holds for creatures of every element. Cougars will draw a crowd where armadillos open to an empty house. The Bengal tiger, to my taste, is the most wonderful spectacle that has ever prowled the Earth. The scaly-tailed rat, known to the connoisseur as the pier rat, is a damn nuisance. As opposed to the tiger, it has a very low fan base.

But it is the creatures of the air that, at their finest, speak to mankind's wish and need to appreciate the beauty and wonder of nature's living marvels. And of these, surely there is none quite so simply impressive as the eagle.

The poet Tennyson has covered this point so very well before me that it would be churlish not to quote him:

The Eagle

He clasps the crag with crooked hands;
Close to the sun in lonely lands,
Ringed with the azure world, he stands.
The wrinkled sea beneath him crawls;
He watches from his mountain walls,
And like a thunderbolt he falls.

All together now: "Yeah! Alfred!"

So, let us return to *The Globe*'s pictures of Thursday morning, of a golden eagle and a marmot—specifically, the dead eagle and the live rodent.

The story was of a clandestine operation by the British Columbia government, which set out the carcass of a dead deer to lure golden eagles to lunch—and then shot six of them. This, because golden eagles, under God's providential assignment of these matters, is a predator of the marmot, and the marmots of Vancouver Island are a dwindling clan. And because, one must presume, under the missionary zeal of ecological "management," some wizards in the B.C. wildlife division felt a little shotgun intervention on the pro-marmot side of the equation was the really sensitive thing to do.

There was even a Gagliano touch to the story. A ministry spokesman indicated that, while the public wasn't told of the kill, neither was it a secret.

I should add, just to gild this bloodied lily, the ministry in question has also "encouraged" the shooting of cougars and wolves under the same demented idea of marmot protection. This may well be the My Lai moment of the endangered-species movement.

There are six dead golden eagles in a refrigerator somewhere in B.C. because official conservationists wanted to spare some weasel's cousin the wear and tear of the wild.

It's a mischief on the same scale as harpooning a whale to "save" the sculpin.

In the civilized nation to the south of us, they have a better sense of priorities. In Bush country, it is a criminal offence to vex eagles; loggers have paid fines ranging into the hundreds of thousands of dollars for cutting down trees wherein they nest.

Lord, let us be saved from the people who care about things. There is no insolence stronger than that which springs from a caring heart.

AL GORE RECYCLED | July 17, 2006

Will Al Gore save the world?

Well, he was on *Larry King Live* the other night, which, as we all know, is the very hospice of our ailing world. When a man has a world to save, where else would he go?

Whenever the great, the rich or the famous feel the itch of social conscience, they head to Mr. King's amicable chat hospital to have it scratched. For us. For the peons who, without their guidance, and a comatose nod from Larry, would not recognize the handbasket of the week in which our green and fragile world is careering to hell.

Bono ends a gig in Amsterdam, say, and remembers Africa is in a spot of trouble. There is no G8 meeting in session, and it's pointless to issue press releases slagging Paul Martin anymore. Gives Larry a call. Appears next night. Africa fixed.

If tubular Dr. Phil fears America is too fat, a quick call to Larry, a fresh set of suspenders, and the alarm is sounded. America shrinks.

And it was only recently that Paul McCartney and his then-loving spouse, Heather, found themselves agitated over the parsimonious earnings from the "cruellest harvest" in the world, the Newfoundland seal hunt. They went to Larry, and now, of course, the ice floes of the North Atlantic are a floating daycare centre, a Christmas on ice, for unmolested seals.

Go on, Larry. Vent. All is well. It's better than a syllogism. It's neater than physics.

The seals are doing fine. Paul and Heather have hit cold water, though. Their marriage is *finis*. The publicity is horrid for Heather, and the sorting out of the marital spoils promises to be nasty. And yet, just a few weeks ago, there they were, cute as squirrels, on Larry's show.

Yesterday, their troubles seemed so far away. And now—well, now it seems they're here to stay. Oh well, it's their business. Let it be.

So, when I saw Al Gore on with Larry, fresh from his jetting to Cannes and hopscotching the globe with his new documentary film/presentation, *An Inconvenient Truth*, I knew—as surely as I know that Liza Minnelli will be a guest again on *LKL*—that whatever state the world is in, we were saved.

Mr. Fixit was on with Larry. The Pied Piper of Global Warming (climate change, for those at the front of the class who have been keeping up) was executing a passionate seminar for our doomed planet and . . . was it just my imagination, or could you feel the ice caps mending? Were perspiring polar bears suddenly high-fiving each other? And was there, finally—thank God—a (recuperative) chill in the global biosphere?

Either that, or I'd left the fridge door open. Again.

Al is on a crusade. The chads are history. The one-time geek who lost to the frat boy has, in the immortal mantra of a million therapists, "put all that behind him." He's found himself, again. He is no longer wooden Al Gore. He is Al Gore the Jeremiah of a planet whose thermostat has gone wacko.

Al is a salesman. He's the doctor, too. *An Inconvenient Truth* is the finest expository opus since Michael Moore caught George Bush reading about a billy goat to school kids the morning of September 11.

Al is everywhere. He's new again. And he cares. Am I skeptical? Do Rice Krispies crepitate?

I know the word is delicate these days, but Al is on a crusade. And of all the causes that are out there, none is so sentimental, so saturated with vague, emotive attitudinizing, fed on soft science and ripe with moral grandstanding, as global warming.

Global warming, precisely because it is so grand and nebulous, precisely because it is that perfect storm of scientism and moralism, because it is so susceptible to demagoguery (however fashionably packaged and presented), is an almost unstoppable cause.

Hands up, those of you who are against "saving the world."

There are the usual rote denials from Gore about a further run for the presidency. But now he's riding the thermal drafts of undreamt-of popularity. He has the approval of all right-thinking people. Hollywood loves him, Cannes gushes, Larry nods.

The only thing between him and a clean shot at the presidency as the Democratic nominee is the ice queen of American politics, Hillary Clinton. And what chance has an ice queen against the Pied Piper of a warming world?

Hillary may want to take a look at *An Inconvenient Truth.* Some truths are more inconvenient than others. The verity offered for her digestion is that Al Gore is back.

CARS ARE SMOKERS, TOO | October 7, 2006

Which city is more scrupulous in enforcing its pollution bylaws: Glasgow or Toronto?

No, this is not a thought experiment. In Toronto, during the manically hyped International Film Festival, the Iraq reporter and sometime actor Sean Penn lit up a cigarette during a press conference at the Sutton Place Hotel.

There are bylaws in Toronto against just this sort of thing, and they carry heavy penalties. I've seen postings in elevators warning of $5,000 fines.

There are bylaws in Glasgow, too. I haven't had a chance to peruse that city's elevator literature, but I'd wager it features equally big fines in similarly small print. In Glasgow, it was Keith Richards who lit up in a public place.

Perhaps, because it is Keith Richards we're talking about, I should be more explicit: he lit and smoked a cigarette. Whether Keith was, himself, lit up, is irrelevant. He wasn't at a news conference—nor, it might be helpful to add, was he up a palm tree.

He smoked, on stage, during a Stones concert.

Here in Toronto, the result was interesting. Sean Penn escaped any penalty. But the Sutton Place Hotel, the venue of the press conference, got hit with a $605 fine. This doesn't seem fair. The hotel wasn't smoking. But, evidently, the hotel's staff had neglected to convey personally to the intrepid Mr. Penn the many prohibitions of the Smoke-Free Ontario Act.

The Glaswegian authorities were more merciful. Neither the company that operated the stage, nor the Great Inhaler himself, Mr. Richards, was fined. In Glasgow, they made a judgment of Solomonic finesse: a "stage" was not an "enclosed public space" in the meaning of the bylaws. Scots are nothing if not subtle. David Hume was a Scot, and he could unravel cobwebs—with his teeth.

It is useful to add that Mr. Penn's defiant fumigations caught the attention of no less a marplot than Ontario Health Promotion Minister Jim Watson, who allowed that Mr. Penn was a "great actor" but, notwithstanding the comforts his great art has brought the world—I'm paraphrasing here—he was not above the law, and that "he could be charged and he should be charged." He hasn't been, and he won't be.

Film festival officials grovelled in perfectly toneless and abject prose: "The festival and our hotel partners make every effort possible to ensure that our guests are aware of and respect Ontario's Smoke-Free Act. We apologize that our moderator did not address the issue during the press conference." I hope none of the PR people are writing movie scripts.

So, Toronto takes its bylaws very seriously. And so does the Ontario government. When a minister scolds a widescreen demigod, you know it's serious. The environment is a big issue in this province, as I hope this comparative study illustrates. Those Scots may be slackers, but Ontario is the dour jurisdiction when it comes to its air.

Just as it's big on global warming. Or so I thought. This is a province in love with blue boxes and a house of great crusaders against the tobacco menace—which no less an authority than Al Gore has recently linked to the global warming phenomenon itself. Except when it comes to areas larger than a pop star's studied show of trivial rebellion, or something a little more drastic than parking the liquor empties in the right-coloured bin.

Consider the statement this week of Ontario Premier Dalton McGuinty.

Rona Ambrose, the federal environment minister, has been talking of imposing fuel-emission standards on automobile manufacturers. Here's Mr. McGuinty: "The one thing we will not abide is any effort on the part of the national government to unduly impose greenhouse-gas emission reductions on the province of Ontario at the expense of the auto sector."

This is the same premier who recently welcomed the news that government-subsidized GM plants would soon be the home for the manufacture of the new "muscle car," the gas-guzzling Camaro.

Fine a hotel for one star-lit cigarette, but welcome the manufacture of thousands of environmentally retrograde muscle cars. And promise not to "abide" any effort to "unduly impose greenhouse-gas reductions." This is a parable of the entire global-warming debate. Those who accept the science of the climate-change projections, who profess to be most anxious over the "greatest crisis" of our times, will say every right word, and pursue the most trivial acts of symbolic environmentalism. But when it comes to action that has any real cost—political or personal—they are as hard-line an opponent to any change in the status quo as the most relentless climate skeptic.

It really is time for those who say they accept the crisis represented by climate change to live up to their professions.

The skeptics can always retire to Glasgow. And contemplate the Scottish understanding of an enclosed space. While having, if it pleases them, a smoke.

NUMBERS GAME | November 4, 2006

The Stern Review on Global Warming was released this week, and once I'd had the chance to catch a few of the headlines it inspired, I thought immediately of Joey Smallwood.

Mr. Smallwood liked big numbers. Especially big numbers preceded by dollar signs. If a road somewhere on the South Coast was about to be paved, a new trades school built, or a new industrial project launched, Joey would wind himself up and find a microphone. "This new road/school/industry is going to cost NOT 10 million dollars, NOT 20 million dollars, but FIFTY MILLION DOLLARS!"

He could find nearly infinite rhetorical variations on a simple number (breaking it down into its constituent "hundreds of thousands"; pluralizing—50 millions of dollars—etc., etc. and etc.). The trick was to bludgeon Newfoundlanders, not accustomed even to the sound (never mind the actual possession) of great amounts of cash, into a state of catatonic awe at the nearly inconceivable heaps of money this project or that was going to cost.

The trick grew stale. After a while, being told how many twenties were in a stack of 50 million dollars became tedious, and the long tease of "not 10, not 20, not 30 but . . . X millions of dollars" became a risible bore. Another failing of the technique was the fading power of the word "million." By the end of his fractious reign, the campaign speeches rang with allusion to hitherto unapproached altitudes of "billions of dollars."

When arithmetic is rhetoric, each new speech must have a bigger number. Let us call it Smallwood's Law.

The Stern report on climate change illustrates Smallwood's Law in a way that would make the old conjuror proud. It projects a cost to the world, if measures are not taken to mitigate or halt global warming, of *seven trillion dollars*. Even in these days of Enron-scale frauds and income trust cancellations, a trillion dollars is an astronomical number. *Seven* trillion summons the galaxies and all their wheeling stars.

I look at that number more as an instrument to arrest attention than as a real figure. If Sir Nicholas Stern had said nine trillion or six trillion, would he have been pounced on by accountants and academics the next day saying, "He's up by two trillion, or down by one?" I don't think so.

When we enter the area of projecting costs in the trillions of dollars, based on the wild variables of planetary weather patterns over the next forty-five years or so, and speculations on the industrial growth of 162 nations over the same period—a marriage, let it be noted, of two roulette tables: weather forecasting and the stock market—any claim of exactitude is at best a mirage, at worst a carny's bark.

I know that skepticism over global warming—or, as it has been more tactically rebranded, "climate change"—is less and less a popular stance. In some quarters, it even approaches being socially unacceptable. On the not-so-far fringes of Gaia-consciousness, to mark such disapprobation, the phrase "climate change denial" is being tested out.

It is a worrisome development. The ardent advocates of climate change are more than a little imperious in their certitudes. Every counterargument or qualification to their view of things is discounted as being "paid for" by the oil industry. Or, it is labelled as being a denial of "the science." They cast yesterday's hurricane as "evidence" of extreme weather brought on by greenhouse gas emissions in the full knowledge that what we now call one "weather event" is, or can be, proof of nothing.

In my view, it cannot be emphasized sufficiently that the climate-change movement is at least as much a subcategory of rhetoric—the art of persuasion—as it is a branch of science. It is at least as much a partisan exercise (partisan in the sense of supporting a cause) as a harvest of neutral experiment and observation.

The science is not complete. The models are not perfect. The projections, economic or meteorological, over the next fifty to two hundred years are most unobligingly and massively complex. Prediction on this scale is necessarily wildly fallible.

Journalistic skepticism on climate change is a rare orchid indeed. Too many journalists are advocates, and that—whatever the cause—is a fatal mixing of mutually exclusive categories.

Most pernicious in this context is the attempt to declare, "The debate is over." It isn't over. That declaration is unsupported assertion. It is rhetoric's oldest trick. Just as declaring the arguments of those who see things differently as being corrupted by other interests is not a counterargument but a commonplace *ad hominem* evasion.

It is in this same territory that I place the Stern review's $7 trillion warning. It is not a number. It is just a gorgeous and late-blooming illustration of Smallwood's Law. How Joe would have worked it—a seven and then that whole mile of zeros.

I can, alas, hear him now.

DESPICABLE MASK FOR A WEAK ARGUMENT | May 2, 2007

It's not just the planet that's warming, it's the rhetoric on the subject of the planet's warming.

Elizabeth May, the Green leader, in a sermon preached this past weekend in London, Ontario, invoked the words of an activist British journalist who has likened the governments of Tony Blair, George Bush and Stephen Harper and their respective responses to global warming as worse than Neville Chamberlain's appeasement of the Nazis. May cited his words, but now claims on the Green website she did not compare Nazi government and the Holocaust to any current issue.

In a purely literal sense, perhaps she did not, but if you are preaching a sermon in a church and global warming is its theme, you are not chatting loosely with friends in a coffee shop. Furthermore, invoking Chamberlain and appeasement in reference to those who do not share your views makes it fairly clear you also wish to invoke the unqualified moral authority of what followed appeasement, the Holocaust, on your side of the rhetorical ledger.

Another noted environmentalist, Prince Charles, has been standing on this same tricky ledge. The Prince has claimed that urgent action is needed on climate change and likened the struggle to do something about it to Britain's battle against the Nazis in World War II. These are not the only occasions. The more fervent advocates of global warming are also far too fond of calling those who disagree with them "deniers," trying to colour a policy difference with the brush of Holocaust denial.

It is a despicable tactic. There are a number of problems with injecting the Holocaust or its shadow into the current political debate on global warming, and the separate debate on what to do about it. For the West, the Holocaust is the absolute standard of evil. It was—maybe the reminder is necessary—the deliberate, conscious torture and inhuman murder of six million people, men, women and children, by the Nazi government because those people were Jews. It is also a historical fact, something that dreadfully has really and already happened. Aside from the most pathetic anti-Semites, no one can or does dispute it.

Political policy on global warming is a choice, from a range of possibilities about what to do in the face of some very serious arguments that mankind is influencing the global climate. Advocates on either side may be claiming absolute certainty for their positions, but precisely *because* we are dealing with the future, approximated by models and estimates, neither side can possess such certainty. Invoking the Holocaust is wrong first on logical grounds. It *has* happened. We *know* it. Global warming policy is an attempt to meet a future contingency. The tactic is also wrong on a much higher level, for it is an attempt to claim, or associate with, the absolute moral authority that belongs to the Holocaust and all who were victims of its torments, and to transfer that absolute authority to the advocacy of a current and contentious issue.

Extreme rhetoric is often a mask for weak argument. It is also very often an attempt to override discussion in favour of a stampede to predetermined and unexamined policies. Surely, with all the science that Kyoto and its advocates have lined up on their side of the debate, dipping into the history of appeasement and the Holocaust is, at the very best, unnecessary.

Too many people, I among them, have noted the overlap, sometimes tending to perfect symmetry, between environmentalism and the more rigid varieties of religious adherence.

For all the most ardent environmentalist's loud prattle about the "science," they show precious little respect for any contest over their views. Scientists don't invoke the Holocaust when there is a quarrel over a line of research, or a dispute in some of the arcane understandings of quantum physics. They do not see quarrels as a form of heresy, or seek to argue down their opponents by questioning their motives and associations.

The most strident of the global warming enthusiasts—and they are many—demonstrate a willingness to be very nasty indeed when it comes to "debating" those who hold a different view from them. And of all their miserable tactics the attempt to picture their opponents as in the same moral domain as Holocaust deniers is the most desperate and despicable. Some scientists.

THE NEW INQUISITION | February 16. 2008

David Suzuki has stirred a minor controversy, recently, by some remarks he made in a speech to six hundred students at McGill University. A report in the *McGill Daily* tells us "he urged today's youth to speak out against politicians complicit in climate change."

"Complicit" is the damning word there. People are complicit only in dark and pernicious undertakings. He went on to suggest the students "look for a legal way to throw our current political leaders in jail for ignoring science," those comments drawing rounds of cheering and applause.

Well, this is a turnaround of some proportions. In the old days, the really old days, it was the foes of science, the enemies of what we have come to call the Enlightenment, who used to call for the rack, the stake and the dungeon to treat those who challenged religion's pre-eminent authority to both speak and know the truth.

We generally look upon it as a backward moment when the Catholic Church put the bridle on Galileo, subjected him to house arrest and the tender rebukes of the Inquisition. So it's at least mildly disconcerting to hear of a celebrated son of the Enlightenment, in the person of one of Canada's star communicators, urging a university audience, no less, to seek to "jail" those whom he perceives as "ignoring science." I think it's fairly clear he doesn't really mean science in general here, but rather a very particular subset of that great endeavour, the contentious and agenda-riven field of global warming.

I am under no illusion about the force of the global warming consensus. It is the grand orthodoxy of our day. Among right-thinking people, the idea of expressing any doubts on some of its more cataclysmic projections, to speak in tones other than those of veneration about its high priests, such as David Suzuki or Al Gore, is to stir a response uncomfortably close to what, in previous and less rational times, was reserved for blasphemers, heretics and atheists.

But wherever we are on global warming, and on the models and theories supporting it, it is not yet the Truth, nor is it yet Science (with a capital S) as such. And to put a stay on our full consent to its more clamorous and particular alarms is not, *pace* Dr. Suzuki, either "ignoring science" or "complicity" in criminal endeavour. Nor is reasoned dissent or dispute on some or all of the policy recommendations that global warming advocates insist flow, as night follows day, from their science.

It's worth pausing on this point. What global warming is, what portion of it is man-made, is one set of questions properly within the circle of rational inquiry we call science. What to do about it—shut down the oil sands, impose a carbon tax, sign on to Kyoto, mandate efficient light bulbs or hybrid cars—are choices within a range of public policy options that have to be made outside any laboratory whatsoever.

Global warming's more fulminating spokespeople are apt to finesse that great chasm between the science and the politics. They are further apt to imply a continuum between the unassailable authority of real and neutral science and their own particular policy prescriptions. (I notice late in the week that something called Environmental Defence has hailed the Alberta oil sands as "the most destructive project on Earth." It goes on to say that "your desire to tackle global warming is being held hostage by the Tar Sands." I'm not sure how they latched on to that "your" there. Is Environmental Defence elected? But let that pass; it is the tactic that is familiar.)

Global warming is the truth. So, shutting down the oil sands is also the truth. If global warming is primarily a "man-made" phenomenon, then what to do about it is a political, discussion before it is anything else at all. If Environmental Defence or Dr. Suzuki thinks shutting down the oil sands is not a political choice, I advise both the group and the man to visit Alberta and acquaint themselves, while they are at it, with the history of the National Energy Program, and what its consequences were for the West and Confederation. Shutting down the oil sands would make the storm over the NEP feel like a soft rain on a sultry day by comparison. It would break the Confederation.

So, far from jailing our politicians if they continue to debate what should be done, I'm in favour of leaving them where they are for now. If that's a soft stance, all I can say is that I favour discussion over imprisonment. Dr. Suzuki will surely agree that truth, like science, is not under the ownership of either any one group or any one man. To argue that those who question a prevailing orthodoxy should, even metaphorically, be tossed in jail is radically inconsistent with the essence and spirit of science itself, the essence and spirit that Dr. Suzuki, in his better moments, so clearly reveres.

We may decorate reports with graphs and charts and huge numbers, and conjure pages of the most exquisite and arcane equations, but the very best we can offer on climate a hundred years from now is a series of sophisticated and ever-ramifying probabilities that are themselves subject to a myriad of unforeseeable contingencies.

Who will undertake the difficult task of sifting the real science from the alarmist advocacy? Who will draw the boundaries between climate activism and cold analysis? Who will present a statement of the case, as close as reason and science today can make it, to what we actually know, and can reasonably project on the basis of what we know?

CANADIAN IDENTITY

WITHOUT HOCKEY | November 20, 2004

We are being tested as a nation. Winter has made its first strikes in a number of regions.

Poor Nova Scotia got belted early, and then Newfoundland got its first real smack. I know down home the weather in any season is a kind of test, but winter assaults mind and body with an almost conscious fury. A Newfoundland winter is an extended torment, mainly, I think, because Newfoundlanders never know when it begins or ends.

Snow on the 24th of May, the great mid-spring holiday weekend, is so regular as to be preordained. We have to *wait* for sunshine and warmth in Newfoundland.

And while we wait and grumble, elsewhere in what was once the great Dominion, flowers whose names I will never know are in blossom. Joggers are in their short pants for months, the Vancouverites—who are climate snobs—are out on the sidewalks, sipping decaf in March, the various chinooks have given Albertans a stay against the long frost, but poor Newfoundland can be up to its (metaphorical, of course) ears in slush, with another blizzard lying in wait—in June.

Some of the weariness of winter, both at home and all over this frigid country, is dissipated by the defences we have built against it. Newfoundlanders of an earlier time were much given to the manufacture of their own diversions. I suspect that half the really good folk songs and all the great stories of my place had their origins by the heat of a kitchen stove, under the glow of a kerosene lamp, as singer or storyteller broke the siege of the winter months by spinning a yarn or honing a melody.

We were great ones, too, for winter concerts. Homebrew, a good violin, a few recitations and the use of the parish hall gave a little innocent (or wicked) entertainment, while the wind howled and the snow drifted high. And famously—at least, famously to us—there was "janneying" of "the mummers," the cross-dressing pastime of the twelve days of Christmas.

Neighbours, in ridiculous or elaborate disguise, visited neighbours. The jannies or mummers were invited in; a guessing game over the identities of the visitors was the next part, and when all were spotted or revealed, a little singing, a little dancing and much rum concluded the visit. It was sweet sport.

Much of this, though not all, faded with the synthetic and vicarious amusements of TV. Sitcoms have quieted more invention than we will ever tabulate. With each "advance" of our remorselessly entertained society—from CDs to GameBoys, Cineplexes to iPods—the urge or the need to amuse ourselves has been tranquillized.

The great national response to winter, and the greatest shield against its many glooms and ravages, was, of course, the invention of hockey. Hockey may be seen, in its earliest manifestation, as a means of turning winter against itself; of giving a very great number of people, who were definitely not masochists, a reason to look forward to the time when all the lakes and ponds were frozen and the wind chill bit the soul. Hooray, we're freezing! Let's play hockey!

I never had the skill, the grace or—truth to tell—the heart for the game, but everyone I have ever known, with the exception of a few as impoverished as I am of all athletic resource, played or were fans or both. From one end of the country to another, from north to south, hockey, played and watched, has insinuated itself into the very codes of the Canadian experience.

The advent of professional hockey was the (pun half-intended) crystallizing culmination of our adoption of the sport. In professional hockey, all those amateurs and fans who knew and loved the game just from their own ordinary experience of it got to see it as it was meant to be.

He who plays "Chopsticks" is not Vladimir Horowitz. But even a little acquaintance with a piano is the perfect passport to really appreciating the miracles with which Horowitz, wizard of the keyboard that he was, sprinkled his every performance. It's a rare delight, watching something you only partially understand and imperfectly execute, taken to its highest expression by a master.

Every boy or girl who has ever laced a skate and chased a puck knows something of that delight. Since there's been a *Hockey Night in Canada*, our legendary virtuosi have been there for all to see and worship, from Richard to Lemieux.

Except, of course, now. We are heading into a Canadian winter minus the thrilling anodyne of professional hockey.

This cannot be a good thing. We are a fragile country. We cannot depend on Tim Hortons and Canadian Tire alone to keep us together. Or infinite reruns of *The Simpsons* and *Law & Order*, the new default Canadiana.

It's going to be a long winter. We may, dear Lord, have nothing but the spare kindling of politics and Ron MacLean subbing as a movie critic to keep us warm. How far away— O June, how far away.

ONE NATION | November 27, 2006

That the Québécois form a nation within a united Canada is, they've been telling us, just words, just symbolism, and, now, merely a "motion."

Well, words are what we live by. They are the foundational marble of our intellectual, moral and civic existence. Some of them—"home," "country," "nation"—constitute the deepest meaning in our lives. As for symbols, well, the flag is a symbol. Symbols are extremely powerful. They are concentrated meaning, the emblems of our deepest common passions.

And as for it being merely a motion, the parliament of the nation of Canada is the ultimate deliberative and legislative body of the nation of Canada. A motion passed with all-party approval in that parliament specifying one group of citizens, the Québécois, as a nation—well, that's the highest imprimatur any words about Canada can have. So trying to brush off as "mere" words the idea of the House of Commons recognizing the Québécois as a nation within Canada is absurd.

The Commons hasn't done anything as significant in years. This is of the utmost importance. It is changing the grounds on which we, all of us, understand our idea of Canadian citizenship, and the idea of the one nation to which we, all of us, give our fealty.

How important? Today a minister, Michael Chong, resigned. By the way, good for him. It's refreshing to see so dignified a stand on a matter of principle and a politician willing to lose cabinet rank because he thinks something is fundamentally wrong. Mr. Chong deserves respectful credit. The motion itself is a train of mischief and ambiguity, as is the entire concept of nominating subsets of Canadians based on their ethnicity or historical associations or geographical boundaries or constitutional past—Newfoundland would be an example—as nations in their own right. But it is particularly mischievous and ambiguous when it sets the Québécois as the community designated for nation status.

What is the Parliament of Canada doing declaring the Québécois a nation? Has that not been the principal aim of the Parti Québécois and the Bloc, the separatists, since their formation? The idea behind this motion has been a mischief since the train was put on the track by Michael Ignatieff in his leadership bid, and as it gained momentum with the Bloc's embrace and Stephen Harper's too-clever response last week, it has become more divisive by the day, igniting the call now by the premier of British Columbia to go one more step and incorporate all aboriginal peoples in another group nation.

There's no reason to stop there. It sets a division within Quebec—who are the Québécois? All Quebecers? Some? French-speaking people across the country—are they part of this new nation too? And this will spark division outside Quebec. Why not a Ukrainian nation? A nation of Labrador? An Alberta nation?

The House of Commons, the House of Commons of Canada, should be underlining only one nation: Canada. We are all its citizens, regardless of height, colour, province, language, history, religion or politics. Canada is the nation, and the biggest quarrel I have with this motion tonight is that our parliamentarians seem to have the courage to declare a bit, a slice, a portion of the country a nation when they are timid about asserting and constantly asserting and proudly asserting that *Canada* is the nation, and all Canadians are already and deeply a part of it. But I forgot, it's only words.

I'M WITH THE BRAND | May 17, 2008

On this Victoria Day weekend, back home in Newfoundland, there will be thousands of people hustling off to cabin or pond to make a day of trout fishing and having a boil-up. Very likely it'll snow, since a snowfall is an almost infallible curse of the first long weekend of Newfoundland spring. In the old days, if there was to be a boil-up and a few trout to be fried, everyone brought along a block of Good Luck butter and three or four tins of York wieners and beans. Had to be York, had to be Good Luck.

Good Luck and York were the brands of choice. Newfoundlanders, for reasons that defy any substantial analysis, bonded with certain brands. Robin Hood flour, a local bread called (excruciatingly) Mammy's, a chocolate bar that was not a bar at all (Cherry Blossom), Klik canned beef—there were a batch of such brand items that simply belonged. I've seen Libby's beans on camping trips, but I knew, and everyone else did, too, that the dolt who brought them was a stranger and an heretic.

Certain items moved into a territory of being more than just commodities. They offered a kind of whimsical identity, a grocery shelf of Newfoundlandia. In the really old days, a plug of Target chewing tobacco was as much a part of a fisherman's kit as nets and lines.

All were more emblems than products.

The same phenomenon can be seen on a much wider

plane today with Tim Hortons. I doubt anyone can locate the moment Hortons stopped being a small doughnut shop serving, at best, indifferent coffee and transmuted into a hallowed piece of Canadiana, but that it arrived no one can doubt. Outside of *Hockey Night in Canada* and—with reverence—Don Cherry, there are few institutions or companies that have blended into the character of the nation so completely as Tim Hortons.

I became a hostage to Boston cream doughnuts so long ago the day is lost in gooey memory. And now, in every town and city across the country, despite the advances of the upscale chains, the aggressive yuppie haunts of Starbucks Corp., the gentrified caffeine oases of Timothy's and Second Cup, Tim Hortons remains the venue of choice for all everyday Canadians. You knew the Canadian effort in Afghanistan had registered with the great Canadian public when Tim Hortons opened in Kandahar. Hortons is not the red Maple Leaf, but it has brewed and baked its way into being an essential piece of Canadiana.

Up to now, anyway. I think Tim Hortons is drifting from its special status. This has nothing to do with the fury of recent weeks over the woman fired for giving away a Timbit to a crying infant—though that incident may be a signal of how the brand has strayed. Nor has it to do, in my judgment, with the consideration that Tim Hortons was, until recently, purely a Canadian company (Wendy's owns it now).

No, the change is more subtle and has crept in by a kind of osmosis.

Perhaps the invisible moment was the first time a Canadian went to a Tim's not for itself, but more because it wasn't a Starbucks. A reverse-preference moment. Perhaps it came when Tim Hortons became conscious that it really wasn't just selling cheap coffee and doughnuts. (That, incidentally, was more than a while ago. Just one old-fashioned plain is eighty cents now; years back, you could buy the whole front counter display case of doughnuts for about five bucks.) Perhaps it was the moment when they became self-conscious, and started to *see* themselves as a symbol.

Something has leaked out of the enterprise. Did the coffee change? Are the doughnuts still as fresh as once they so proudly boasted they were? I'm not sure what it was or is, but, for me anyway, the zest has gone out of the transaction between chain and customer. Their "roll up the rim" is a farcical gimmick. The signature phrases—"double double" being the most familiar—gall more than they please. Their ridiculous lineups—in some places it takes longer to get a coffee than to pick up a licence at a motor vehicle registration office—have lost the kind of self-congratulatory charm they had some time back. People used to smile at each other for the silly indulgence of lining up for a not-very-good cup of coffee. They don't smile as much anymore. They mutter.

Most of all, people don't feel the loyalty they once did. It is no longer a traitorous act to wander into Second Cup—though, it must be noted, treading into Starbucks is still a barista too far. All in all, I think Timmy's—another unfortunate coinage—is past its best-before date. The romance has wilted. The coffee has cooled. It has had its crowning moment as a badge of this great white north, but unless something in the chemistry between coffee and customer changes, real soon, the days of Tim Hortons as an essential Canadian experience are dwindling and few.

HANDS OFF HORTONS | January 9, 2009

Unlike the Americans, we don't have a written pledge that guarantees our right to the Pursuit of Happiness. But over time, we've evolved. I think it's now generally agreed that, while the founders of the Canadian state were a little slack in spelling things out, that ordinary Canadian has determined that a morning visit to Tim Hortons, and the prospect of the first fresh Boston cream doughnut makes up for any defects in our Constitution—and places the pursuit of happiness right where it should be: in the salivating reach of all.

We hold this truth to be self-evident: that the Boston cream doughnut is the acme of human civilization as we know it, and that the only experience better than an early coffee and a Boston cream is an early coffee and *two* Boston creams. Isn't mathematics wonderful?

The Boston cream doughnut—paradise with a chocolate coating. Now, I have seen people at Tim Hortons who've actually ordered a danish. But then, that's what they were—Danish, I mean. Once, I even saw a guy ask for the tea biscuit. But he doesn't count. I think he was a nutritionist.

However, there's alarming news on the Timmy's front. Back home in St. John's, I hear some cabal is trying to ban the drive-thrus. Trying to slow access to Tim Hortons in . . . Newfoundland? Shut down the Seal Hunt, why dontcha? Ban Flipper pie? Make accordion-playing a public offence? What is going on in my home and native land? Have they all become Diana Krall fans?

Mark my words, this is the Chapters crowd, with their Starbucks "emporia," and their *Chicken Soup for the Soul* "literature"—and those inedible splodges Chapters/Starbucks offer in place of the honest doughnut. Have you ever tried to eat something at a Starbucks?

That crowd are either all come-from-aways, or they should be. Furthermore, what's this prissy attitude about Tim Horton drive-thrus? Too downmarket for you? Too pickup truck? Too—horrors!—Don Cherry? Michael Ignatieff, I hope you're paying attention here.

But there's a bigger issue, too. We're about to throw a hundred billion or so out the window in the next federal budget—now there's your drive-thru—for businesses that don't work. And here's the one business in Canada, up to its knees in cash—the most loyal clientele on the face of this hungry earth—and some damn town councils want to see if they can knock it down. Have you seen the boat that the guy who used to own Tim Hortons just launched?

He's not going to be looking for a bailout—unless it's from the marble hot tub.

Canada is a vast geographical expanse variegated only by Tim Hortons outlets—our coffee-shop parliaments, which offer coffee in cup sizes people can actually understand, where using white sugar is not a crime, and where the person serving you—thank God—would die if you called her a barista. Canada is one huge drive-thru for Tim Hortons.

It's bad enough we're in a recession/depression. It's bad enough Stephen Harper has been scared into opening the federal spigot on January 27 in a way we haven't seen in a generation. But, for godsake, there's only one thing still working in this country. Tim Hortons. Leave it alone. If you want to read Wally Lamb or *The Life of Pi* next to the Oprah's Picks stand, you know where to go. But leave Tim Hortons out of it.

SCANDAL

COMPLETELY FOXED | March 15, 2008

William Blake saw visions. But not even Blake, pottering about naked in his back garden chatting with angels, as he was wont to do, could have fantasticated something as alien to the age he lived in as the Emperors Club, with its diamond-rated *filles d'hôtel*, available at rates of one to five thousand dollars an hour, ordered up as easily as pizza.

Which is not to say that Blake was ignorant of purchased pleasure. Prostitution, as the glib axiom testifies, is the oldest profession, and from drab to courtesan, camp-follower to *fille de joie*, the variety of its practitioners is one of its enduring characteristics. Rather, the poet was more progressive than the age in which he wrote, sensed more keenly the misery that brought women to traffic in their flesh, and the miseries that traffic imposed.

Indeed, poor, old, crazy, wise Blake, in his poem "London," penned a verse of much pity and anger on the subject:

> *But most thro' midnight streets I hear*
> *How the youthful Harlots' curse*
> *Blasts the new-born infant's tear,*
> *And blights with plagues the*
> *Marriage hearse.*

Between prosecuting and patronizing upscale cat-houses (a neat trick, in both senses), Eliot Spitzer probably didn't have much time for poetry, but he may want to check Blake now.

There was something in the face of Mrs. Spitzer, called to stand twice with her self-disgraced hypocrite husband at news conferences, that said she understood the force of Blake's phrase "marriage hearse." And Mr. Spitzer himself might have a less self-centred idea of the damage he's done from another of Blake's warning couplets. Contra the theme of enlightened argument, prostitution is not a victimless crime, but a social toxin:

> *The harlot's cry from street to street*
> *Shall weave old England's winding sheet.*
> *A governor who rents women is complicit in the state's*
> *decay.*

Blake's wisdom is perhaps too crisp and emphatic for our relaxed age, where pimps—at least in certain venues—have more currency than pastors. Pointing to the moral

and social dimension of Governor Spitzer's bedroom trans-
actions, via Blake or anyone else, is probably gauche, or
even worse, judgmental.

After all, following this "personal tragedy," as, unfailingly,
it is called, Mr. Spitzer must have time to "heal." The warm,
moist towelettes of pop therapy must be laid on his troubled
brow, distillations of Deepak/Oprah chatter sluiced on his
injured esteem. Let us pray there's a spa where he can "confront his demons" guided by selected readings from the
Book of Charlie Sheen. After which, he can, of course, "move
on," "put it behind him" or, if he is truly heroic, "reach out
to others," "repair his relationships" and appear on a call girl-
themed edition of *The View*, gushing apologies and bleeding
"authentic" recovery from every self-exhibiting pore.

There aren't really many original observations to come
out of the Spitzer train wreck. That the powerful are arrogant is the weariest of commonplaces. That a crusading
prosecutor would commit the very crimes he prosecutes
would not startle a six-year old. Lear railed against that pre-
cise hypocrisy four centuries ago:

> *Thou rascal beadle, hold thy bloody hand!*
> *Why dost thou lash that whore? Strip thine own back;*
> *Thou hotly lust'st to use her in that kind for which*
> *thou whipp'st her.*

I have some admiration for those who named the call-
girl enterprise The Emperors Club. What could be more

appealing to the egotism of the clientele, the brassy over-achievers of politics and commerce? Real emperors, alas, do not lurk in hotel rooms under aliases or pseudonyms. Napoleon would never check in as "George Fox," which was Mr. Spitzer's *nom de whore*. The name, incidentally (besides being that of the seventeenth-century founder of the Quakers), is that of one of Mr. Spitzer's closest friends, which must have pleased the real George Fox when it raced around the world in every newspaper and on every TV station. Mr. Spitzer was digging a pit for maximum accommodation. Was ever a man so intent on making sure that, should he be caught, everyone—friend, foe, neutral or intimate—would have a reason to despise him?

I have some sympathy for the young woman. Before, her body was the commodity. Now, she has entered a version of Monica Lewinsky's world—her self, her breath and being, are product. Talk shows, late-night monologues, stalking paparazzi, tell-all articles—poor young "Kristen" may even mistake it for celebrity.

They'll pick her up in limousines and bring her to grand hotels. *Entertainment Tonight* and its tacky peers will burble at her approach.

Then the moment will pass and she won't be able to flag down a cab.

Which offers a fearful symmetry (another Blake caution) with the profession she probably thinks she's left.

BERNIER'S GIRLFRIEND | May 27, 2008

Well, that was a short run. Not everyone gets to be minister of foreign affairs for a great nation, but Maxime Bernier's gaffe-tormented tenure was more of a touchdown than a stay. But even butterfly-brief, what a touchdown it was. More a touch of Peter Sellers's Clouseau or one of the more exotic episodes of *Friends*—Ross meets the biker chick—than *The Diary of a Statesman*.

There's nothing intrinsically wrong with dating the former girlfriend of a Hells Angels cavalier, but it would be a sign of minimal gravitas, if you happened to be one of the highest-ranking cabinet ministers of a national government, to fish from a less tumultuous pool. Even in our antiseptic, determinedly non-judgmental age, a man in the position of representing his country abroad should probably have sought a soulmate with less flamboyant associations than with the Quebec chapter of a continental biker gang. That would have been what an earlier age called simple good sense, or maturity.

When Mr. Bernier's associations were raised by the opposition, Mr. Harper, his boss, dismissed their questions as those of busybodies and issued a further statement that belonged more in the patronizing mouth of Dr. Phil than a prime minister: that Bernier's private life was no one's business.

High office demands responsibility and judgment, and it is often in the very terrain of private life that those virtues are most exercised. Instead, Mr. Bernier, as numerous photo ops concur, acted more like a high school kid parading his cheerleader date than a high officer of the Canadian state. And to cap it off, yesterday's revelations that he forgot some sensitive documents at Madame Couillard's apartment. What could have made him so forgetful?

But that was not the icing on this tawdry cake. That came with her—need I say inevitable—TV appearance following the breakup, in which she keened that Mr. Bernier had destroyed her life, a lament she tried to retail to the *Toronto Star* for fifty thousand bucks. Ruin and grief have their price. What's more, she retailed to her Quebec television audience that Maxime was her wardrobe consultant and he picked the much-commented-on dress—no state secrets there—worn at his swearing-in last summer, and revealed something of his dating philosophy in words that will surely end up in a book of wisdom for the ages. Said Mr. Bernier, "I can't switch girlfriends like I change shirts." Hasn't got the ring of "For better or for worse, in sickness or in health," but it will do.

No private life is worth anything these days until it's all unravelled in full confessional mode to an audience of millions on television. The only commodity not on display in this gruelling farce was a smidgen of dignity. Mr. Bernier obviously thought his private life had a consequence higher than his public duties, or he would have been more scrupulous about seeing that the private did not intersect with the public.

The office of foreign minister for Canada is less dignified today than it was some months ago, and Stephen Harper, for all his seeming austerity of manner, showed very little prudence and minimal judgment in setting this whole farce in motion with the appointment in the first place. The scorned busybodies were right, and Canada's affairs of state are now just a sorry soap opera of Hells Angels, forgotten documents and the prime time confessions of a jilted lover.

Our scandals are, usually, much tamer than the U.S. ones. We don't have—thank every god—Nancy Grace or Dr. Phil to lend their graceful intellects to the parsing or reportage of the moral defaults of our public performers. Nor do we have the full echo chamber of the tabloids and Internet sites our brethren to the south employ for the amplification of every nuance and the relentless detailing of every awkward titillation. We also lack the full uninhibited appetite for the stuff, the relish of it. I think there is still some remnant of reserve in the Canadian temperament, which makes us a little less eager to pry over the wall, or peer into every window when occasion offers a spurious licence to do so—as every so-called public scandal does.

The Couillard book, it is encouraging to note, did not do very well. If Spitzer's pay-for-play young business-woman were to put pen to paper, I suspect the resulting book would scale the alpine peaks of *The New York Times* bestseller list with the agility and rush of a frightened cat.

CANADA AND THE U.S.

HOW WE FLAGGED THE AMERICAN BULL | March 5, 2005

Busy as a bee is the folkloric tag, and of all bees—those of the meadow or those that toil in more metaphorical hives—Martha Stewart is the very busiest. I've read that, within days of her going to jail, she was at work on a floral arrangement for a recently deceased corrections officer, and "fashioned a beautiful topiary, trimmed with pampas grass."

Just too good, that last detail—"trimmed with pampas grass." How Martha. Your run-of-the-mill detainee would probably have stapled a few buttercups together, rubber-banded a few posies and called it a day. But put Martha on the job and, behind bars or not, that "topiary" will be "trimmed with pampas grass," even if she has to grow the damn pampas to get it—a little bit of Argentina just under the guard tower.

The Wall Street Journal says she also gave yoga lessons, kicked off a lecture series and "offered pointers for a prison weaving class." A longer sentence, and the world might now have a second Taj Mahal constructed from Popsicle sticks. Bordered with pampas grass, undoubtedly.

Martha is out now, more prosperous than ever, and more compelling as a news magnet than before the hit from the prosecutors. I tremble in the writing of this, but I believe she may be, as they say, "bigger" than Oprah.

I wonder if Frank McKenna, freshly installed as our U.S. ambassador a mere day or so before Martha's exit from her industrious durance, had the instinct and the courtesy to send her a thank-you card. It's a test of an ambassador to know the moment, know whom to signal and what to watch.

He arrived, to put it mildly, at an awkward time. George Bush is not returning our prime minister's phone calls, there has been some temporizing on the timing of Secretary of State Condoleezza Rice's visit, and the air in the U.S. is, unwontedly, thick with abrasive comments on us, the usually invisible, congenitally nice neighbour to the north.

In a U.S. Senate debate on the subject of reopening the border to Canadian beef, I heard a surly tone about Canada that was very nearly shocking. The worst came from Democratic senators. Democrats in Washington and Liberals in Ottawa are not exactly the Bobbsey twins ideologically, but insofar as either may be said to think, they think more or less alike. Harsh scolding from Democrats is not the predictable rant of Pat Buchanan ("Canuckistan"), say, or the comic bristling of Bill O'Reilly, the cranky tribune of all that's "fair and balanced."

I am sure Mr. McKenna saw and heard more of that Senate debate than I, and probably shivered more from its acrimony than its actual result—a resolution to continue the ban on Canadian beef, which we are perhaps unrealistically confident that the president will veto when it reaches his desk.

Even before the Senate debate, our new ambassador was offering his reflection that the recent, and badly conveyed, Canadian decision on missile defence was very likely coloured, the "temperature" of relations raised, by the stalemates on mad-cow disease and softwood lumber. He more or less claimed that Paul Martin's call on missile defence grew out of the Americans' stubbornness and intransigence on trade matters.

It's a rational reading, but I doubt it. I think the decision on missile defence, from our government's perspective, had less to do with beef and timber than with raw political considerations. Signing on to missile defence carries, for many Canadian voters, the dread stigma of that vilest carnality—climbing into bed with the Americans.

Mr. McKenna is right. Canadians—certainly, cattle ranchers and people in the softwood lumber industry—are very angry. But the bigger anger, because of its clout, is actually that which is starting to drift from the U.S. to Canada.

The temperature, as Mr. McKenna has it, is rising. When Canada's "free ride" on continental defence makes it to the news billboards of CNN, when Lou Dobbs gives his precious attention to our defence budget, when the cable channels have a round of Canada-bashing—why, yes, things are getting hot for us. If cattle and defence weren't linked before, they are linked now. Our stand on missile defence definitely caught the U.S. media spotlight.

Fortunately for us, and our ambassador, its intense beam is fitful. What is mad cow and softwood lumber to measure against the allure of the iconic Wonder Woman of aspirant yuppiedom and the release (fringed with pampas grass or not) of Martha Stewart?

For Frank McKenna, perhaps even more than for Martha, it was a very good thing.

P.S. Make sure, Mr. Ambassador, that the card is one of a kind. Parchment with calligraphy would be nice.

HOME TRUTHS FOR BOTH COUNTRIES | September 24, 2005

Paul Cellucci's tenure as U.S. ambassador to Canada may be described as a one-mission assignment. It was early in the term of his appointment that nineteen al-Qaeda terrorists hijacked four airliners to work their murderous intent. The destruction of the twin towers, the scarring of the Pentagon, the appalling loss of life—all broadcast in real time to the television screens of the world—necessarily radicalized the United States' sense of its vulnerability, and utterly transformed its conduct toward the rest of the world from that moment on.

Mr. Cellucci quotes Prime Minister Jean Chrétien remarking after the towers fell that "the world has changed." Chrétien was correct. From September 11 on, the world's only superpower elevated the matter of its own security, the safety of its citizens at home and abroad, to the fundamental priority of its foreign policy. Everything was subordinate to that objective. Mr. Cellucci's task was to translate the imperatives of that elevation in the particular arena of relations between his country and ours.

Even in normal times—if, in a busy, chaotic world, "normal times" is a sustainable concept—the position of U.S. ambassador to Canada calls for formidable delicacy, nuance and sensitivity. We are friends and neighbours, have fought together in the two great wars of the last century, and the United States has been, up until a bare two weeks ago, Canada's largest trading partner (China now owns that distinction). Canadians are immensely aware of the economic and cultural giant on our doorstep. We are grateful she is pacific toward us; 1812 is a buried memory.

But we are acutely aware that the sheer cultural and economic mass of the United States almost inevitably has an impact on our way of life, and we therefore examine every interaction between our two countries with great self-consciousness and rigour, lest some portion of our statehood, our way of life and identity, be diminished, obscured or even obliterated. We are on a jealous watch up here.

The spectrum of our sensitivity is a broad one. There is the blind contempt and overt disdain for all things American, from its president to its pop culture; there is pure and visceral anti-Americanism, which fuels the passion of the hard Canadian left, of which Carolyn Parrish's occasional spiteful outbursts ("Damn Americans. I hate those bastards.") are such obnoxious examples.

Then, too, in polar reverse, is the worship of high capitalism and reverence for the great heroes of American republicanism, which warms the dreams of the hard Canadian right and has, as its fitful vehicle, the Conservative Party.

In the middle, there is the sane appreciation of the Americans as neighbours and allies, and a reasonable admiration for their undeniable achievements and goodwill. This is coupled with a cautious recoil from the excesses of their sometimes unhinged and shameless culture, even as we mimic its more vapid splendours (witness *Canadian Idol* or the "Canadian" edition of *Entertainment Tonight*) or even export a few of that culture's grossest exponents (Céline Dion, Tom Green).

Whatever the Americans do—and sometimes whatever they do not do—as it refers to us, is put to a scrutiny and analysis of rabbinical finesse. They haunt us continually. What Pat Buchanan thinks, or what *The Wall Street Journal* on any given day may say, does not alter the temperature of the universe, and whether we are mocked or praised on blog or pundit panel should, by now, be a matter of the greatest indifference to us. But, of course, it isn't.

It was into this chamber of heightened cultural and political sensitivity—a sensitivity amplified on both sides of the exchange by the great horrors of September 11—that Mr. Cellucci wandered when he accepted the post of U.S. ambassador to Canada. After that day, from the Americans' point of view, there were some messages that had to be delivered raw. There was neither time nor inclination for the more serpentine volubility of a traditional diplomatic approach.

Which is probably why Mr. Cellucci's memoir is titled *Unquiet Diplomacy*. His mission to us was the very plain one of making sure that we understood how serious, post–9/11, the Americans were. That, regardless of our long tradition of neighbourliness and the historic casualness of our cross-border relationship, there was nothing that would be allowed to impede or interfere with the Americans' redrawing of their national priorities.

We shared a continent, and the United States had enemies. It was at war. So, from the U.S. point of view, if there were deficiencies in our security that they felt would have an impact on *their* security, if our military's anorexic state indirectly jeopardized their sense of safety, if our border controls did not measure up to their standards of strictness—then he, the new ambassador, was going to tell us. Straight out.

His memoir is a chronicle of the key episodes during which he unfolded this message, and the events and issues that intersected with it. We Canadians first began to hear the new tone when Mr. Cellucci began "advising" us on the strength of our military. An interesting sidelight on this contentious issue is that Cellucci was specifically enjoined by Secretary of State Colin Powell to perform this task. It was the first and only specific injunction he received from Powell. Quite naturally, a fair portion of the Canadian public and our politicians were not pleased—either with the advice itself or that the ambassador was "lecturing" us on our affairs.

He made it clear very early that in the changed world, "Security trumps trade." This pithy formulation had an edge of threat. Canada's economic fortune hangs—even in these mixed days of softwood lumber disputes—on the easy flow of goods between our two countries. What Cellucci was underscoring with his formula was that even his relentlessly capitalist country would not nurse trade at the expense of security. That unless Canada tidied up its house, monitored its borders and ports with renewed zeal, showed that we had a determination equal to the Americans' to forestall future attacks, the economic nexus between our two countries would be broken.

The issue of continental defence, specifically its anti–ballistic missile component, was the most troublesome and annoying, according to Cellucci, to the Americans and President George W. Bush. On the system itself, the Americans did not understand why we wished to exempt ourselves. It was not going to cost us anything. We were already partners in NORAD—indeed, on the day of the terror attacks, Canadian Air Force General Rick Findley "was in command at Cheyenne Mountain . . . and scrambled the jets in response to the President's orders."

Further, they did not appreciate the description of missile defence, which so appealed to the critics of the system, as "the weaponization of space." Finally, they were disappointed not only that Canada did not "sign on," but that the Canadian government had been confusing in its signals on this issue, temporizing over its resolution and then adding another disappointment with "the clumsy manner in which it was announced." Pierre Pettigrew communicated the decision to Condoleezza Rice, while Prime Minister Paul Martin, who was actually with Bush (both men were attending a NATO meeting), didn't tell *him*. As Cellucci notes, they "were standing side by side. But not a word was said."

It's a subtheme of these memoirs that the Americans found our government's method of communicating policy choices more annoying than the choices themselves. Cellucci gives solid evidence that he grew to learn of the complexities of Canadian parliamentary politics, especially in its current "minority" phase. He is aware of the inescapable perils that visit Canadian leaders if they are seen to be "too close" to the Americans on some issues, or—sprinkle the holy water—actually get chummy with their presidents. Brian Mulroney singing "When Irish Eyes Are Smiling" with Ronald Reagan at the so-called Shamrock Summit evoked a national cringe that probably registered on the Richter scale.

But Cellucci hints, more than once, that even with those complexities, a stronger leadership and some daring on the part of the two prime ministers he has dealt with, Jean Chrétien and Paul Martin, might have led them to make wiser choices than they did, and might also have worked to raise and reinforce Canada's standing in Washington and the world.

We in Canada wish to have leverage on world affairs, to work the reins as a respected middle power. We diminish our possibilities in these areas when we define our diplomacy with Washington primarily or only in relation to its Canadian domestic political consequences. If by our words and actions we instruct the Americans that, finally, we are not really serious about these matters, then they will, perhaps with some disappointment, conclude that we are not serious. That will have far greater consequences for us than for them.

The ambassador more than hints that the two major issues—missile defence and the invasion of Iraq—where the Canadian government and its chief spokesmen gave confused signals, led the Americans to believe we would be onside. Then, both times we backed out and followed up with less than helpful remarks, either on the policy or on Bush himself.

On Iraq, following the failed attempt to get a "second resolution" from the UN, Chrétien announced that Canada would not be joining the United States. The Americans were disappointed, but they were offered the mollification that, "although Canada would not participate as an active party in the war coalition, once the war began, our government would say positive things about the United States, and negative things about Iraq."

That assurance barely survived the time it took to phrase it. Chrétien, on the very day after the invasion, chose to implicitly rebuke the United States by saying that such actions as the invasion had to be authorized by the UN. And on the heels of Chrétien's barb, National Resources Minister Herb Dhaliwal chose to offer the public a personal assessment of George Bush as "a failed statesman."

Cellucci was very angry in both instances, and while he did not see the prime minister recanting, he thought the words of the minister merited a trip to the woodshed. It was not to be. "Mr. Dhaliwal's insult to the President went unchallenged and uncriticized."

Meantime, just to appease the gods of irony, Alberta Premier Ralph Klein had sent a letter thanking the United States for "its leadership in the war on terrorism and terror." For this, Premier Klein received "a stern rebuke from the Canadian government." Mr. Cellucci comments: "Ralph Klein was not the only premier to publicly express his support for my government in Iraq, although he was the only one to receive a dressing-down from the federal government."

In both cases, what I take from Cellucci's account is that, while the Americans were disappointed and even surprised at Canada's decisions, and in the case of missile defence actually perplexed, what soured them and made them angry were the petty verbal pile-ons before and after the decisions had been made. Françoise Ducros, Chrétien's communications adviser, had opined that Bush was "a moron"; Carolyn Parrish had a small franchise of witless anti-American insults and Bush-bashing; then Mr. Chrétien voided the understanding that he was to "say nice things" and Dhaliwal, a full cabinet minister, gratuitously degraded the American president.

I suspect that in diplomacy, tone is as important as substance, and respect between leaders and nations more important than either. I take from what Mr. Cellucci has written that both he and his masters in the White House could live with Canada's taking its own line, but were thrown off balance and genuinely astonished that representatives and spokesmen of their neighbour and ally were so liberal and earthy in jabbing the president and deriding his policies.

Neither Cellucci nor the Americans are stupid. They know that occasional spasms of anti-Americanism, or "standing up to the White House," offer an easy harvest of electoral popularity. Why did we stay out of the war with Iraq? Was it because we thought it wrong? Or was it because the Chrétien government could not, politically, contemplate going along with the Americans? I'd say the second was a more puissant recommendation than the first. Decorate the choice with a few anti-Bush comments, and you've hit the sweet spot of Canadian politics.

But did the manner hurt us on other fronts? Mr. Cellucci, for all his professed candour, doesn't oblige with a real answer. It is almost impossible to believe that, if the Americans thought we were gaming them on Iraq—

depreciating the "legitimacy" of the invasion, avoiding missile defence, not on the merits of these cases, but on their "optics" for Canadians—they would not respond on other fronts. Softwood lumber, for example. We pay for our posturing, and anyone reading *Unquiet Diplomacy* will understand why.

Did his message get through—that this is a changed world, and that the U.S. has elevated its own security to the status of an absolute and incomparable imperative?

First, if it did not, it is not because Mr. Cellucci failed in delivering the message. He found ample occasions and eager ears, and he had the necessary manner. But did it get through to Canadians with all the force and priority Mr. Cellucci intended? I don't think so. Mainly because there remains a gulf between the two countries—the gulf established by the cruel acts of September 11. They were attacked and we were not. We may have stores of empathy for the Americans, and the more imaginative of our citizens and leaders may have formed some idea of the shock the Americans felt. But there is an unbridgeable psychological distance between us and them: their country was hit, the empire was attacked; we were sympathetic witnesses. September 11 is another strand in the evolving myth of that country—it has contoured the imaginations of all its citizens.

Which leaves a gap between us. The Americans have a greater intensity on matters of defence and, when necessary, aggression. They are not waiting for another blow to fall. Right or wrong, they are going to intervene in the world, and they will look both for allies to support them and, in our case, neighbours who, in matters of border security, defence and intelligence-gathering, will be as intense as they are. But we do not see things in an equally dire light. A majority of Canadians probably feel that the Americans are overreacting. And, occasionally, some Canadians will scold and even mock the Americans for the post–9/11 intensity.

Which means not only will we at times not be on side, we will also at times be seen by them as posing, as haughty and preachy. And they will see that as hypocrisy—since, as Mr. Cellucci made clear in one of his early speeches on the topic of Canada and the United States post–9/11—they would take our fears at face value.

They would automatically come to our aid.

In the sense that *Unquiet Diplomacy* opens a window on U.S.-Canada relations, it is a naturally interesting book. Mr. Cellucci is on most things, I think, a straight shooter. You don't have to decode his remarks. But having been a diplomat, he has learned the diplomat's art of always holding something back, or allowing certain things to speak for themselves, or of supplying enough by way of tone or example to let readers form larger judgments than he himself is willing to supply.

He likes Canada and he likes a lot of Canadians, and he loves the country itself. He survived Cape Breton and the Calgary Stampede. We could wish he were a better stylist, but not every ambassador is John Kenneth Galbraith, and perhaps that's a blessing. *Bon mots* are best in after-dinner speeches anyway. This is a tidy memoir, mercilessly unembroidered and stuffed with home truths for both countries.

OUR CAMP COFFEE | January 12, 2008

Stumbling around the Internet, I came upon the delightful revelation that coffee, according to legend, was discovered by an Abyssinian goatherd who chanced upon his goats dancing happily around after their having eaten berries from a coffee bush.

Encouraging as it is to learn that *espresso macchiato* has its Eden myth, and that Abyssinian goatherds, sages that they are, know a happy dancing goat from a sad one, the story cued me to the changing fortunes of our caffeine-fortified times.

Is the sun setting on the Starbucks empire? Well, as the ancient maxim has it, there is always hope.

There's a memo Starbucks chairman Howard Schultz sent last February to the now-ousted CEO of the bean empire. Actually, it's less a memo than a *cri de coeur*. Nothing as pathetic as this had been penned since poor, incarcerated Oscar Wilde, brooding on his ruin, wrote that immortal lament *The Ballad of Reading Gaol*. It was Oscar's conclusion, rendered in highly melodramatic tetrameter, that "all men kill the thing they love." The big guy at Starbucks doesn't quite have Wilde's gift for epigram and *le mot juste*, but the story he tells is the same: Starbucks is doing in Starbucks.

Mr. Schultz is worried that, having gone "from less than 1,000 stores to 13,000 stores and beyond" in ten years, the company had made "a series of decisions that, in retrospect, have led to the watering down of the Starbucks experience." I don't think that, when he speaks of "watering down," he literally means watering down. He is really speaking of what he likes to think of as the aura of Starbucks—the "Starbucks experience," as he charmingly puts it. The coffee, I suspect, is as strong as it has always been.

He's worried that some people may now be going to the yuppie salons just to get a cup of coffee. He reflects on Starbucks' decision to bring in "automatic espresso machines" and notes that the choice was a good one in terms of "speed of service and efficiency." But the machines displaced the La Marzocca models (which bore a passing resemblance to some of the alien spaceships shown on *Star Trek*, if you can imagine tackily drawn spaceships with three or four pump handles).

Further, the new machines now blocked the "visual sight line" of the Starbucks customer, who could no longer see the coffee being made. Which (give my regards to Broadway) removed "much of the romance and theatre that was in play with the use of the La Marzocca machines." And, ultimately, led to customers no longer having their "intimate experience with the barista." Well, pimp my *grande latte*!

The memo reaches its crisis moment when Chairman (and now CEO) Schultz lets cry from out of the depths (cue the pan flutes): "I am not sure people today even know we are roasting coffee." As the old epitaphs used to say, "Reader, stop here, or gently pass."

Now, speaking as one who can't claim—and would go some considerable distance to deny—"an intimate experience with a barista" and who couldn't distinguish a shade-grown, free-trade organic coffee bean from a turnip, I can't honestly say I feel Chairman Schultz's pain. Starbucks has always carried the aroma of a trumped-up exercise in lifestyle pedigree, hawking a faux pedantry over brews and beans, and overripe pseudo debates on the superiority of the Ethiopian product to its Moroccan congener. They're beans, folks.

I suspect that the wonderful success Tim Hortons has had over the years came, in part, from the rise of the lifestyle coffee chains such as Starbucks. Even though Tim Hortons may have begun earlier than most of them, it picked up some commercial propulsion and swelled its constituency by offering, so self-consciously, the very opposite of what the newer coffee lounges stood for.

Tim Hortons is a lifestyle coffee, too, but Tim Hortons is, or used to be, aggressively unshowy. Line up, grab a Boston cream and a double-double, retire to the corner, slurp, and (in the good old days) smoke. Tim Hortons was Don Cherry: direct and unadorned. I'd guess a lot of people went to Tim Hortons as a way of saying they wouldn't go to Starbucks. And a lot went to Starbucks to demonstrate the reverse.

Lately, I wonder whether Tim Hortons, though with less torment than that exuded by the Starbucks memo, has forgotten what it's about. The crowds are still there, the lineups interminable. But I sense it's more the inertia of habit that's drawing them now. And, alas, a certain campiness.

It's "in" to go to Tim Hortons—which is as much a contradiction of why people went there in the first place as the loss of "theatre" and "intimacy with the barista" is a reason for the Starbucks' downturn. It's enough to make an Abyssinian goatherd, dancing or otherwise, weep.

For more on Boston cream doughnuts and the Tim Hortons experience, see "I'm with the Brand" (page 221) and the item that follows it, "Hands off Hortons."

HUMAN RIGHTS

SAUDI JUSTICE | December 22, 2007

It flashed around the world, with only minute variations, and has to be one of the oddest sentences ever written, as a headline or otherwise: "Saudi king pardons gang-rape victim."

You know you've entered a strange country of the mind when the same sentence contains *pardon* and *victim* as verb and object. But you have found a passport to some utterly arcane territory indeed—a mix or compost of the absurd and sinister—when *pardon*, the verb, governs (as used to be said in those now archaic grammar lessons) as object this most grim noun phrase: *gang-rape victim*.

With victim we might associate verbs other than pardon: treat, sympathize, commiserate, care or pray for. These are the obvious candidates.

Saudi king offers deepest sympathy to gang-rape victim— no one would start at that sentence. Or *Saudi king pledges all possible support to medical treatment of gang-rape victim*. I don't think that would leap off the newspaper page as something extraordinary. The world would read it, very likely think a little better of that Saudi king, and then go about its business.

But *Saudi king pardons gang-rape victim*. This sentence, as we say now, simply does not compute. We do not know a world in which gang-rape victims are the ones seeking or receiving pardons, from Saudi kings or other potentates either less or more exalted. We know instead a world where those who have been raped, and most especially those who have endured the near-unendurable torments and dehumanizing outrages of gang rape, inspire the most profound sympathy and concern.

Not so, it seems, in the petroleum kingdom, where a gang-rape victim receives a pardon from her king.

The headline springs from the story of a most unfortunate nineteen-year-old who was charged with the "crime" of being in a car with a man who was not a relative, when both were set upon by seven men, both raped—she most violently, for two hours, by all seven, and more than once. She was reduced to numbness, shock and near-suicide and suffered horrific psychological and physical trauma.

But in the *Alice in Wonderland* meets Kafka meets *1984* world of Saudi Arabia's *sharia* jurisprudence, the gang-raped nineteen-year-old had to appear before her Islamic judges and be tried for the crime of sitting in a car with a man. At first, her sentence was, by the standards these judges set for themselves, considered lenient—a mere ninety lashes and some months in jail.

She—poor, tormented woman—seems to have had both the dignity and simple force of character to protest this monstrous verdict, and sought appeal with the help of a lawyer of some courage and resource. He—brave soul—protested the infamy of putting to the lash a woman who had already been gang-raped. For this noble and worthy exertion, he earned for himself severe reprimand and the threat of removing his right to practise law—such as the law is, and such as it is practised there—in Saudi Arabia.

She, for the temerity of appealing a mindless and barbaric sentence, and for the publicity that was the result of her appeal, had her sentence increased to two hundred lashes. Sharia justice is very scrupulous of its own honour, and the tenets of Islamic law as it applies to the monstrous horror of a woman being in the company of a man not her relative, will not be mocked by appeals to mercy or sense. Hence, two hundred lashes and six months in jail—the six months presumably necessary to give the stripes from the whip time to burn into scars.

The world at large found this excessive and, to be truthful, both odd and cruel, too, beyond even the odd and cruel bounds of the ancient codes that, sadly, still are imposed on so many of the women in so many countries.

Through her lawyer, with the help of some genuine human-rights organizations, the case was not allowed to rest on the pronouncements of the three-man tribunal that upped her lashes from ninety to two hundred. I expect the Saudi king felt the wave of revulsion and contempt that followed on the world's press coverage of this outrage, and thus it came to pass that a nineteen-year-old who had been raped, shamed and tormented by seven men was relieved of the further shame and torment of two hundred lashes and incarceration in a Saudi jail for half a year of her young sad life. But "King pardons gang-rape victim" remains, in my mind, anyway, an atrocious declaration, a simultaneously absurd and mean statement.

He has no pardon to give her; she none to receive from him.

An apology, that is within his gift: for the fact that he presides over a kingdom where laws still exist to punish a woman who has been brutally raped, and where they multiply the lashes if she has the strength or character to decry such insanity.

Such a king should be seeking clemency, not confusing himself with the delusion that he has the moral or political authority to exercise it.

FLAGRANTLY ISLAMOPHOBIC | January 3, 2008

Time was when "human rights" was a truly large and noble idea. I associate the concept with, and its birth out of, some of the great horrors of the past century: the bestial depredations of the Nazis, their "race science" and death camps, the horrors of unbridled totalitarianism—under which, the whim of the rulers was sufficient warrant to mutilate, torture and destroy lives, collectively or individually or send millions to arctic slave camps—and the debasement of internal exile and psychiatric rehabilitation.

More currently, I associate real human-rights advocacy with the case of a young Saudi woman who was repeatedly gang-raped and then she—the victim—was charged and sentenced by a Saudi court to two hundred lashes and six months in jail for being in a car with a man not her relative. The sentence, after international protest, was voided—but that young woman's case represents a real example of the violation of basic human rights.

What I do not associate with this deep and noble concept is getting ticked off by something you read in a magazine—or, for that matter, hear on television—and then scampering off to a handful—well, three—of Canada's proliferate human rights commissions, seeking to score off the magazine. This is what four Osgoode Hall law students and graduates—a very definition of the "marginalized"—under the banner of the Canadian Islamic Congress have done after reading an excerpt from Mark Steyn's *America Alone* in *Maclean's*. The complainants read the article as "flagrantly islamophobic."

Maclean's magazine? Well, we all know what a hotbed of radical bigotry and vile prejudice *Maclean's* magazine has been. Go away . . .

For what seems like a century, *Maclean's* was no more "offensive" (that is the cant term of choice these days) than a down comforter on a cold day, and if Mark Steyn's article offended them, so what? Not every article in every magazine of newspaper is meant to be a valentine card addressed to every reader's self-esteem. *Maclean's* published a bushel of letters following the article's appearance; some praised it, others scorned it. That's freedom of speech. That's democracy. That's the messy business we call the exchange of ideas and opinions.

But where does the B.C. Human Rights Commission, the Ontario Human Rights Commission or the Canadian Human Rights Commission come into this picture? Has anyone been publicly whipped? Has someone or some group been hauled off to a gulag? Is there a race frenzy sweeping the land?

Why is any human rights commission inserting itself between a magazine, a television show or a newspaper and its readers or viewers? Is every touchy, or agenda-driven, sensibility now free to call upon the offices of the state and, free of charge—to them, not their targets—embroil them in "justifying" their right to write and broadcast as they see fit? The *Western Standard* magazine, during the so-called Danish cartoon crisis, got hauled before the Alberta Human Rights Commission for publishing the cartoons that all the world was talking about. The action drained the magazine's resources, but it was free to the complainant.

Meantime, real human-rights violations—threats of death against Salman Rushdie, riots after the cartoons, death threats against the artists, the persecution of Hirsi Ali, the assassination of Benazir Bhutto—neither inspire nor receive human-rights investigations.

Maclean's and its columnists—especially of late—are an ornament to Canada's civic space. They should not have to defend themselves for doing what a good magazine does: start debate, express opinion and stir thought. And they should most certainly not have to abide the threatened censorship of any of Canada's increasingly interfering, state-appointed and paradoxically labelled human rights commissions.

REAL RIGHTS AND RIGHTS COMMISSIONS | November 14, 2008

Jennifer Lynch, chief of the Canadian Human Rights Commission, participated in this week's ceremonies at the National War Memorial by laying a wreath. It's nice to know the commission honours Canada's veterans and the cause for which so many fought and died.

The cause, distilled to its fundamental point, was freedom. The Second World War framed that cause in the starkest form imaginable. It is impossible to conjure up an example more pervertedly perfect of the odiousness (Churchill's term) of tyranny than Hitler's regime. There was only one freedom in Hitler's Germany, as there would have been only one freedom in Europe or the world should Hitler's insatiable nightmares been realized: his freedom to cancel every freedom of everyone else.

One lesson that grieving millions took from that war was that the only certain antitoxin to the "after-Hitlers"—those lesser or greater avatars of tyranny an always-changing world will almost certainly force on us again—was freedom. The second lesson was how massive the cost, how massive the sacrifice, to extinguish tyranny once it's taken hold in one country and marches on to others.

This is what makes Remembrance Day so solemn—remembering those costs, those sacrifices, that are tallied in millions of dead and wounded. Freedom does not fall from the air. Freedom (ask the vets) is never free.

At the heart of this freedom the Second World War taught us so dearly to cherish is the notion of the individual's intrinsic or, as we say now, human right to think, speak and write as he sees fit, circumscribed only by certain time-tested laws (defamation, libel, public safety) evolved over centuries and subject to the oversight of a trained and independent judiciary.

The essential point is that the most basic rights, those of freedom of thought, speech and expression, belong to the individual. That is why we call them intrinsic or human rights. They are rights that inhere in our basic status as human beings. They are our most profound rights, belonging to our character as human beings. And, for that reason, we neither multiply them trivially nor dilute their force and meaning by placing them in piecemeal cohabitation with less fundamental accommodations. Like the right not to wash one's hands while working in a fast-food restaurant, or the alleged right to strip past a certain age, or the right not to be offended by a Mark Steyn article.

These "cases" may have merits, and some wild-eyed philosopher may articulate those merits. But they do not abide, as rights, on the same plane as freedom of thought, speech and expression. They may be something, but what they are will not be inscribed on any cenotaph: They are not human rights.

Human rights, the real ones, are ours from the beginning. They are not bestowed by the state, because the state does not "own" them; they are not a state's or a ruler's—or, for that matter, a human-rights commission's—to give. It equally follows that they are not a state's or a commission's to abridge, circumscribe, tamper with or make a toy of.

The concept of human rights, real human rights, has been long with us. But only in modern times did we learn what immeasurable darkness falls on the world when they are nullified. The butcheries of Auschwitz and Buchenwald followed as a straight and bitter line from Hitler's assumption of absolute power in 1933 and his cauterization and extinction of the concept of freedom in the German Reich. Nothing less than the Holocaust underwrites the modern understanding and appreciation of human rights.

Human rights are as profound and central a concept to the democracies of the world as we have. They constitute the core of human freedom. They are the antidote to tyranny. They are fundamental.

Of late, however, in Canada, this most painfully acquired

understanding has been utterly unmoored. The various provincial human rights commissions and their federal godfather have been cutting away at the core of, and extending into utter fatuity, the term "human rights." They are capricious, agenda-driven, a great mishmash of political correctness and "right thinking" bulldozing away at the basic freedoms of thought, speech and expression while they, under some osmotic impulse, investigate, prescribe and torment with zealous and self-righteous abandon.

Which is why I find Ms. Lynch's presence at Remembrance Day ceremonies odd. Because Canada's human-rights commissions are diluting and trivializing and thereby offending the very core of the concept that gives them their name. And a Remembrance Day ceremony is an awkward occasion to be reminded of that.

A BLOT ON DEMOCRACY | January 12, 2008

I read in Thursday's newspaper of Finance Minister Jim Flaherty's determination to declare Bill C-10, dealing with tax credits that support the making of Canadian films, a matter of confidence. C-10 is an attempt to tie which films receive tax credits to certain government-determined standards with respect to violence and sex.

Bill C-10 has, to my mind, rightfully inflamed what we often refer to as the artistic community. It is not quite, as is argued, censorship, but it is close enough to it to be worrisome. When it comes to the making of films, the matter is best left, however imperfectly, to the judgment and skill of the writers and filmmakers who will actually make them. Mrs. Grundy and her prissy avatars should be kept out of the screening room.

I'm still puzzled, however, that Mr. Flaherty—and, by unquestionable extension, Stephen Harper—should make this a matter of confidence. Should a government fall over an argument about tax credits and whether a film is too "sexy" for its overseers? Good luck with the next election.

Were Mr. Harper, however, looking for an issue centred unequivocally on a matter of the most profound principle, I think we would have heard from him by now on the wretched intrusion of human rights commissions into the domain of this country's free expression and free speech.

These commissions have stealthily migrated from their original and defined mandate to prevent discrimination in housing or employment, from deeds of discrimination, to an activist and capricious role of monitoring speech or thought. Under the hopelessly elastic and malleable rubric of "any matter that is likely to expose a person or persons to hatred or contempt," they investigate and rule on everything from bishops to magazine editors, from genital surgery to hand-washing protocols at McDonald's.

A single complaint triggers their attention and zeal. Their procedures conform to a pattern known only to them. They leave those complained against to endure the process entirely on their own resources, while those who originate a complaint are nursed with all the resources of the state. They travel wide waters. Their writ runs from letters to the editor to the furthest reaches of the Internet.

Complaints may be started and then idly dropped by the complainant, dropped without penalty, or indeed, remark, from the commissions concerned. This was the case just recently when one of the complaints against former publisher Ezra Levant, for printing the controversial Mohammed cartoons, was withdrawn by the Calgary imam who first brought it. Mr. Levant, for nearly a year, bore the cost of the aborted "investigation" and wore the shadow of having been under investigation for exposing people to hatred and contempt—not a pretty allegation for a citizen of an exemplarily tolerant country. And then, poof, the process ends, without comment, apology or compensation. Eerily, another on the identical issue still continues.

The rulings of human rights commissions have the flavour of an agenda. They seem to have a problem with traditional religious organizations and religious speech. They are the very hall prefects of "progressive" political correctness, answerable in their judgments and methods, it seems, only to themselves.

These commissions have wandered so far from their original purpose as to be, in these matters of speech and expression, disowned by the respected civil libertarian Alan Borovoy, who, more than any other man, brought them, in their early restricted mandate, to birth. They are, in their very real capacity as censors and judges on what is to be said and not to be said, a blot on the central dynamic of any self-respecting democracy.

Yet Mr. Harper, with all his tactical prowess, has let the controversy over human rights commissions go on without so much as a comment. The Ontario Human Rights Commission, outlandishly, can decline the now-celebrated complaint against *Maclean's* and then proceed to mercilessly slag *Maclean's* in public, and Mr. Harper's Tories sheepishly let the whole mess pass by without a word.

He will have Mr. Flaherty say that an election will be triggered over the grey question of tax credits and film content. But he is mute as a beach rock over a fundamental offence to democracy. So, too, it should emphatically be noted, is one of Pierre Trudeau's successors as leader of the Liberal Party, Stéphane Dion. Liberals used to have regard for free speech.

Real Liberals—take a bow, Keith Martin—still do. Dr. Martin has presented a motion calling for the repeal of the most noxious provisions of the Canadian Human Rights Act. Dr. Martin still knows what a real parliament is about. Mr. Harper, and Mr. Dion, should adopt his cause and tame these commissions.

CATASTROPHE

SPIRIT BEHIND THE GIVING | January 8, 2005

It's not a contest, but were it to be, it's the right kind of contest. The tsunami relief efforts of so many countries, and so many people, is something of a phenomenon in itself.

The speed with which the citizens of so many countries are making donations to aid those struck by the tsunamis is astonishing. As are the amounts (in most cases) being raised. Governments around the world are acting with equal celerity and generosity. Australia is an astonishment. The government of John Howard has pledged $800 million (U.S.) toward assisting victims of the disaster, most particularly the citizens and government of Indonesia. Mr. Howard has a fine ear, as displayed in his comments announcing the aid:

"This is a terrible tragedy for mankind. But what we are saying, to the people of Indonesia particularly, is that we are here as your friends. There's an old saying in the English language that charity begins at home. Our home is this region and we are saying to the people of our nearest neighbour that we are here to help you in your hour of need."

It is worth remarking that "giving" has its canons of tact and delicacy. How people give is as important sometimes as what they give. Whether on a public or a private scale, people can be aggressive or blunt in their charity—help can come with a snarl of superiority or rancid with condescension.

It is one of the finer moments of our time, in which there are so few fine moments to begin with, that the response to the present catastrophe is so little stained—as these words of Mr. Howard demonstrate—by the wrong spirit behind the giving.

The Americans, God bless 'em, are acting with their usual dispatch and generosity. Who would have guessed that an aircraft carrier, the nuclear-powered USS *Abraham Lincoln*, would be among the first and most vital contributors to the tremendous challenge of offering succour and relief to the survivors of Sumatra?

It will take all the desperate and jaded ingenuity of the genetically anti-Bush crowd to turn this marvellous example of benign intervention into a parable of imperialism and Yankee hegemony. But I have faith in them. I am sure they will. I look forward to the speculation that Halliburton had the contract for the *Lincoln*'s propellers, and Dick Cheney's aunt's getting a dollar for every helicopter takeoff from the carrier. Very likely, Michael Moore has a documentary in the works proving that the invasion of New Zealand is the real object of this exercise, and Naomi Klein is even now readying to pen "Let's bring Sumatra to Seattle," or some equally fastidious essay on the perfidy of American goodwill. "No quinine for oil" might strike the right note.

Those less hospitable to the anti-Bush monomania see this wonderful conjunction of an aircraft carrier and the crisis in South Asia as being just what it seems to be: America being generous, and quick with its generosity when it counts.

George Bush himself has been engagingly alert to this disaster from the beginning. When we see him asking his father and Bill Clinton (!) to be joint fundraisers in the private relief effort, we know he's not posturing. Anything that could unite Bush the First with "Elvis," under the sponsorship of Bush the Second, goes beyond even the scripted fantasies of *The West Wing*.

The Canadian public and government are reacting with a wide spirit and an open pocketbook. I agree with a number of people who point out that we seem to be feverishly self-conscious about what we're doing, and that there's far too much self-congratulation in our response. Even that criticism can go too far. The itch to be seen as benignant is a hell of a lot better than studied neutralism of indifference. An anxiety to be seen to be doing good is a stress we can live with, especially as it is a prompt to the actual doing of that good.

Our wish to act is circumscribed by the chronically reduced circumstances of our military. However bountiful the spirit of Canadians may be, what we can actually do depends, in very large measure, on having the mechanical and logistical resources to act. Depends, in other words, on how well-equipped and prepared of a military we are ready to support.

A military is never just a war-making machine. It is always the only ready instrument for practical and trained intervention in a time of catastrophe. We cannot short-fund the military and simultaneously extend our reputation as a benign and humanitarian nation.

That seems like a paradox. But so does a nuclear-powered aircraft carrier on an errand of mercy.

ON OUR BLINDNESS TO DISASTER | September 10, 2005

> As when the Sun . . . from behind the Moon in dim
> > Eclipse disastrous twilight sheds
> On half the Nations, and with fear of change
> > Perplexes Monarchs.
>
> —John Milton, *Paradise Lost*

The word "disastrous" is a more choice or Latinate version of "ill-starred." The word evokes an old idea of fate as the influence of a star—a famous and easy example being the story of Romeo and Juliet. The play itself tells us they were "star-crossed."

Belief in astrology, that the juncture and rotation of

the planets is meaningful to one's life, is a feeble, though durable, idiocy, often accompanied by a taste for wind chimes or the equally melodious gurgling of PBS's pet mystic, Deepak Chopra.

The etymology of "disaster" is useful in one particular. It speaks to the dark grandeur and enormity of a given calamity. For, if a mischance or calamity is on such a scale that it speaks to the operation of menace birthed in the cosmos itself, then the mischance, the catastrophe, must be mighty indeed.

Certainly, Hurricane Katrina was, and is, a disaster— nature at her most violent and devious. The scale of devastation and misery entailed is not something, let us thank our stars, we on this side of the world are much familiar with.

The great devastation the hurricane wrought is truly a horrific and heartbreaking visitation on our good neighbours the Americans. They deserve every good wish and support we Canadians have to offer, because they are undergoing a real disaster—an event out of proportion to all human efforts, even in the puissant West of the twenty-first century, to forestall.

I think a portion of the meaning of this terrible word, disaster, has left the consciousness of North Americans. It may be a terrible sentence to write, but we don't expect cataclysms, real disasters, to happen in *our* part of the world— they are not "natural" here. We have become inured to a heartless exceptionalism: that whenever a typhoon, hurricane, tidal wave, famine or earthquake occurs, when the dead number in the thousands or tens of thousands, it is only "natural" if it occurs somewhere else.

But when a natural disaster of the scale of Katrina does hit our side of the world, its devastation carries a psychological magnification. We have all but given up the belief that such events can happen to us.

But they can, they do and they will. And there is nothing that wealth, technology or government can do to stop a disaster—however much all three can do to circumscribe everything but its central impact. It is in this area, in the area of deploying the abundant resources of a powerful state to check and reduce the human tragedy incident upon every disaster, that the furious debate over Katrina now rages.

There was no stopping the hurricane itself, and most likely no staying of the terrible flooding that followed. Floods are as old as Noah; the whirlwind spoke to Job.

But there were deficiencies of planning and response, from the mayor's office to the White House, and the incidents of sheer recklessness and criminality during a time of crisis are sufficient to fill an anthology of incompetence and willfulness.

The failures of planning and response may, in part, be set down to that sense of immunity to disaster, our sense of favoured exceptionalism, that has seeded itself in the West. The recklessness and criminality on display from some in New Orleans perhaps belongs to some territory beyond explanation. Both factors have made a horror more horrible.

However, there is one aspect of the debate that is a very troubling signal of the state of American politics now. The ferocity of unstoppable partisan frenzy, which began with the first news of Katrina's landfall, is, I fear, almost too much for the American political system to contain. For the antagonists of George W. Bush, there is nothing too grotesque or outrageous by way of insinuation or allegation to lay on his doorstep. Of which the charge that racism "explains" whatever shortcomings the U.S. federal response may have displayed is both the most vivid and toxic.

A great natural calamity is just another stick to wield in the partisan wars. American politics is, day by day, more a continuous fever of accusation, irrational hostility and destructiveness. Partisan combat knows no limits. A democratic system cannot be sustained under such a pitch of opportunism and cynicism.

The dead have not been numbered, grief has not been given its time—and, yet, partisanship rages on. This may be Katrina's second drear gift: the eclipse of American politics.

I wrote here about partisanship as "toxic." If there is anything that will finally dismantle the modern democracies of the West, it will be found in the ever more total, fervid, blind and angry reduction of politics to the hyper camps of left and right. Nothing is off-limits to real partisans. Foreign policy, natural disasters, personal life—these were once the territories where decency feared to tread. Politics has become total; any weapon will do; decency of argument is a museum relic. The American system is supersaturated in hyper-partisanship; ours, being smaller, has not reached the white-hot and hateful depths of our burdened neighbours. But it has its moments and spaces of rival ugliness. Left and right are the new fanaticisms for some.

THE BLEAKEST DAY | July 1, 2006

Newfoundlanders are as exuberant as everyone else about Canada Day, but, in my province, it has been an abiding irony since we joined the Confederation that the national birthday coincides with the bleakest day on the entire calendar of Newfoundland history.

That's a large claim to make. Newfoundland history is streaked with calamity and loss of life. Those who have any familiarity with the long, sad course of the contentious seal hunt are aware that its pursuit has been scarred all too frequently with appalling catastrophes. Indeed, it was on the very eve of the First World War that seventy-eight sealers from the SS *Newfoundland* were caught away from their ship in a savage storm on the northeast coast and died a gruesome death.

Outport existence and fishing on the wild waters of the North Atlantic were always a wedding with danger and peril. How many, over the generations, went out in the morning not to return at end of day is probably impossible to tell. It is enough merely to note that Newfoundlanders are not unacquainted with grief.

Modern times are no different. The boon of offshore oil had a terrible inauguration with the *Ocean Ranger* disaster. On February 15, 1982, under the assault of 100-mile-an-hour winds and massive waves, the *Ocean Ranger* went down, and all her eighty-four-member crew with her. I remember that day. Newfoundland is a small place. It blackened the entire province, as everyone seemed to have some connection—family, neighbour, friend—with one of the lost.

Grief strikes hard in a concentrated space; it echoes longer in the common memory. For every rollicking ballad of the likes of "We'll Rant and We'll Roar Like True Newfoundlanders," a song intoxicated with the delight Newfoundlanders take in the rough, wild place we call home, there is another pitched in a minor key.

There is an undernote of keening in all Newfoundland history. That keening was never sharper than after the morning, ninety years ago today, when the 801 members of the Newfoundland Regiment left their trenches and went "over the top" toward the German lines at Beaumont Hamel. So many, and so young, they went to death or maiming. Of those 801, only sixty-eight were present for roll call the next day. For the Newfoundland

Regiment, for Newfoundlanders back home, it was, to summon up a biblical name, Aceldama, the field of blood.

If Newfoundland, in terms of population, is a small place now, it was an even smaller place then. The young men of Beaumont Hamel (we would surely call many of them boys today) had come from every corner of the country (as then it was). Not an outport nor a town but sent someone, not a family hardly but was to bear the terrible cross of a favourite they were never to see again.

They had gone with that mix of motives with which young men have always gone to war. Adventure beckoned some, escape from the too-familiar others; honest fealty to "King and Country," which probably seems a little *outré* today, likely spoke in some measure to all.

But it surely ripped the heart of all of Newfoundland that, in the very first minutes of the great Battle of the Somme (in less than half an hour, they knew doom was upon them), on a perfect summer day, so many of her sons in that battalion, nearly all, were dead or mangled. The Newfoundland Regiment fell under a brutal hammer stroke of concentrated machine-gun fire, mortar and sniping. They were, for that time, alone on the field. The Essex Regiment, which was to have simultaneously advanced, in the confusions of that morning, had not.

It was the most brutal day in Newfoundland history.

The regiment received the honorific of "Royal" from King George himself, the only such designation that was awarded during the entire war. But for me, the most affecting

memorial comes not from the ceremonial designation—
the Royal Newfoundland Regiment—or even from the care-
fully tended battlefield, which today will host the first
return of the regiment as a unit since that awful day ninety
years ago, but from the words frequently cited of some of
the wounded survivors of that terrible morning: "Is the
Colonel pleased? Is the Colonel satisfied?"

There is a ferocious loyalty in those words. And a ferocious innocence as well. They are empty of every cynicism.

NEWFOUNDLAND

LAST DICE GAME

Winston Churchill once set up a meeting for Joey Smallwood with the legendary Rothschilds. Mr. Smallwood had been trying to put together in the early 1950s a consortium to finance his dream of harnessing the great falls of the Hamilton River (renamed Churchill to honour the statesman, in part for this intercession). The aging Mr. Churchill was impressed by Joey, who had a volubility only second to that of the great lion himself, and arranged a luncheon. The upshot was the Rothschilds became one of the key financial mediators in the development of this huge engineering miracle. Mr. Churchill, like Mr. Smallwood, was taken with the scale of the enterprise. He called it (Mr. Smallwood never tired of quoting these words) "a grand imperial concept."

It says how long ago all this was that at the time of this celebrated utterance, "imperial" was not a pejorative. It's another index of those long ago days that the main draw of the development, at least for Mr. Smallwood, was that it would immediately create jobs, thousands of jobs.

I have often thought that Mr. Smallwood's economic understanding was unduly influenced by the example of the pharaohs (John Crosbie might argue the influence extended to Joey's style of government). If a project was massive, grand, monumental, it had intrinsic appeal. And jobs. These twin allures may explain, in part, why the deal wasn't closely examined as to benefits after the project went on stream. Or at least as closely as any project should, that once it was up and running was under a ninety-nine-year contract.

No one dreamed then of OPEC, or escalating oil prices. "Energy crisis" hadn't entered the lexicon. No one, at least on the Newfoundland front, glanced a few decades down the road to insert a clause in the power contract that might allow for some flexibility in the selling price of Labrador power, should the world demand for energy alter over the near century of its term.

The rest is history, and from the Newfoundland side of the equation, miserable history at that. Mr. Smallwood got to cut ribbons, hobnob with the wealthy and powerful, and see himself as a true titan of Newfoundland's economic development. He got, as well, the lengthy and frequent pleasure of retelling his story of the meetings with Sir Winston and the Rothschilds. Mr. Smallwood was his own Homer.

Churchill Falls was the first big project. There would be others, and a truly mixed record they have. Remember Come-by-Chance: By the time offshore oil loomed on the economic and political horizon, it occurred to Newfoundlanders that this was probably the last one. Mines, paper mills, petrochemical complexes—they had all in succession been shrouded in the promise that this one would be the one development that would unshackle Newfoundland from its economic chains. The dependence on the fishery, and mainly the fishery, which was always a mixed and frequently tragic mainstay, would finally be broken.

Well, all the world knows the Churchill Falls deal now as a very poor trade. A lot of labourers went to Labrador when the project was in construction, but the gold of Churchill Falls has been a shower into the Quebec treasury ever since, and will be for decades more. And all the other big-ticket items were either a mess from the start (Come-by-Chance) or never really delivered on their promise.

It is grandly ironic that, at least from Mr. Smallwood's day, the search for economic development was always conceived as something to supplement or counterpoise the historic Newfoundland fishery. Never to replace it. That was unthinkable. The fishery would always be there but it would never on its own be enough to draw Newfoundland into its full potential, keep young Newfoundlanders home, and offer anything like real economic parity with the mainland.

But fate, or careless management, which in Newfoundland's case is fate's twin, intervened, and the fishery died. This was an arrow to the heart. The province has been reeling ever since. Its faith in its own future, in the best of times a tenuous, anxious emotion, has been very nearly exploded altogether.

No wonder, then, that on the question of the offshore, on the disposition of its revenues, and on the issues of equalization and "clawback formulas," the citizens of Newfoundland and Labrador are exercised as they rarely have been. It's very much The Last Chance syndrome. The offshore is seen, almost by one and all, as our last chance to secure an economic viability—the last great project that might rescue Newfoundland from five hundred years of just hanging on.

In the long shadow of the collapse of the fishery, this is not just another routine Ottawa-versus-St.-John's conflict. For my crowd, it's the moment of truth.

It was a puzzle to me on the day it was officially announced that the Newfoundland cod fishery was to be closed that there was so little public outcry, and it has been even more of a puzzle since. I do not mean to say there was no notice of it, that it wasn't huge news, or that it wasn't the talk of just about everyone in Newfoundland at the time. There were a couple of "noisy moments" during the actual announcement, by then-fisheries minister John Crosbie. But there was nothing like any full manifestation of outrage, no giant demonstrations, nothing—to my mind anyway—that measured up to the scale and significance, to the meaning, of that announcement.

It was, in effect, the suspension of the defining social and economic activity of all of Newfoundland since there has been a Newfoundland: that day marked the first moment, since there was a Newfoundland, that Newfoundlanders were stopped, by law, from drawing on the resource that brought it in to being, sustained it, and stamped its whole historical and unique culture.

The thought has teased my mind ever since that Newfoundlanders, perhaps defensively, perhaps for reasons too subtle or profound to offer easy articulation, were attempting to defer a total acknowledgement of the significance of this despairing milestone.

They—we—knew what it meant, but it was too large and deep a blow for an immediate commensurate response.

VICTIMS OF STEREOTYPING | January 15, 2005

"I like Newfoundlanders. I really do."

My esteemed colleague Margaret Wente wrote that in a recent column on Newfoundland. Twice. Well, let me say at the top of this one: "I like Margaret Wente. I really do." But I fear her repeated assurance—and I wish I wasn't writing this—leaves me unconvinced.

After all, if you write a column describing Newfound-landers as "picking the pockets of Chinese dry cleaners and Korean variety-store owners who work ninety hours a week," describe them as "surly" ingrates, "gobbling" cod tongues while they luxuriate in a great "scenic welfare ghetto," and, in general, put down everyone in Newfoundland as part of a set of lazy, self-indulging, whining spongers, rote-chanting "I like Newfoundlanders" doesn't salvage the piece from being one sour, willful, collective putdown.

It's a nasty cast of mind that traffics so generously in stereotypes. The Chinese are dry cleaners; Koreans know only convenience stores; Newfoundlanders are shiftless pick-pockets. It's a spurious contrast she sets up, and she knows it.

If the point Margaret was hoping to insinuate—that it is only "hard-working" new immigrants who actually "pay" into the revenues that provide equalization; that it is only the most industrious being extorted to pay for the least industrious—then she has so bizarre a conception of the Canadian tax system, and the principle of equalization, that it is beyond my ability and, more to the present point, my desire, to rescue her from it.

She makes other scattershot observations that are insult trying to dress as candour. Newfoundlanders have a "sense of victimhood that is unmatched." Dear Lord, the global industry of professional victimhood has landed on many shores, and infested whole multitudes of causes and groups like a plague, but if one were seriously to look for a few places where the posture and cant of "the victim" is considered unseemly and unworthy, Newfoundland would be one such place.

For all the social clichés and easy characterizations of "pogey" and "handouts" that seem to teem in Margaret's "I like Newfoundlanders" brain, any real acquaintance with Newfoundland would have introduced her to a strain in my province's character that is the radical opposite of her wildly gratuitous calumny.

I've known people so hostile to every notion of something for nothing, they wouldn't trouble a neighbour to borrow a cup of milk. I've known legions of men and women who put in a lifetime's work of a kind that those of us who spray words for a living should be embarrassed to stand next to.

Try going to Long Harbour, or Burgeo, or Lamaline, or St. Anthony or Port de Grave and meet with some of the men and women who have worked, really worked, for a living, Margaret, and try telling them to their faces they're the spoiled delinquents of your furious imagination. Try telling the same to those who, after a life of work, have nothing, and have abandoned their homes and history to find work elsewhere.

We have our louts and layabouts—point me to any region of any country that doesn't. But where you come up with the notion that Newfoundlanders—of all people—are the artists of victimhood is a trawl too confused for me to fathom.

Then there's this business where Margaret writes of Newfoundlanders blaming "us" for the collapse of the fishery.

Who's this "us"? The citizens of Canada didn't collapse the fishery, and no one in Newfoundland even dreams they did.

The only point on which any blame is being assigned is over the stewardship of the resource since Confederation. That was federal. No one argues otherwise. And it is surely fair, and not victimhood, that if the government that had control failed in its stewardship, then it should bear some responsibility for so failing.

As for the money being poured into Newfoundland while we guzzle cod tongues and stare out the scenic bay, keep in mind the billion dollars a year going "outward" from the Churchill Falls hydro project that alone nullifies the equalization "debt."

Her last shot was as carelessly aimed as all the rest. You can keep all the gas and oil revenue, she says, but pay us (there's that enigmatic "us" again) back what we've sent down. Well, say I, not so fast.

Restock (and return) the Continental Shelf, turn back Churchill Falls and, one last thing, rescind the contemptible practice—which obviously has appeal to very limited natures—of dealing in caricature and stereotype and maligning an entire province on the basis of little more than ill-acquaintance and condescension.

Shut down the Newfie joke industry, of which, it mildly saddens me to say, Margaret Wente's column is an extended and singularly hostile example.

That said, I like Margaret Wente. I really do.

THE PEACE OF TWILLINGATE | August 12, 2006

Less than a week ago, I was fortunate enough to spend a few days, under perfect skies, driving through some of the resolutely beautiful communities of Newfoundland's northeast coast.

Twillingate is a spectacular setting at any time. But under a summer sun, with smog-free air, this outport on the very edge of North America will easily lead even non-Newfoundlanders to believe that the world's great vacation spots—the Caribbean islands, gaudy Maui of the Pacific, famous others—are greatly overrated as ecological marvels.

And this is not even to make mention of Musgrave Harbour. Not perhaps as celebrated as Twillingate among the cognoscenti of the mainland, Musgrave Harbour is the very jewel of the northeast coastline. The people are friendly, solicitous to be hospitable but tactful in its dispensation. Musgrave Harbour's stretch of sea and beach would send pangs of bitter envy through the most devoted fan of Tofino, way over on the other side of the country.

The northeast coast is quite a place. It has produced a sturdy, hardy, generous band of people. Perhaps never more so than a few generations back, when the towns and villages of this part of the island brought forth the "iron men" who set their teeth to the howling gales and tempests of brutal North Atlantic winters and sent forth such local heroes as Abraham Kean, the greatest sealing captain of all time, to the exigencies and unimaginable deprivations of the Labrador ice in midwinter.

It was also the nursery of quite possibly even more formidable heroes, their epic wives and mothers, who gave birth, raised families, took sorrow and hardship as it came, and endured absences laden with continual and surely heartbreaking anxiety each year the hunt was on.

These towns and outports are, naturally, less riven now by the strict and unforgiving imperatives of the pre-Confederation era. And since Confederation, the commanding spirits that would once have assumed prominence in the limited channels of the fishery, politics, the church or local commerce have turned their energies to the wider world of Canada or beyond.

The outports remain, but now, especially since the collapse of the cod stocks, they are less busy, and the harbours, inlets and coves are more slenderly trafficked. Some fishing remains, the glory of their setting remains, some trickle of tourism is solicited and received (Newtown, Bonavista Bay, is a wonderful stop—try the jam!), but, at least to my imagination, there is a glow of melancholy nostalgia over them even on the most luminous summer's day.

Still, they are peaceful and tranquil—certainly so to the visitor. I mean to be neither condescending nor fulsome when I say they radiate a sense of remove and shelter from the gathering whirlwind of our too modern world.

All of which is the context for when, on leaving this

slice of rock, ocean and charm, I caught up on the news of the remaining part of the world.

Another (alleged) plot by mad jihadis, this time to murder thousands high in the sky on intercontinental flights leaving London; talk of "liquid bombs" and "disposable camera flashes" as detonators. We are getting very close to an absolute definition of "sinister" here. If the allegations prove true, this is a bitter plate some very evil men were about to serve on the innocent and unsuspecting.

How fragile we've become, how fragile the modern world, when, in its great capitals, you must not take toothpaste or hair gel as you make the transit from the terminal to the airplane. How much more anxious would millions of people be today, if the diligence of British and Pakistani agents had not revoked the planned slaughter, if a dozen great jets and all within them had been destroyed by murderous fanatics.

Sixty or seventy years ago on Newfoundland's northeast coast, people worried about storms, shifting ice, the perils of direct encounter with an imperious Nature as they pursued a livelihood. Now, people may be going to a convenience store in London, or walking to a beach chair in Bali, or working in a great office tower, or just taking a subway home, and a percolating menace surrounds us and all we do.

I am not sure, in one sense, which was the more challenging life.

I agree with those who say we are in combat with desperate, determined and artful forces, and that—in our typically overprivileged, casual, Western way—we do not take what threatens us with the mortal gravity it deserves.

One thing is certain: the quiet and peace of Twillingate and Musgrave Harbour, the sense of sanctuary I tasted in those places for a few sunlit days, seem to have departed the world forever.

METEOROLOGICAL MADNESS | April 15, 2006

Weather is the starting-motor of almost every conversation, the oil of every new acquaintance, the life preserver of all our awkward moments. A few of the great humorists were weather connoisseurs. Twain said some fine things about weather. I rather like his telling of how cold it once was: "Cold! If the thermometer had been an inch longer we'd all have frozen to death!" And Twain generally gets the credit for "Everybody talks about the weather; nobody does anything about it."

Weather is always more than just weather. That's a rule of life. Shakespeare knew this. He sketched it in *The Tempest*, but saved his finest stuff for *King Lear*. Lear comes to terms with himself only after coming to terms with the weather—storm therapy. Lear on the heath, caught "unaccommodated" under the furious elements, is Shakespeare at his best: "Blow, winds, and crack your cheeks! rage! blow! You cataracts and hurricanoes, spout . . ."

William knew his weather.

My crowd in Newfoundland are certainly the very scholiographers of weather, Nature's own and very finest band of weather-readers. Lear would have had more than a few buddies in Newfoundland. Weather, back home, is talked about with greater frequency, with mixed and strained affection or savage, raging hostility, than I have ever noted anywhere else in this country. In Newfoundland, "weather" means "bad weather." And that, alas, is mainly true. Bad weather we usually get, and always expect. If someone says "there's a bit of weather coming on," they inevitably mean a lot of weather's coming on. All of it bad.

The main problem with Newfoundland weather, however, is not how bad it is, but when it's going to happen and what form it will take. Newfoundland weather veers and oscillates, shoots up one bay and down another, crashes from snow to rain to fog, drizzle and sleet, and back again through every conceivable and mortifying combination, with dazzling unpredictability and precocious variety.

Whoever coined the term "weather system" never visited Newfoundland. There is no "system." I've been in houses on the South Coast, down around Marystown, where there was a warm front on the porch and a blizzard in the kitchen. (Wasn't going upstairs. God knows what waited up there.) Lear wouldn't have lasted the night on the South Coast.

System? Randomized torment, maybe. But system? Ha!

The Liberals, a few years back, in the high noon of their genius, decided in the face of the sheer, God-defying impredictability of Newfoundland weather, that taking all forecasting off the island and out of the province was a good idea. They shut down the weather office in Gander, and decided it somehow made more sense to guess, from a weather station in Halifax, at next morning's blizzard in Joe Batts Arm on Fogo Island.

No more forecasting from Newfoundland itself was the principle. They could just as easily have chosen Winnipeg or Hawaii, for the logic involved. In any case, there wasn't a man, woman, boy or girl in any bay or harbour, city or town of all Newfoundland and Labrador that had the slightest idea why the bunch in Ottawa thought Halifax, the capital of another province, should be asked to utter prophecies on "the weekend weather" in Newfoundland.

Gander, after all, was at least "in" the weather it was taking a stab at projecting. Do people phone Calgary when they are going camping in Kelowna?

It defied sense. It defied reason. And it produced a massive protest, culminating in what was, I'm told, the largest petition ever signed in the province—more than 125,000 names, to haul the weather centre back from Halifax and moor it again on the drenched, blizzard-ridden, fog-tormented soil of the home province.

It was bad meteorology; that was indisputable. But it was stupid politics incarnate. Weather is the currency of every Newfoundland conversation, and it may be a misery, but it's our own misery. Outsource the weather—why, that's Newfoundland blasphemy!

This saga has an interesting end. On Wednesday, the day after introducing the Accountability Act in the Commons, Stephen Harper visited Newfoundland—his first trip there as PM. He gave a speech in St. John's, but he announced the reopening of the weather office in Gander. The Harper boys are already looking toward the next campaign, is what this tells me.

The Liberals had better tidy up that leadership business real quick. It's no time to be dallying when Mr. Harper, only two months in, is scoring points on "fixing" the weather in Newfoundland.

Michael Ignatieff, quick: Blow, winds, and crack your cheeks.

ONE VOICE THAT COUNTS | August 25, 2007

It's a Danny Williams year back home in Newfoundland. The Hebron oil field is on again.

Mr. Williams has played a hard game with the big boys and he's won. That is the near-universal verdict, and in politics there is nothing quite as attractive as winning. It's a victory that has a bigger charge or echo in Newfoundland than it would have in perhaps any other province. That's because, almost since Confederation became a reality, the

Newfoundland record on setting the terms for the exploitation or management of its resources has been such a dismal one.

It all goes back, as does almost all modern Newfoundland politics, to Joey Smallwood's reign—and that term is chosen advisedly. Smallwood had many attractive qualities, but among them we may not include either prudence or prescience. In the presence of big-name promoters or industrialists, hard man Joe purred with obsequiousness, starstruck and infatuated from mere proximity to the rich or the great.

His economic development policy can easily be seen in retrospect for what it was: a series of manias. Starting small, it went from hockey stick factories to a chocolate bar company, a rubber boot plant to a strange and darkly comic essay in cattle ranching. Alas, Newfoundland never did catch on as Wyoming north. From there, it ricocheted to greater and grander schemes, many of them midwifed by dubious promoters or downright fraudsters.

Smallwood's formula was a basic one: huge government subsidies in exchange for jobs up front. Combined with what can only be understood as an absolutely positive thirst for snake oil and a worshipful gratitude for those who relayed it, by the tanker truckload, to his eager throat: this was not a solid business plan.

The greatest scheme was the Churchill Falls development. It married Smallwood's mania for job creation with his ego-besotted lust to be associated with a "great" enterprise.

Seeking to get that project off the ground brought "the little fellow from Gambo" into the chambers of the fabled Rothschilds, and even to an audience with the very hero of the twentieth century himself, Winston Churchill.

To say such encounters placed Smallwood's judgment on sabbatical implies that, on the matter of Newfoundland's economic development, he had judgment to begin with. But, alas, that was not so. Having met with the great, he began to believe he was one with them, floating above mere mortals on the hurricane currents of his own deeply aggravated self-regard. By this point, Smallwood was so popular politically, without challenge either in the House of Assembly or within his own cabinet, that he was less a premier than the Pharaoh of the North Atlantic.

This was the psychological context in which the deal to develop Churchill Falls was brewed. Its most irresistible characteristic was an immense upfront payoff: thousands of construction jobs for Newfoundlanders. And in Newfoundland politics, jobs, then as now, are better than gold—they are platinum. Where was the cold eye to look over the contract for the long term, to weigh immediate benefit against long-term and catastrophic inequity? In the climate of the time, in the near-delirium of this "great imperial project," disinterested scrutiny was a phrase in a dictionary no one owned.

And so, as Newfoundlanders, to our woe, have long recognized, we signed on to one more megaproject—the greatest of them all—only, over the long years since, to see the substance of its benefit, the billions of profits teeming from the Upper Churchill till 2045, flow to another jurisdiction.

This is the backdrop against which Premier Danny Williams's obstinacy (as it is perceived out of province) on so many matters plays. Most particularly, it is the background on which his hardball with the offshore oil companies is perceived. No wonder the deal has elevated his already stratospheric political stock, and no wonder, either, that, as he approaches a provincial election, he is a one-man juggernaut. He's right to have been so strenuously resolved that an economic mischief of heroic proportions for Newfoundland not be repeated.

His very success, however, is building a worrying symmetry. In Newfoundland right now, Mr. Williams is unopposed and unopposable. In the authority he has over Newfoundland politics, and in the scale of his current eminence, he is stronger and of more sway than even his historic predecessor, Joey Smallwood.

He is neither as fitful nor as naive as Smallwood, which is a mercy beyond all thankfulness. But he is so powerful at a time when the future of Newfoundland (the offshore success notwithstanding) is so precarious, that there is only one voice in Newfoundland that really counts.

There's the symmetry. And that is a peril, both for us and for him.

THE ELUSIVE FLAVOUR OF OUR POLITICS | October 13, 2007

There have been many books on Newfoundland politics, but none that captures all, or even a flare, of the grim, manic, impulsive, compulsive, erratic, exultant and heartbreaking flavour of the sport.

Newfoundland politics is emphatically not one-dimensional. True, like the politics of other provinces and places, it does, on a democratically periodic basis, concern itself with a collective assessment of the villains and scala-wags in office and allows for a contest to refresh the mix. You know these events as elections.

But the real flavour of Newfoundland politics can't be picked up from some post-election scoresheet. It's in the tone and byplay of the campaigns, the anecdotes from elections past, legendary nomination battles—all the great tidal wave of political minutiae that has never made it to the headlines outside the province, and not that often within.

One famous election, Joey Smallwood's last as pre-mier, ended up in a near tie: Liberals 20, Conservatives 21, New Labrador Party 1. To add to the tangle, several indi-vidual districts were won by extremely narrow margins—the narrowest by one vote. In that district, there was a polling station in a village roughly halfway between Cow Head and Baker's Brook by the name of Sally's Cove.

By the morning following this closest of elections, it was learned that all 106 Sally's Cove ballots had been burned. (Legend has it the ballots were used to start a fire.

They surely did.) The fate of a whole government hung on incinerated ballots, atoms of ash swirling in the fog-choked winds over the wild coastal shoreline of the Great Northern Peninsula. Democracy cremated.

The burning of the Sally's Cove ballots—an incident by turns as ludicrous as a Monty Python sketch and as sinister as a John Le Carré fable—left all Newfoundland in suspense as to which party—Joey Smallwood's or the young Frank Moores's—was to rule, while a perplexity of judges and a conundrum of constitutional experts wearied their brains and souls in an attempt to sort out the mess.

All this played to a counterpoint of relentless skulduggery being practised on a number of backbenchers, through bribes, booze and bombast on a scale unknown since the days of Tammany Hall. Picture, if you will, a garage sale of backbenchers, a flea market of the fickle. Some were bought, then rebought. One was bought so often it was impossible, on any given day, to determine who owned him.

One loose cannon was put "in storage" in a St. John's hotel room with enough booze to secure him for a few months and keep him away from the lures and guiles of the other side. And one of Frank Moores's successful candidates promptly quit the Conservatives because Mr. Moores wouldn't publicly offer him a cabinet post even before he, Mr. Moores, knew, or could know, he would be premier.

I cannot remember a wilder farce, and nothing I've seen on the mainland—and I've been to British Columbia—compares with it. I remember another close election in which a Liberal candidate won a tight race on the strength of a story about "losing the family rosary beads." That was, alas, ever so long ago, and it is questionable now whether there are many candidates with rosaries to lose, and certainly none with the wit to make a story of the loss.

Of the most recent campaign, that of this week, in which Danny Williams won record approval—an almost frightening popular endorsement—it was so intensely focused that it was almost "dry" of those splendid moments and adventures that diversified the many that preceded it.

Mr. Williams has acquired, in a very short time, superlative campaign skills, and those, in combination with his superbly vocal "standing up for Newfoundland" in various contests with prime ministers and oil companies, have turned him into something of an instant local hero. But it was not just the theme of standing up for the province or his theatrical repertoire that got him the landslide.

There is an undercurrent of deep apprehension about the fate of Newfoundland, over the survival of the main currents of the singular culture produced by a long and unique history. That apprehension emerges, even amidst the current so-called oil boom, from the gradual emptying out of Newfoundland's outports, the spectacular social erosion brought on by the collapse of the historic fishery.

Mr. Williams was seen as the only figure large enough to at least address this apprehension, and it was to the tender hope he could stave off so grim an outcome to Newfoundland history that he owes so much of the endorsement that he received. Newfoundlanders are far from sure that he, or anyone, can really meet this challenge, but they are quietly praying it may be so.

Maybe, in its way, this is yet another story about rosary beads after all.

DANNY WILLIAMS HAS GONE TOO FAR | September 13, 2008

It's too bad Loyola Hearn, who was the Newfoundland minister in the Harper government, is not running again. After a long career in politics, he has decided to leave the game.

Mr. Hearn is a very decent man, a product of the great coastal stretch outside St. John's we call the Southern Shore. He is an "outport" man, just as Danny Williams is a "townie." The health of Newfoundland has always, by some peculiar chemistry, depended on a dynamic equilibrium of its outport and townie components.

Today, after the collapse of the cod fishery and with the near-coincidental explosion of offshore oil, the outport dimension of Newfoundland is almost in ruins, while St. John's and its suburbs are rich and active as never before. There are two Newfoundlands. The capital city and environs are in a fever of development, while vast stretches of coastal communities are inert and underpopulated, mere phantoms of what once they were.

Mr. Hearn's retirement deprives Newfoundland politics of a necessary voice, one suited by temperament and background to speak on the overwhelming subject of the accelerating extinction of Newfoundland's quintessential outport heritage. It deprives the province of an authentic countervoice to the extremely present Premier Williams.

This is not the only unhealthy imbalance in the province. There are forty-eight seats in the House of Assembly, and Mr. Williams owns forty-four of them. The Liberals, with three, are the rump of a rump, and the NDP, with one, is a vapour. The numbers tell it: Mr. Williams is King of the Rock, the most powerful politician since Joey Smallwood. The scope of Newfoundland politics has shrunk to oil and Danny Williams.

There are only two ways of doing politics now: Mr. Williams's way, or no way at all. Those who cross him, in what he sees as "Newfoundland's interests," are given short shrift and none too subtly derided as working against Newfoundland. This was a Smallwood turn, and the least attractive aspect of his quite mixed political qualities. In Mr. Smallwood's last and bitter days, he turned Newfoundland politics into a one-man show incarnate.

That's why it was so very unfortunate that, when Mr. Hearn—who, while he may not be as good a politician as Mr. Williams, is at least as honourable a Newfoundlander—said he was retiring, Mr. Williams issued this statement: "The one thing that my cabinet ministers have done throughout is stood up for their constituents, for the electorate and the people they were elected to represent and they have done that. And it's unfortunate in the last few years that Loyola hasn't done the same thing."

Oh, cut it out. This "standing up for Newfoundland" palaver is best administered in small doses, if at all. And it never fits the mouth of the person doing the "standing up." Furthermore, a difference of opinion, a clash of party interests, should never be categorized as a clash of patriotism. There is a jingoism of small places as well as of large, and Newfoundland is more susceptible to it than most. Newfoundlanders are ferociously fond of Newfoundland, but that very affection can play havoc with our judgment and our politics.

The idea that Mr. Hearn, because he disagreed with Mr. Williams, acted with less than honourable intent toward Newfoundland is ludicrous. Mr. Williams, in fact, is a much better man than his own statement would have you believe.

And now that the federal election is on, Mr. Williams has thrown himself with gale force into the campaign. He sent an email to his entire caucus to determine whether they were onside in his campaign against "Steve." And out of the forty-four, there was only one spine. It belongs to Elizabeth Marshall, who earlier—this is the distilled version— quit her cabinet job because she wasn't going to put up with the premier running her ministry for her. Ms. Marshall alone didn't respond with the ovine bleat, "Yes, sir, yes sir, three bags full." All the others signed on.

It's not Mr. Williams's quarrel with Stephen Harper that's at question. It's hauling into that quarrel all the rhetoric of "disloyalty" to Newfoundland, stirring the jingoistic fevers and characterizing those on the other side as unworthy. Newfoundlanders have been lucky in past decades that, when we had strong premiers, we had strong ministers in Ottawa.

Danny Williams has reached such supremacy, however, that he has effectively become the only voice in Newfoundland politics. Mr. Hearn is gone. John Crosbie is in honorific heaven. And now there's only Danny. That's bad for us. It's bad for him, too, should he care to think about it.

He should look over history's shoulder and take in what happened to Joey Smallwood, a great premier who subtracted from his own legacy by succumbing to the vanity of power, the great, corrosive self-flattery of believing that being in charge is the same thing as always being right.

The "fights" with Ottawa get all the news. The feud that Premier Williams has very much personalized with Prime Minister Harper is a certain headline grabber. At time of writing, its latest instalment, over the January 2009 federal budget and its impact on Newfoundland's federal revenues, is part of the chain of challenge and counter-challenge between the two.

And Premier Williams's highly successful ABC—anything but Conservative—campaign in the most recent federal election, while it was emphatically a great tactical success, came attended with at least one full-scale irony.

Newfoundland now, for the first time since Confederation, has no minister in the federal cabinet. This is more than a minor deficiency. Newfoundland has had, almost always, strong personalities representing her interest at the big table. Jack Pickersgill was a wizard of federal politics—he was "our boy" for a while in the Smallwood years. And was there ever a more emphatic presence in any cabinet than John Crosbie?

Now, during a worldwide recession, retreating oil prices, jobs being lost in the oil patch, and the feud with Ottawa in full swing, we have no one at all.

FAITH

PLAY MYSTIC FOR ME | September 18, 2004

It's uplifting to learn that Madonna is on a five-day pilgrimage (if that's quite the right word) to Israel to deepen her understanding and commitment to Kabbalah.

My understanding of that ancient and esoteric discipline is not much greater than that of another of its accessorized devotees, the spiritualist Britney Spears. Britney, incidentally, in imitation or homage to Madonna has gone all mystic, too.

For those who can't afford a stretch limo to the House of Wisdom, and therefore have to travel a thornier path to this great subject, let me recommend the book of books on the subject: *Kabbalah*, by the last century's greatest scholar of that tradition, Gershom Scholem. Scholem has been described as the very "master-spirit" of this difficult and subtle field. *Kabbalah* and his other books are triumphs of faithful scholarship. I don't know if Mr. Scholem did any videos.

Scholem is a monument to the ardours and austerities of the highest intellectualism, a very type of the idea of patient and courageous intellect.

George Steiner has written a one-sentence cameo of Scholem that catches that temperament very well: "That Voltairian mien, the needling eyes, the bat's ears ever alert, the lips given to sardonic display, composed a mask of reason . . ."

Scholem's study was his life's whole work. I cannot say whether our two celebrity exegetes are out to surpass Scholem or merely surf in his monumental wake. Nonetheless, when the minds and vocal cords that gave us, respectively, "Like a Virgin" and "Hit Me Baby One More Time" unite in any one enterprise, the world has reason to quiver in expectation.

Madonna's path into mysticism has led—somewhat by analogy to Prince, who wore for a long and fruitful inter-lude the luggage sticker "The Artist Formerly Known as Prince"—to her taking a new name. Madonna is now Esther. Britney is still Britney, though. However, should the pop princess pupate namewise, now that it's available, maybe she'll take "Madonna." That way, there'll always be a Madonna even though Madonna is Esther. This mysticism is tricky stuff.

Britney is, I think, more of a "sampler" than Madonna. Her last big religious flip was the quickie wedding—or wed-ding quickie, the relevant divines have yet to rule on the distinction—in a Las Vegas house of worship. The famous eight-hour marriage with the appropriate Las Vegas vow "till death or a hangover do us part." From which we may take it that young Ms. Spears is a daring eclectic. Anyone who seeks to absorb the sacramental in the satin chamber of an Elvis chapel on the Vegas Strip, in earshot of Wayne Newton and Céline Dion cauterizing the eardrums of the supper-club crowd, has bowels of brass.

I find from a story in the *Daily Telegraph* about the pilgrimage that Madonna has taken to wearing "a red thread on her wrist to ward off the evil eye." Considering some of the videos Madonna has appeared in, she could mummify herself in red thread and some eyes, evil or otherwise, would still be glaring.

Britney is not slacking off on the insignia, either. She's been spotted with her crimson bracelet, but a red thread worn anywhere on Britney, apart from its mystical potency, probably also counts as a wardrobe surplus.

Madonna is reportedly very irritated that her new-found adhesion to this profound and complex tradition is regarded by some "as a celebrity fad." The jaundice of petty minds, say I. I'm sure there were days that Thomas Aquinas emerged from the scriptorium to jeers of "modish monk."

Madonna has left herself a little open to the same charge. Over the long arc of her spiritual odyssey, she has shed personas so frequently that it's difficult to keep the file current. I know there was a yogic period, and of course her incubation as the Material Girl is a station of everyone's cross. But for the life of me, I can't remember whether her marriage to Sean Penn was in her Sex Crusade phase, or her Under the Moon of the Conic Bra period.

Any surly consideration that it's mere faddism, Kabbalah-lite, vanish into pixie dust when we learn she's with a posse of fellow seekers. There are two thousand other novitiates from the Los Angeles–based Kabbalah Center with her. When was the last time two thousand Californians and a sprinkle of celebrities got caught up in anything trendy? "There are energy vortexes," intones one of their guides, places people "can go and recharge [themselves] with positive energy." Verily, a Ninth Beatitude.

If you can spot a hint of vaporous trendiness in that clotted nugget, I'm Dr. Phil.

TOLERANCE MUST FLOW TWO WAYS | September 23, 2006

It is not often that lectures on the finer points of theology and philosophy, delivered from so retired a venue as the University of Regensburg, turn the world, or at least a good part of it, on its ear. But it must be said as well that not every lecturer is the Bishop of Rome.

Pope Benedict XVI's lecture may be fairly characterized as both subtle and erudite, a typically scholarly exposition from a man who was a scholar before he was a Pope. A few words of that lecture, however, and the consideration that it was the Pope who spoke them made it one of the most explosive addresses of our time.

Most of the Pope's address was a nuanced exploration of the relations between reason and faith. A good sense of the tone and nature of his talk, which is readily available in full on the Internet, may be taken from this sentence, which contains, as I see it, its central thesis: "Is the conviction that acting unreasonably contradicts God's nature merely a Greek idea, or is it always and intrinsically true?"

Hardly a red-flag item, even for the most excitable bull.

It was the few words of that address cited by His Holiness to assist in the illustration of his elegant argument, a quotation from a fourteenth-century Byzantine emperor, that ignited, or at least has been the occasion for igniting, a great storm across parts of the Muslim world. The quotation and the words leading to it are these: "He addresses his interlocutor with a startling brusqueness, a brusqueness which leaves us astounded, on the central question about the relationship between religion and violence in general, saying: 'Show me just what Mohammed brought that was new, and there you will find things only evil and inhuman, such as his command to spread by the sword the faith he preached.'"

That one-sentence quotation of an ancient emperor, within an otherwise quiescent address, has set off a fury of anger and outrage. Churches have been attacked in the West Bank, there have been demonstrations elsewhere, and the Pope has been reviled by some Muslims as another Hitler or Mussolini.

Following the tumultuous response, Pope Benedict has invited Muslim envoys for talks, and has twice expressed his regret for the reaction to his lecture, but—and this is not the same thing—he has not apologized for his talk. Nor should he.

The fury in the Muslim world following the Pope's talk seems similar in two respects to the greater fury that followed the publication of those now-famous Danish cartoons. The first similarity is that the volume and spread of outraged response gives every evidence of having been mobilized or concerted. That there is here, in other words, a "determination" to display outrage, less as evidence of a genuinely wounded religious sensibility, than as an act of political leverage against the West.

Not that I question some Muslims may well have taken deep offence at the Pope's words, but the offence taken has been magnified, and perhaps manipulated, for secondary motives.

The second point uniting these episodes, the point I think the more consequential, is the expectation from some Muslim authorities that their sensibilities and beliefs are owed, *as of right*, a singular respect and immunity from all negative comment and remark. It is more than curious that those who do not believe in Islam should be expected, by some believers, to uphold the same codes of respect toward it as those who do.

There attends this expectation, which is sometimes phrased as an actual demand, a further one: that, should "offence" be taken, whatever violence does ensue—be it rioting, the burning of churches or death threats—must be laid at the door of the parties who "insult" Islam, rather than those who have undertaken the actual violence in response.

These considerations are troubling. First, because the respect and privilege claimed by some Muslims from societies that are not Muslim is not afforded religions other than their own in societies that are Muslim. There is a magnificent mosque in Rome close to the Vatican. Do I need to say there is no basilica in Mecca? One religion should not claim rights it will not afford to all others. In too many Muslim countries, Christianity is institutionally—and this is a very kind word—disadvantaged.

Secondly, the rhetorical violence visited on Christianity and Judaism ("apes," "pigs," "crusaders," "infidels") by various Muslim spokespeople is both fervid and frequent, and in some of its expression utterly eclipses in its ferocity and deliberateness, either the bywords of the Pope here, or the famous cartoons.

Tolerance, like its elder, respect, is very much a current that flows equally between two parties. I cannot see how burning churches—as happened in the West Bank—or crude attacks upon, and threats against, the Pope, provide any foundation to calls for "greater sensitivity toward Islam."

There are precious things in the West, too, two of which are freedom of speech and critical analysis. Storms of outrage, and almost predictable violence after every perceived slight, leaves me feeling that the cardinal values of the West will wait a long time for a portion of that respect that parts of the Muslim world insist upon, immediately and in full, as their due.

THE JAMES CAMERON CODE | February 27, 2007

Hollywood is an inverted religion. Like most, this week I watched bits and pieces of that great orgy of idolatry and self-worship, the Academy Awards. What we call superstars are the gods and goddesses of our decadent time. Their church: fame, luxury and immense, obscene wealth.

Al Gore was called in as the pastor of a more austere calling, environmentalism. *An Inconvenient Truth* was given an Oscar to show that Hollywood can take a spell from narcissism and ally itself with something a little more substantial than surgically crafted cleavage and insane self-obsession. Al Gore is Hollywood's carbon pope. We may not need popes much longer.

The awards were barely over when one of the titans of big film, no less than James Cameron, he of the bloated budgets and blockbusters *Terminator* and *Titanic*, two milestones in the history of Western art, announces that he's about to release a documentary that will expose the last two thousand years of Christianity as a feeble sham, explode the central mystery of the Christian faith, the Resurrection, and while he's at it, prove even beyond the diligence of Dan Brown—book sales be upon him—that Jesus Christ was married to Mary Magdalene, died a natural death and was buried with Mary to boot. So much for the Incarnation.

James, you see, has picked up the old story. There's this tomb, see. Cue Angelina Jolie. And having watched enough *CSI* to bring himself up to speed, Mr. Cameron has gone all David Caruso on the bones, done the DNA research and, hey, presto, the central faith of the Western world, two thousand years of belief and scholarship beyond even the reach of Céline Dion, has, may I say it, hit an iceberg.

The world is wrong. Hollywood producer, archaeologist, Academy Award winner, self-appointed king of the world James Cameron has unlocked the greatest mystery in the history of the world. Better than Geraldo Rivera at Al Capone's vault. I expect the Vatican to apologize and close its doors within a week. Haul down Notre Dame, board up Westminster, give over all the cathedrals and churches to Starbucks. It was all a scam.

If what Jim has on film is true—and he's a formidable ecclesiologist—Christianity is for dupes. I have a minor question: Do you think we'll see any documentaries of like attempt and equal impertinence from James Cameron on Mohammed or Islam?

To ask the question is to answer it. Hollywood is only daring with Christianity. Why does Hollywood, which worships only money and itself, feel so blithely free to mock, degrade, toy with and abuse the sacred story of billions of people and offer the gospels no more respect than they would the script for *Showgirls?* Probably the answer to that question is that the minds that produced *Showgirls* are so radically vulgar they are incapable of realizing any distinction between the two.

That frame of mind will prostitute anything—the life of Christ, other people's religion—for a stale press conference and a fresh buck. It's that simple. It also explains Al Gore's Oscar. Having toppled one messiah, Hollywood wanted a shallow facsimile in the wings.

THE PATH TO POWER

DION BURIED ALIVE | October 18, 2008

It is an ancient and sage observation that politics is mean and harsh. Consider the cruel and enlightening example of Stéphane Dion.

Hold the grief counsellors, cue the vultures. The body is not yet cold—good grief, it hasn't even hit the floor—before the dissection begins and the post-mortems offer up their verdicts.

In Mr. Dion's case, the anonymous voices of the backroom, the "high-placed insiders" of the Liberal Party, hymned an instant chorus of his failings, an instant call for his ouster. And not to avoid what cannot be denied, we in the press are equally eager to spur and participate in the instant demolition. Personality always trumps politics—the human drama of a leader undone is worth a thousand panels on Afghanistan.

The latest word is he'll announce his resignation on Monday.

Dion wears his party's loss. After all, he would have been showered with hosannas had he won. At the leadership level, politics is an all-or-nothing game. Leaders have been bathed in praises to make a pharaoh blush for presiding over electoral victories for which they, the leaders, had as little to do as the fall of a leaf.

They were just there when it happened, when the public turned like an angry beast on the party that was in, and would have elected a party with a sick and ugly dog for a leader to send a measure of their disgust. Be the leader in one of those moments, and prepare to be extolled as a genius, a Napoleon of the ballot box. The sycophants and camp followers will crowd the throne room and every tongue will chirp his greatness.

Mr. Dion is on the underside of this phenomenon. It was the centrepiece of his platform—the Green Shift—that, more than any other item, obstructed the Liberal Party's performance. His personality, likewise, was a poor match for uncertain and anxious times. And he was the least able communicator of the very team he headed. Yet, for all that, there is still something unseemly, bordering on cruel, about the speed with which he is being marked as rubbish and consigned to the bin.

He failed. Bury him quickly. Disregard or ignore the sensibility of the individual caught in a moment of awful transition.

A decent interval to let him gather himself might have been a signal that politics has a heart, that party politics can permit a moment of composure to one of its leading figures and thereby indicate the game isn't always everything. In other words, that it could, however briefly, allow some respect for a particular human being and his human circumstance.

That is, of course, a hope far too large for politics as we have come to know it, and I fear being regarded as hopelessly sentimental—or, what's worse, antiquated—for merely introducing the thought.

The other personality at play is Stephen Harper's. He won—not the majority he hoped for, but still, he won. He remains prime minister—that is the crucial, the essential, consideration. Those disappointed that some of his performance was less than it should have been, that he misjudged the issues in Quebec, that he offered "stock tips" during a time of plant closings and financial anxiety, will muffle their criticisms. The well-oiled knees of those hoping for favour will genuflect at the rumour of his presence.

Which is too bad—for him. Mr. Harper needs to listen to those who would judge him coldly. Not the "Harper is Bush" mob, who think a slogan is a thought. But those who are willing to hazard a frown from their master in the cause of delivering some delayed truths to his attention. Among those truths, perhaps the most startling one is that he needs some of the very qualities of the man his party mocked and brought down. An occasional gust of charm, for starters. He needn't make it a habit. A more frequent willingness to speak without a prompt sheet from the polls. To speak in the voice of who he really is. To give some glimpse of his real feeling—outside those dreadful TV ads—about the arts, how he sees the country, what he thinks of the times we're in.

There's a hard truth in the consideration that many Canadians don't trust Mr. Harper, and I think it's because they see *he* doesn't trust *them*. His guard is always up. The brain locks in gear before the mouth stirs.

That's where, surprisingly, he could learn from Mr. Dion. He should note that, though Mr. Dion lost the election, there is still so wide a feeling at some level of Canadian appraisal that it was too bad he did. He was not the leader Canadians wanted, but his openness and "exposure" implied a trust, a faith in the people whose support he sought. Loss notwithstanding, that was admirable.

Stéphane Dion, for the most part, let Canadians see him. Stephen Harper should study that example.

COALITION FOR A DAY | December 13, 2008

Just twelve days ago, on Monday of the past week, there stumbled into life what all of us now remember as the coalition.

Three men—two leaders of national parties, one leader of a Quebec separatist party—held an official "signing ceremony." The coalition was all ready to become the government. Stéphane Dion would be its prime minister; Jack Layton's NDP would have six of its cabinet ministers; the

Bloc was guaranteed something called a "formal consulting mechanism" during the promised eighteen months of the agreement. Only the delay of an imminent confidence vote, and the subsequent prorogation of Parliament, stayed the coalition's swift and lofty ascent to power.

I'm summarizing what everyone already knows, because in the hectic, stormy politics of the last two weeks, events of twelve whole days ago feel like something you might catch only on the History Channel. It really does seem like years have passed since those two or three days when Mr. Dion really looked like he was going to become prime minister after all. But it was only just last week. As T.S. Eliot once sagely observed, "History has many cunning corridors," and as if by way of illustration of this maxim, last week's PM-to-be is this week's backbencher. The governor general had barely finished sipping tea with an imploring Stephen Harper before the Liberals jettisoned Mr. Dion and placed Michael Ignatieff in his job.

Where are we now? Last week, the coalition had everyone in the country mesmerized. There was talk of nothing else. Open-line shows, comments on web pages, editorials—there was a wave of popular and media response of a volume unseen since the wrangles of Meech Lake and the Charlottetown Accord.

And where is this coalition now? What is it? Does it even still exist? Mr. Ignatieff hems and haws about "a coalition if necessary, but not necessarily a coalition," which is what a really fancy mind comes up with when it wants to say yes and no to the same question. Equivocation in a tuxedo, but pure equivocation nonetheless.

One would think the brand new leader of the Liberals could give a direct answer on something as plain as whether his party still has an agreement with the NDP and the Bloc; that all three are, like the fabled musketeers, all for one and one for all. That, as per the agreement between them and the signing ceremony that announced it, come January 27, when Parliament returns, it's out with the Harper imperium. But on the few occasions that Mr. Ignatieff has been pushed to clarify the most central question in all of Canadian politics—Is the agreement to bring down Stephen Harper still in force?—the most erudite washing machine in Canadian politics goes into full spin cycle.

And out tumbles yes, no and maybe as if they were synonyms.

Even the NDP, which I think has the first claim to pride of authorship in this matter of a coalition, seems more than a little hazy on its current status. Its most dulcet-toned deputy leader, Thomas Mulcair, reminds Mr. Ignatieff that he was "one of 161 MPs who signed a letter to the Governor General asking to form an alternative government with the NDP."

But when pressed on the matter of whether his party and the Liberals are still in concert, still determined to do what that coalition was set up to do—form that alternative government—out comes the tepid "I have every reason to believe in his sincerity and in the sincerity of his Liberal colleagues."

Let's try that again: "I have every reason to believe in his sincerity and in the sincerity of his Liberal colleagues." *There's* a trumpet blast. More "let's do lunch" than "give me liberty or give me death."

Are the Bloc still in this thing? No idea. Do they still have that wonder, detailed in the signing ceremony, of a "formal consultation mechanism?" Is Michael consulting with them? Is Jack mechanizing? Haven't heard.

This is all very strange. Just twelve days ago, we had the boldest, most dramatic parliamentary manoeuvre in a generation, a formal alliance between three opposition parties, a signing ceremony of their leaders giving birth to a new entity and an "alternative government." This week, the once-explosive notion of a coalition is a shimmer in some phantom zone of yesterday's politics. No one who had anything to do with it wants to admit it's dead. They want it to fade away all on its own. If it weren't for that signing ceremony and the wonderfully retentive powers of videotape, I'd almost bet some of its backers would deny it ever existed.

There won't be any more rallies for the coalition. It was the fevered product of a moment's opportunism, a political house of cards. Five years from now, it'll be a good question for Trivial Pursuit.

The idea that a coalition underwritten by an agreement with the Bloc Québécois had a legitimate claim to form a "national" government was an offensive

> contradiction from the moment of its opportunistic conception.
>
> The coalition was almost instantly reviled by a majority of Canadians, in large part because a majority of Canadians simply could not digest the notion of a federal government owing its existence to the one party in the House of Commons that rejects the idea of a federal government. I don't know if Canada is the only country in the world that funds its own separatist party, but I am fairly certain it is the only country in the world that contemplated (as in the coalition) asking a separatist party to be the guarantor of its national government.

GRIT MIRACLE | December 20, 2008

Michael Ignatieff is good news for the Liberal Party.

It was good news when they *didn't* pick him at the leadership convention two years ago. He was then too fresh to the party and too fresh to Canada. He needed some time to wash the scent of the Harvard common room off himself. Needed time to establish some bona fides with the country he hadn't lived in for most of his adult life. Needed time for that big brain of his to wrap itself around the issues and rhythms, both subtle and complex, of Canadian politics.

Well, wrap itself it has, and the odour of Harvard has been duly subdued by the more manly fragrances of Question Period and the Liberal caucus room.

He stayed on after that first loss. That, of course, was critical. He stayed on and played the good soldier during the torments of Stéphane Dion's (let us be Christmas kind) uneven stay as Opposition leader. Two years ago, he was a resumé. Today, he's a politician, almost "one of the boys."

And here he is, leader of the Liberals. Precisely how he managed this during the political convulsions of the past few weeks is almost mystically perplexing. If Mr. Dion had been in focus on the night of December 3 (I'm referring here to the infamous late video), Mr. Ignatieff might not be leader today. Let's just say that chance and tumult co-operated.

Now that he's leader, he has restored morale. He generates interest. People, non-politicians, find him interesting. No, he's not our Barack Obama or Pierre Trudeau redux, but he looks good opposite Stephen Harper and he clearly outshines both Jack Layton and Gilles Duceppe. Check out the Liberal front bench these days. They're smiling again, and it isn't the forced rictus of the past two years.

There's already talk that Mr. Ignatieff is visiting Quebec early, hoping to pick up where Mr. Harper clearly struck out in the last election. And where many say Mr. Harper has further damaged himself by the vigour of his attack on the participation of the Bloc Québécois in the horror the country came to know as the coalition. Wooing

Quebec under these circumstances is no less smart for being the obvious thing to do. Mr. Ignatieff will do fine there. A high brow and a patrician manner, a little flavour of the cosmopolitan, is not an unfamiliar combination to Quebecers.

All this, I'm sure, cheers the Liberal Party. But the best news for the Liberals comes in what some may have seen as throwaway lines at his early press conference as leader. Mr. Ignatieff—no Horace Greeley fan, I'm sure—spoke of going west.

The Liberal Party has long treated western Canada as some kind of political Ultima Thule, or, if I may maul a familiar phrase from *Hamlet*, an "undiscovered country from whose bourn no Liberal MP returns." The smartest thing Mr. Ignatieff did at that first press conference was to pay tribute to the West as the "beating economic heart of our country's future."

Westerners have become all too familiar with eastern politicians ignoring them or treating them as afterthoughts, or less. There has been a mighty strain of condescension built into this country's politics toward the West, and it has infected the Liberal Party in particular.

There's no need to bring up yet again the great nightmare of the National Energy Program to illustrate this point. That policy burned the house of Liberalism in the West to the ground. Mr. Ignatieff is the first Liberal leader I've heard since the dread days of the NEP to make clear acknowledgment of the resentments and mischiefs it inspired. These were the words he used: "I want us to reach out and hope that western Canadians forgive and forget, to be very blunt, some of the errors the party has made in the past."

That's smart. And, if he means it, wise as well. There was also considerable wisdom in holding himself somewhat at arm's length from the coalition. Because, despite conventional wisdom, what ticked off the West about that jerry-rigged fabrication wasn't so much the Bloc's inclusion but that it nullified, by backroom deal, the West's huge representation, by the ballot, in the Harper government. All those western MPs and cabinet ministers were suddenly going to be patrolling the corridors of opposition, just because Messrs. Layton, Duceppe and Dion had cooked up a deal to shunt them there. Many westerners saw themselves once again being dealt out of the power equations by eastern politicians.

So, Mr. Ignatieff is good news for the Liberals. And no more so than that his radar is tuned so early into turning the party's fortunes around in the one region of the country that most of his recent predecessors barely acknowledged was on the political map.

Mr. Ignatieff will fish in Mr. Harper's waters. There's a turnaround. The season of miracles, indeed.

COALITION OF UNINTENDED CONSEQUENCES | February 7, 2009

So much begins with the wonder and farce we came to know as the coalition: the pact, deal, improvisation between Messrs. Dion, Layton and Duceppe, that for a heady moment seemed destined to overturn the Harper minority, install Stéphane Dion as prime minister, and place Jack Layton with five other New Democrats in the federal cabinet. Gilles Duceppe and his Bloc were then, metaphorically, to ride shotgun on this tidy arrangement, by guaranteeing it would be impervious to confidence measures for a year and a half.

Merely saying that it didn't fly is a serious understatement. But so wonderful a combination was not without its effects. If the coalition had not reared its various and confusing heads, Mr. Dion would still, in his manner, be leading the Liberal Party. Canadians were rightly staggered that a man who had, more or less, already been told by his own party that his days were numbered was, by this piece of artfulness, soon to be their prime minister.

The Liberals were forced to confront a fairly strong objection to this outcome. He had been found wanting, was on his way out in fact, but would do nonetheless as prime minister for a while. Logic of this kind is why the word perplexing was first invented.

Skipping all the glorious details, this is why, without a full convention, Michael Ignatieff is now Leader of Her Majesty's Official Opposition. The fury that roiled public opinion after the triple signing—Dion, Layton, Duceppe—forced the Liberal Party to confront its own leadership problems. Dominic LeBlanc dropped out first, Bob Rae conceded, and Michael Ignatieff slid ever so gracefully into its leadership.

The always snarky gods of irony turned the coalition from an instrument to unseat Stephen Harper as prime minister into an instrument to install Michael Ignatieff as Liberal leader. "Last to sign on, first to be king" should be the Ignatieff family motto.

The coalition gave cover to Mr. Harper to explode eighteen of his finest loyalists into the Senate. Eighteen senators in a single day. It enabled Mr. Harper, with minimum fuss, to go from ardent Senate reformer to a chartered member of the "If you can't beat 'em, join 'em" club. The coalition gave Mr. Harper his very own patronage Christmas.

That's had its benefits. In the case of Mike Duffy, it put a merciful end to the longest audition in Canadian history. It ferried Mr. Duffy from an interviewer's stool outside the Commons to a more accommodating perch on the stuffed velvet cushions of appointment paradise, the Red Chamber.

Early on, by the way, Mr. Duffy is showing signs of being Mr. Harper's most inspired choice. His maiden speech (strange) had elements of pornographic fantasy. The scene called up was all about premiers Danny Williams and Robert Ghiz in bed together, with such flourishes as "when one is in bed with Danny Williams, he will come out on top" and "where that will leave PEI in the end." Is there a cover charge to listen to Senate debates now? *Mike Duffy Live* takes on a whole new meaning.

But however much Mr. Harper may be gratified to have Mr. Duffy as an apprentice standup comedian turning riffs on Danny Williams and Robert Ghiz sweating under the sheets, it can be as nothing to his satisfaction on hearing Senator Duffy's ardent and blush-free tribute to him.

In a passage of exquisite piety, Mr. Duffy recalled that, in his days as a journalist, he "learned one cannot be a successful leader without sound political judgment and the courage to make tough decisions despite determined opposition." This was followed by a sublime moment of sycophancy dressing itself up as candour: "I am here to tell honourable Senators today—this is where the hard part begins—Stephen Harper has both that judgment and that courage."

So that was the hard part. Praising the prime minister who put him there. We have the coalition and its tormented aftermath to thank for that fresh page in Canadian political folklore.

The most immense transformation that grew out of the doomed coalition, however, was the complete conversion of Mr. Harper as a fiscal conservative. The budget just brought down is a great scattershot of huge spending, put together we may safely assume in the panic-laden days following the threat to Mr. Harper's staying in power. It embraces deficit financing during a recession with a fever that has Bob Rae chuckling in the op-ed pages. Chuckle he should and may.

Were Mr. Harper in opposition facing a Liberal government bringing down this budget, he would be on it like Savonarola rounding up heretics. This is a budget that would have made Jean Chrétien proud.

The coalition as a tactic was a massive failure. The coalition as an event has precipitated radical changes, pushed a dogmatic Conservative prime minister squarely into Liberal territory, and finessed the arrival of Michael Ignatieff into the leadership of the Liberal Party. And, of course, elevated Mr. Duffy.

IT MIGHT HAVE BEEN | February 21, 2009

John Greenleaf Whittier—it's a great name for a poet. Love the Greenleaf. With that as a middle name, were he around today, it's hard to think he wouldn't be flogging his Muse in the great cause of global warming, penning odes to windmills or versicles for Al Gore. If he's known at all any more, it's for a mournful little couplet that earned almost proverbial status in years long gone by. I thought of it this week during the visit of His Obamaness:

> *For of all sad words of tongue or pen,*
> *The saddest are these: "It might have been!"*

The rueful maxim popped into mind during Barack Obama's session with Stephen Harper. Were it not for the wisdom—as I see it—of Governor General Michaëlle Jean's decision to give the prime minister the prorogation he so desperately needed during the coalition crisis, Mr. Harper might not have been standing there Thursday with the gloriously popular Mr. Obama. Instead, Canada would have been "turning its lonely eyes" toward Prime Minister Stéphane Dion and coalition partner Jack Layton doing the diplomatic equivalent of a fist bump on centre stage with the world's most popular leader.

And Mr. Harper, glowering as only he knows how to glower, would have been ferrying himself as opposition leader out to Ottawa airport for a more rationed *tête-à-tête* at the tail end of the presidential visit.

But it was mainly Jack and Stéphane that summoned J. Greenleaf's fortune-cookie melancholy. They could have been basking in the starlit moment, sharing the wave to the crowd, having the private lunch with the Western world's newest hero. Alas, "it might have been."

Aside from these purely fanciful speculations, I was taken by another, purely subsidiary, aspect of this week's visit. This was the question, which got considerable grinding in the press, of how many minutes Michael Ignatieff was to receive for his "face time" (odious phrase) with Mr. Obama.

Depending on the day or the press release, it was to be thirty minutes, or fifteen minutes, then back up to twenty minutes; at one (surely ominous) point, it was only ten minutes.

The Ignatieff camp was plainly determined to have its due, reaching back to Mr. Harper's time as opposition leader during the 2004 visit of George Bush. That, said Mr. Ignatieff, was a "good and extended meeting." He continued, and the tone was almost Churchillian: "I will expect no less, and I'm sure I will receive no less." There's a lot of Harvard in that sentence.

In any event, it all turned out sweetly for him. He not only got as much of the clock as could be hoped for—a full 30 minutes—but was able to include Bob Rae in the picnic. Outside of the extempore visit by Mr. Obama to the beaver tail hut in the ByWard Market (that's one shop that will survive the recession), I consider the resolution of the face-time-minutes crisis the human-interest highlight of the trip.

Mr. Ignatieff's real coup in the last little while, however, is far beyond the hyped and specious drama of how much time he was going to get with the new president. The Liberal leader has been making speeches in the western provinces that, in their tone and substance, signal he does not intend to simply accept what has been one of the iron laws of Canadian politics for a generation or more: that the Liberal Party hasn't a hope in hell of winning any real support out West.

Mr. Ignatieff has been speaking up for Alberta as the economic dynamo of the country, he has moderate words for the oil sands and he talks about the Liberal Party's past sneakiness (that's my paraphrase) of "running against the

West"—all in all, he gives every evidence of trying to put the Liberals into serious play in the deepest Harper territory.

This is a good thing, a very good thing. No parts, regions or provinces should be "owned" by any one party. The result is complacency and stagnation. Mr. Ignatieff is right to reject the lazy cliché that "the West" will never go Liberal.

His timing is opportune as well. Mr. Harper injured himself in the coalition crisis, and hasn't helped himself greatly since with the budget, in the minds of very ardent Conservatives. Mr. Ignatieff's pitch to a presumed monolith of Conservative support—and give him his due, the clarity of that pitch—comes at a near perfect moment.

A few more visits, a few more speeches and perhaps by the time Canadians face another election, Mr. Ignatieff may have removed some of the tired and regressive predictability from how Canadians vote. By that time, who got to wave with Barack Obama or how long they chatted will be one with the memory of John Greenleaf Whittier's other verses.

There were others.

EXTRA! EXTRA!

PALIN CONNECTS | November 24, 2009

There are two great political speakers in America today. Sarah Palin is the other one.

Barack Obama's speaking skills are his signature talent. He's a platform performer, a speechmaker in the great tradition, a kind of teleprompter Cicero. The campaign to become President owed more to Mr. Obama's oratorical mastery than to any other element. His speech on race in America, necessitated by revelations of the ugly thoughts and sentiments of his hometown preacher, Rev. Jeremiah Wright, was the most important event of his campaign. If it had failed, his candidacy would have been doomed. Under pressure—the great test of the real speechmaker—he delivered.

The other great speech of the U.S. campaign season was Sarah Palin's on receiving the vice-presidential slot on the McCain ticket. This was a speech delivered under even greater pressures than that of Mr. Obama. John McCain's choice of Ms. Palin had been early and widely criticized, and in some quarters ferociously reviled. She had never really been under the national spotlight before. The entire media were focused on her with an intensity almost unseen in the annals of vice-presidential politics. If she'd been just "okay," or messed up, John McCain's campaign was over. It was the highest of high-stakes gambles.

Did she deliver? She soared. She was the very acme of self-confidence and ease. She mixed a natural charm with a mischievous edge of sarcasm toward her opponents—even daring the unthinkable by pinging The One himself. It was her "first serve" on the national stage and she delivered an ace. Not only did she not sink the McCain campaign, she gave it the only real vitality and spark that gloomy, tight, fussy little campaign had from start to finish.

Her speech, in fact, was the rhetorical equivalent of Mr. Obama's crucial one. They do not as speakers, it is obvious, share the same idiom. Mr. Obama is utterly composed, deliberate down to gesture and word, very conscious that he is a "figure" on a stage. Mr. Obama "bestows" himself on an audience. Ms. Palin has none of that. She will never speak in front of faux Greek columns. She walks on the stage much the same way she'd stroll into a coffee shop. But she's shrewd in her choice of themes, has a marvellous feel for her audience, and a confidence that will never be confused with arrogance.

They are, in the way fate or the mysteries of politics sometimes offers such things, curiously equivalent or parallel figures, polar opposites but equals. Ms. Palin connects;

Mr. Obama inspires. She's a latter-day frontier figure, impulsive, instinctive; he's pure urban cool, highly deliberate, even detached. Both have real charisma.

It will make Obama fans perspire to hear this, but Ms. Palin has a more forceful bond with her supporters than he with his. Mr. Obama offers a kind of self-flattery to his worshippers. They feel exalted that they have the intelligence or sensibility to see how remarkable their man is. But he remains remote. Ms. Palin works close up. She offers those much invoked, but actually neglected figures, "the ordinary Joe or Josephine," a real sense that she does represent them.

Ms. Palin is in the hurricane's eye again with the publication of *Going Rogue*. The Associated Press assigned no fewer than eleven reporters to "fact check" Ms. Palin's memoir, a concentration of scrutiny AP would never presume to exert over the man who's actually in the White House. Elements of the press mock and scorn her with a fury that is near inexplicable. Rather fewer extol her gifts. But pro or con, the media cannot get enough of her.

Professional feminists despise her, view her with unhinged contempt, as witness this classic assessment of academic Wendy Doniger: "Her greatest hypocrisy is in her pretense that she is a woman." Dutiful "progressives," otherwise windsocks of sensitivity and nuance, revile her in the crudest, most extravagant terms. The intensity of their hostility, its unbridledness and dreadful tastelessness (the speculations on the birth of her Downs syndrome child) is an unwitting measure of her power.

A truly dumb and witless person would not have the demure columnist David Brooks hissing dismissively, angrily in fact, on a Sunday morning talk show that Sarah Palin "is a joke." Poor Mr. Brooks gets intellectual hives just thinking about her. Empty vessels do not inspire such venom and fury.

Ms. Palin is a real and evolving element in the great story of American politics. She is the "other half" of the Obama moment, and she may be in the ascendant. Mr. Obama is losing his lustre, his appeal is dimming, at the very moment the Alaskan outsider is staking her claim. Those who call her a joke are expressing an anxious hope not offering a rational description.

Ms. Palin has rare gifts and stamina enough to give them play. She is the second most outstanding figure on the great stage of American politics.

THE SCIENCE IS NOT SETTLED | December 3, 2009

When Jon Stewart, the bantam rooster of conventional wisdom, makes jokes about it, you know Climategate has reached critical mass. Said Stewart: "Poor Al Gore. Global warming completely debunked via the very Internet [he] invented."

Stewart was half-joking, but Climategate is no joke at all. The mass of e-mails from the Climate Research Unit of East

Anglia University, let loose by a hacker or a whistleblower, pulls back the curtain on a scene of pettiness, turf-protection, manipulation, defiance of Freedom of Information, lost or destroyed data, and attempts to blacklist critics and skeptics of the global warming cause.

The CRU is not the only climate science advisory body, but it is one of the most influential, and feeds directly into the UN Panel on Climate Change.

Let's hear no more talk of "the science is settled," when it turns out some of the principal scientists behave as if they own the very question of global warming—when they seek to bar opposing research from "peer-reviewed journals," to embargo journals they can't control, when they urge each other to delete damaging emails before Freedom of Information takes hold, when they talk of "hiding the decline," when they actually speak of destroying the primary data, and when, now, we do learn that the primary data has been lost or destroyed.

They've "lost" the raw data on which all the models, all the computer generated forecasts; the graphs and projections, are based. You wouldn't accept that at a Grade 9 science fair.

These emails demonstrate one thing beyond all else: that climate science and global warming advocacy have become so entwined, so meshed into a mutant creature, that separating alarmism from investigation, ideology from science, agenda from empirical study, is well nigh impossible. Climategate is evidence that the science has gone to bed with advocacy, and both have had a very good time: that the neutrality, openness, and absolute disinterest that is the hallmark of all honest scientific endeavour has been abandoned to an atmosphere and a dynamic not superior to the partisan caterwauls of a sub-average Question Period.

Climate science has been shown to be—in part—a subbranch of climate politics.

It is a situation intolerable even to serious minds who are onside with global warming, such as Clive Crook, who wrote in *The Atlantic* magazine about this scandal as follows: "The stink of intellectual corruption is overpowering."

Climate science needs its own reset button. And Climategate should be seen, not primarily as a setback, but as an opportunity to cleanse scientific method. To take science away from politics, good causes, and alarmists, and vest climate science in bodies of guaranteed neutrality, openness, real and vigorous debate. And away from the lobbyists, the NGOs, the advocates, the Gores and professional environmentalists of all kinds.

Too many of the current leadership on global warming are more players than observers, gatekeepers, not investigators, angry partisans of some global reengineering rather than the humble servants of the "facts of the case."

Read the emails. You'll never think of climate "science" quite the same way again.

WHICH STEPHEN HARPER? | February 6, 2010

It's time to get out the blue sweater again. Or, brush up on some more Beatles tunes. Anything except *Mean Mr. Mustard*—if the Liberals are smart they're practising that classic themselves. The Conservatives' rather comfortable lead in the polls, where they were hovering interestingly close to a potential majority, has disappeared like mist in the sun.

Some, if not most, will ascribe this to the prorogation half-storm. No one, however, seriously believes that Canadians have prorogation as such at the top of their minds. The mechanics of the parliamentary schedule, or the procedural niceties of the House of Commons, do not besiege the attention of the Canadian voter. Prorogation may have been the occasion for the Conservatives' fall in the polls; it was not, in itself, the cause.

The cause, as always in the fortunes of the Tories, is Mr. Harper. He makes them or he breaks them. It is as simple as that. He does not have a star-studded or even a flamboyant front bench. There are no John Crosbies, or Shelia Copps, or (to go back a fair bit) Jack Pickerskills. In the main, the few spokespeople the Conservatives have at their disposal are bland or less. None seems to have developed an independent standing as a Conservative "star." For example, who's the Bob Rae of the Conservative party at the present time?

Mr. Harper has had his successes. Successive victories,

however slim and contentious, have given his party minority government, and him the prime minister's seat for four years.

Power has educated him. I don't think it can be denied that he's learned a lot since becoming prime minister. He "carries" the job well now. He has, every comic caricature to one side, a dignified and respectable presence. Abroad he fits the part; seems at ease with, and a comfortable equal to, other leaders. And Stephen Harper has learned to modify or subdue his (perhaps) wilder ideological leanings, temper his personality and his politics, the most necessary lesson if he wishes either to stay in power, or strengthen his hold on it.

Call it pragmatism of opportunism, but Mr. Harper has, in the words of a famous formula of T.S. Eliot's, "modified his sensibility" since becoming prime minister.

Why then, are he and his party still stuck in a tie with the Liberals—especially now? After all, Mr. Ignatieff has had a run of six months or so as gruelling as any opposition leader—including Mr. Dion—in recent memory. It all, once again, comes down to Stephen Harper. A goodly portion of the Canadian electorate doesn't trust him, or has an indefatigable disposition not to like him, or have fixed an image of him as an ultimate doctrinaire hard right winger. And blue sweaters and Beatles songs, while they may temporarily moderate those negatives, do not banish them.

And then there are those games he plays, of which prorogation is but the latest in a series, in which he hands critics and those citizens who are predisposed not to trust or like him one more great signal that the "crafty" "plotting" "hidden agenda" Stephen Harper is still inside there lurking under the soft blue wool cover. Every time he issues one of those "reminders," it's back to the starting gate for the Conservatives. Every time he lulls Canadians into a sense of ease with his performance or persona, he finds a way to start the alarms all over again.

As long as there is this "edge" to Stephen Harper, as long as a good swathe of the electorate has this visceral distrust with where he may want to lead the country, and he by tactic or tone feeds it, his ability—even in this period of weak and uncertain Liberal fortunes—to gain a true majority is greatly circumscribed.

What must be nerve-wracking for his fans and followers is the consideration that the one person who most frustrates that ever-so-enchanting possibility is Mr. Harper himself. He did it with prorogation. It signaled to those who are wary of him, and see him in a threatening light, that "nasty" Harper is still busy, and he must be constrained.

It fed, fairly or not, the preconceptions of those disinclined to support him. That's what those polls are saying.

SWIFTER. HIGHER. STRONGER. DUMBER. | February 13, 2010

There have been a few odd, pre-Olympian moments of late, offering interesting aperçus on the eve of the official opening of the Vancouver Olympics.

It turns out some ninety buses rented from California were judged not to be quite capable of making the grade up to Cypress Mountain. What did they expect—they're California buses, probably all very green, with the carbon footprint of a ball of lint and emission standards lower than a rock. California buses don't have engines: They have pedals.

The IOC—high Lords of Olympus—forbade a sixteen-year-old Australian figure skater, Cheltzie Lee, from competing while wearing "a tiny good-luck charm bracelet she wears in memory of her dead friend": A teenager's honest sentiment fails to move the marble gods of the world's greatest exercise in harmony and the formation of good character.

The IOC claims the memorial bracelet comprises a form of "sponsorship," and I guess to the myopic wizards of Olympic bureaucracy it is difficult to distinguish a memento on a sixteen-year-old wrist from the corporate billboards of the world's voraciously advertising megamarketeers.

Swifter, Higher, Stronger gives way, to Dumber, Meaner and Downright Inexplicable . . . which latter triune brings me inescapably to the broad and deep insights into the Canadian soul on full display recently in *The New York Times*.

The Times (All the stale sociology (un)fit to print) has a story about how the Olympics are a Canadian attempt "to rewire the national mindset"—which is downright bizarre. Are we, is Canada, a ham radio?

The flood of tosh swells ominously with the observation that Canada is "a vast country run in many ways like a small town." I guess "Mayor Harper" couldn't be reached for comment because he was busy at the hardware store sorting gyprock for the spring sale.

The nonsense reaches full deluge when we are told further by the panjandrums of *The Times* that the wish to win a few medals at our own games is "nakedly ambitious," and that the slogan "Own the Podium" is making many Canadians "uneasy" because of our "collective inferiority complex."

Dear Lord, where do they get these dim people— probably ferried them in on those California buses. There's better straight reporting on *The View.*

To think we gave that country Celine Dion (and threw in Pamela Anderson as a freebie). Is this the thanks we get from the journal of the "educated class" in Obama's America? We're in high anxiety that we might win something at the Games we're hosting . . . so what? How does such freshman balderdash claim ink in the "paper of record"?

I blame it on global warming. Swells the brain but reduces capacity—it's the humidity.

The worst nonsense in the article comes in the observation that some "left critics" of the games see our "unseemly" wish to win as "connected" to "Canada's aggressive, overly American-like presence in Afghanistan." Who knew figure skating was so martial? Snowboarding a trope for the imperial impulse?

Yes, I know, all that effort to build schools and help young girls in a desperately poor and shattered land, an altruistic effort that has cost dearly in Canadian lives, springs from our emulation of desperately "aggressive" Amerikkka.

I know when I'm watching the bobsleigh next week I'll see Dick Cheney's face on all the hard turns.

Tomorrow's *Times* headline: Host Country Aspires to Win Medals: Unseemly National Pride Sweeps Nation—Is This the Beginning of Canada's Tea Party Movement?

Well, let us all park our inferiority complex, and crowd around over by the town post office, turn on the old Don Messer tapes, while we cheer on all those "uppity" Canadians as they make a bid for a spot on the podium. Try not to be "uneasy." We might distress the *New York Times* reporter . . . but let's chance it. No one ever said winning gold would be without its awkward moments.

Harper . . . you finished pricing that gyprock yet?

HYMN AND HER | MARCH 6, 2010

The Harper government took a lot of heat for prorogation. Was it worth it?

Well, if the justification for taking a break was to refresh their intellectual batteries, then on the evidence of the prose of the Speech from the Throne, either the break wasn't nearly long enough, or those batteries are beyond all charging. It had more platitudes per square inch than a fortune-cookie factory, and its every grey platitude a garment of the dreariest cliché.

"In taking responsible steps to reduce the deficit, our Government will not repeat the mistakes of the past." Poor

Michaëlle Jean—does she get hardship pay for having to voice such vacuous tosh? Not all her formidable charm or energy could infuse this poor sad pudding of relentless banality with a spark of life.

"To succeed in the global economy, Canada must keep step as the world races forward." Something in the nature of a health alert should be issued to the nation's high school valedictorians. Keep away from this speech: It will narcotize your brain.

Not everyone in the circle of the government's advisors could have been unaware that the 58-minute prose purgatory they were unleashing on the nation was a major dud, something worthy of Mark Twain's immortal dismissal of another high-minded document as "chloroform in print." And it was probably with that perception in mind that the call went out to find something, some idea, some project, some suggestion to insert into this flattest of pancakes to diversify its otherwise Saharan tedium.

This is, plainly I admit, purely speculation on my part, but such a line of thought may explain the Harper government's eerie dip into '70s feminist linguistics, i.e., the Throne Speech's surprising announcement that the Conservatives were looking to gender-neutralize—I can think of a more vivid verb—the national anthem. Of all the problems and dilemmas now facing our country, offering dutiful feminist repair to a phrase in our national anthem is not so much at the very bottom of the barrel, as buried an embarrassingly good few feet in the earth underneath it.

Confirmation that its overture in this area was empty and cynical came yesterday afternoon when the government gave up on the ludicrous experiment. Stung by the reaction of the public—the wave of common sense that swept the land—the drive to gender-neutralize the national hymn has been abandoned. Not much of a hill to collapse on.

Still, I cannot help but note that their sortie into this dubious territory was a couple of decades (I'm working from memory on this point) behind a similar effort on the part of no less a firebrand than Sheila Copps. The redoubtable Ms. Copps found the masculinist pretensions of "all thy sons command" an offence against inclusiveness, and spoke out on the same. At the very least, we can say that Ms. Copps' opinions on the subject were both heartfelt and genuine, and of a piece with her political philosophy. But when, as in this week's Throne Speech, we found Stephen Harper attempting catch-up with Sheila Copps on gender politics and politically correct language, we're in a very strange, and not to say contrived, moment indeed. Stephen Harper: the last feminist.

After staying the nation's business, the Tories produced a monumentally dull speech: so they needed a distraction— that's the best I can come up. Toying with the anthem was a reliable sparkler. And if Mr. Harper and his colleagues wanted something memorable to come out of the Throne Speech—albeit trivial, irrelevant and empty as the anthem flare is—they got it. Got it and had to throw it out two days later. Yeah . . . they needed a longer break.

Which leads to another point. When is Stephen Harper going to raise a storm on a real issue, one which is genuinely concordant with his party's philosophy, the dear wish of most of his supporters, and many who are not, as well—that of stripping the Canadian Human Rights Commission of its democratically injurious superintendence and prosecution of free speech?

If the Prime Minister was looking for something to animate this week's slab of dim bromides, why not a signal that he has finally heard the voices of thousands from coast to coast on those wretched inquisitions conducted under the provisions of federal and provincial HRCs?

Why not a statement in the Throne Speech on the value of free speech? Why not some expression of where he and his government stand on the increasingly invasive, procedurally wild, frequently ludicrous, unfair, selective and ideologically driven tribunals and inquiries?

A real government, and a real prime minister, wouldn't have ignored the issues of free speech, free thought and free press wrapped up in this question. But on the HRCs Stephen Harper has been a perfectly mute sphinx.

I suppose it is too much to ask, even after the long siesta of prorogation, that the government show some flash of courage on a matter of real principle and genuine import. Better instead this confected tempest on a non-issue, the factitious "sexism" of our national anthem. It would be a final and just irony if some fatuously aggrieved complainant took the government before the Human

Rights Commission on the distress caused by "all thy sons command."

Maybe if Mr. Harper and his buddies were caught in the menacing toils of the HRC process, they'd finally get the point and find some minimal courage.

ACKNOWLEDGEMENTS

Thank you to:

Tim Rostron, editor at Doubleday Canada, for his diligence, cheer, patience and intelligence, who has been the shepherd of this enterprise, and who summons this slightly antique tribute to mind: *A Man of Taste, to great applause, he read the daily news/ And kept a close acquaintance with the Muse.*

Mark Harrison of CBC's *The National*, a man of rare even-temper and fine judgment.

Alexandra Tomescu of *The National*, a woman of judicious mind and dauntless industry, who produced many of the Points of View included in this volume and gave very necessary assistance in the early trawl of columns and POVs.

The great mix of other people who, over the years at *The National*, have been involved in the various stages of producing *Point of View.*

The cheerful and welcoming crew at the *National Post*— of Doug Kelly, Jonathan Kay and Marni Soupcoff, sherpas all of tolerance and grace.

Speaking of artful guides, Nicola Makoway, publicist for this book, should get medals for patience and persistence.

Bruce Westwood, my genial and efficacious agent.

Erin Cooper, the very able caricaturist, for the book's cover and title page horror (it is, I acknowledge, kinder than a photograph), which has brought much amusement to co-workers and friends.

And my brother Tyrone, whose reserves of scorn and dudgeon so far superior, in volume and variety, to my own—a whole Alpine range of unslaked *indignatio*—leave me feeble with wonder and breathless from vain emulation.

ABOUT THE AUTHOR

Rex Murphy was born in Carbonear, Newfoundland, moved at an early age to Freshwater, Placentia Bay, and grew up in the province during the tenure of its greatest political impressario, Joseph R. Smallwood. During his university days, an early collision with the formidable Joey happily confirmed an innate disposition to look upon politics and politicians as an unacknowledged branch of entertainment, a perspective that has served well to the present day.

He drifted into the world of near-journalism (commentary and opinion) first at VOCM, St. John's, and then for various stretches at CBC, initially at *Here and Now* in St. John's. He is the weekly commentator on CBC TV's *The National*, host of CBC Radio's *Cross Country Checkup* and writes a Saturday column for the *National Post*.